5 CROISIÈRES EN SCANDINAVIE
ÉTÉ 1955

M Stella Polaris

CLIPPER LINE

WARD LINE S·S·MORRO CASTLE

S·S·ORIENTE WARD LINE

PLAN OF PASSENGER ACCOMMODATIONS

1963 INDEPENDENCE Springtime Cruise
(Minimum fare – $1245)

ITINERARY

New York	Mar. 14	5 PM
Casablanca	Mar. 21	8 AM-Mdn't
Palma	Mar. 23-24	8 AM 2 AM
Messina	Mar. 25	8 AM 4 PM
Alexandria	Mar. 27 29	8 AM 2 PM
Beirut	Mar. 30-Apr. 1	8 AM 1 AM
Haifa	Apr. 1-3	8 AM-Mdn't
Dardanelles	Apr. 5	8 AM (in transit)
Bosphorus	Apr. 5	3 PM (Cruising)
Istanbul	Apr. 5-6	6 PM 7 PM
Piraeus	Apr. 7-8	1 PM-6 PM
Venice	Apr. 10-11	11 AM-5 PM
Dubrovnik	Apr. 12	8 AM 1 PM
Kotor Fjord	Apr. 12	3 PM (Cruising)
Naples	Apr. 13-14	6 PM-7 PM
Leghorn	Apr. 15 16	8 AM-1 AM
Cannes	Apr. 16	8 AM-8 PM
Barcelona	Apr. 17	9 AM-7 PM
Lisbon	Apr. 19-20	9 AM-4 AM
Madeira	Apr. 21	9 AM-6 PM
New York	Apr. 27	8:30 AM

CONSULT YOUR TRAVEL AGENT

Printed in U.S.A. Sept. 1962

S S INDEPENDENCE
1963 Springtime Cruise
to the Mediterranean

AMERICAN EXPORT LINES

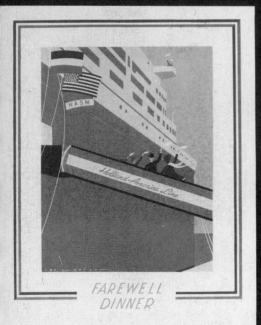

FAREWELL
DINNER

No. C. 177. May 1927. (Cancelling previous issues)
(SUBJECT TO CHANGE WITHOUT NOTICE)

COSULICH LINE
MEDITERRANEAN
ADRIATIC
SERVICE
CABIN RATES

EXPRESS   TWIN SCREW
S.S. PRESIDENTE WILSON

REGULAR SERVICE
BETWEEN
NEW YORK
AZORES-LISBON-NAPLES
RAGUSA-GREECE & TRIESTE

PHELPS BROS. & COMPANY
GENERAL AGENTS
17 BATTERY PLACE, NEW YORK

PRINTED IN U.S.A.

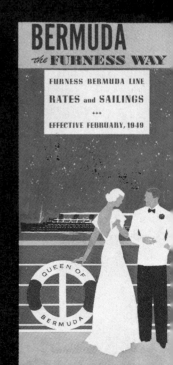

BERMUDA
the FURNESS WAY

FURNESS BERMUDA LINE
RATES and SAILINGS
+++
EFFECTIVE FEBRUARY, 1949

QUEEN OF
BERMUDA

A grand painting of Great Britain *fitting out for service by* Samuel Walters *(courtesy of the SS Great Britain Project).*

FIFTY FAMOUS LINERS 2

Frank O. Braynard FRS & William H. Miller

 Patrick Stephens, Wellingborough

First published 1985
Second impression 1987

British Library Cataloguing in Publication Data

Braynard, Frank O.
Fifty famous liners.
2
1. Ocean liners
I. Title   II. Miller, Bill
623.8'2432   VM381

ISBN 0-85059-751-X

For
DORIS BRAYNARD
from a loving husband and a fond admirer

*Patrick Stephens Limited is part of the
Thorsons Publishing Group*

Printed and bound in Great Britain

Contents

Introduction I

When Bill Miller and I wrote the first *Fifty Famous Liners* we urged our readers to write in with suggestions for a future book of the same type. Now it is our pleasure to offer a new set of 50 ocean liners, many of which were suggested to us in hundreds of kind letters. Thank you all for the response and do not hesitate to write again with more names, for we confidently anticipate a third book of 50 famous liners! Help us make it happen. Honestly it must be admitted that for each worthy ship we include we miss four or five equally worthy liners. Choosing the ships to go into a book like this is terribly difficult and just plain arbitrary — no question about it. Take the French sea queen — *L'Atlantique*, 40,000 gross tons. Most certainly she should have been here, but we just do not have good photographs. Gentle reader, loan us pictures of this wonderful but tragically short-lived ship for volume three.

It is particularly pleasant to be able to use the photos in my collection for this series. My enthusiasm for saving liner memorabilia began even before I started school. Various aunts and uncles instilled in me a passion for travel and ships. I started by pasting clippings in scrapbooks and had over 100 before I turned to steel cabinets as a safer way to store my ship news. My scrapbooks are card indexed by ship, person and line. Today my cellar is jammed with fifteen 27-drawer steel cabinets, fifteen others with large drawers, plus an assortment of tables, bureaus, bookcases and boxes. So you can see what a lifetime of pleasure my love of liners has meant.

Now, thanks to the *Fifty Famous Liners* volumes, I am fulfilling the dream of my youth and really putting to use these treasures gathered over nearly 70 years of collecting. Let's hope there will be a demand for many more books in this series. I look forward to covering 500 liners: there have been some 8,000 built, and a series of ten books like this is easily possible! For me it would be a most gratifying experience. Please help me by suggesting more favourite liners for inclusion in forthcoming volumes.

Frank O. Braynard
Sea Cliff, New York

The Empress of Scotland, *completely restored after wartime service, with the CPR house-flag on her three perfectly proportioned stacks.*

Introduction II

What a thoroughly wonderful, exciting, but sometimes excruciating opportunity—to select 50 liners for a second volume on these famed ships. Frank Braynard and I have received a good number of letters since volume one, suggesting several hundred different entries for this sequel. Every one of them had a right to be included. But, there is—once again—a limit to just 50. We tried for a diverse, varied lot.

As always, Frank is a totally jovial, supportive and inspirational co-author. He has been my single greatest spark (and help) with other books. Working with him (and making good use of his enormous and legendary collection) is more than half the fun. Once again, we pored over news clips and vintage brochures, files of photographs and then, when stumped, we turned to other friendly collectors. We are very grateful for their most important help. A most unique dimension to this work and the previous volume has been, of course, Frank's superb sketches. As the world's master maritime historian, he has a special interest and fascination for each of the ships and these are reflected in his drawings.

Many of these grand ladies have a distinct recollection for me as well. For example, I was aboard the former *Malolo*, then named *Queen Frederica*, as she raced to Bermuda, belching the thickest, blackest smoke from her one 'working stack.' She was 40 years old at the time. My very first cruise was aboard the beautiful *Hanseatic*, the one-time *Empress of Japan*, and I particularly recall the hotel-style revolving doors that connected the outdoor promenades to the indoor foyers. The *Caronia*, in her distinct shades of green, always had a prominence, even when berthed among ten or so other liners along New York's 'Luxury Liner Row.' There are so many other flash thoughts and glimpses: the quartet of knobs (a set for fresh water and a pair for saltwater) for the tubs on the *Queen of Bermuda*; the enormity of the Lanai Suites on the former *Lurline*; the precision German service aboard the *Bremen*, ex-*Pasteur*; the towering majesty of the *Oriana*; the eye-catching beauty of the historic counter stern of the *Independence*. All of these ships are special, indeed *Fifty Famous Liners*.

William H. Miller
Jersey City, New Jersey

FIFTY
FAMOUS LINERS 2

Savannah

The *Savannah* of 1819 was the first vessel ever to cross any ocean using steam. Her 29-day voyage was made from Savannah, Georgia, to Liverpool. During the crossing she used her steam engine on 12 different days to test it in all kinds of wind and weather. Because of her small size she could carry only 25 cords of wood and 75 tons of coal. On the other legs of her voyage to St Petersburg she used her engines considerably more because her fuel could be replenished at ports on the way.

This is the achievement of the steamship *Savannah*, known in her day as 'the elegant steam ship' because of her elaborate passenger accommodation. Everyone knew her as a steamship. The public and the press called her a steamship. Suppliers of equipment for her billed it 'to the account of the steamship *Savannah*.' Even before her launching she was described as a steamship. These assertions may sound unnecessary, but, believe it or not, there are still writers who tend to underrate this historic little vessel and give credit to other, much later crossings by other steamships. Some historians seem to enjoy demeaning her, calling the *Savannah* an auxiliary steamship because she used sails. The public does not remember that sails were used on steamships right up through the end of the 19th century. In fact the specifications for the great liner *Vaterland*, completed in 1914, spelled out that her masts were 'not to be fitted for sails'. So much for the controversy, and now a few words about the *Savannah*'s remarkable master, chief engineer and promoter— Captain Moses Rogers.

Captain Rogers was born in 1779. He was a sixth generation American and early developed a love of ships and the sea. In 1807 he helped Robert Fulton with his steamboat known to most people as the *Clermont*. Two years later he took the *Phoenix*, Colonel John Stevens' rival to the *Clermont*, down to Philadelphia to establish a passenger service on the Delaware River. Over the next decade he had many other steamers under his command, the last of which was on a service terminating at the fast growing Georgian city of Savannah. Here he was fortunate in meeting Stephen Vail, steam engine specialist. He also got to know the 'merchant

prince' of Savannah, William Scarbrough. These three men laid the groundwork for the building of the *Savannah*. Their Savannah Steam Ship Company was formed 'for the laudable and meritorious experiment ... to attach either as auxiliary or principal, the propulsion of steam to sea vessels, for the purpose of navigating the Atlantic and other oceans.'

The *Savannah* was laid down as a coastwise sailing packet at the Crockett and Fickett yard on the East River, New York. She was acquired by Rogers at least several months before her launching in August 1818. A pre-launching news story published in the *Liverpool Advertiser* could hardly believe what it had learned from sources in New York. It ran a story about the new vessel on August 17 1818, six days before the launching: 'It is stated in an American paper that a ship of about 375 tons was ready to be launched from one of their shipyards which is actually to be fitted up with a steam engine and apparatus as a steam packet for crossing the Atlantic.' A story about the steamship *Savannah* noting that she was being built to cross 'the Western ocean' was also carried in *The Times*, of London.

Even before her launching the *Savannah* was referred to as 'the elegant steam ship' because of the great excitement over her luxurious passenger accommodations. She would have full-length mirrors, rosewood panelling, tufted couches in a Ladies' Lounge and private 'state rooms' for 32 passengers. The author (FOB) chose 'the elegant steam ship' as the sub-title for his book about the *Savannah*, published in 1963 by the University of Georgia Press and now out of print.

Great care and the best brains in New York went into the building of her power plant. She would have twin boilers built by Daniel Dod. Her steam cylinder was built by James P. Allaire at his Speedwell Iron Works in New Jersey. Years later this same cylinder would be put on exhibition at the famed Crystal Palace and would be lost forever in the great fire that destroyed that fabled structure. The *Savannah*'s engine boasted all of 90 horsepower. She would have a tall smokestack with a swivelled top segment which could be

The elegant steamship Savannah—*a model of the historic ship made for The Mariners' Museum, Newport News, Virginia, USA* (courtesy of The Mariners' Museum).

turned this way or that to direct the smoke and sparks away from the sails. Her twin paddle wheels would be linked together with chains so they could be collapsed and brought on deck in very bad weather. Her crew came to be very adept at this and could do it in 20 minutes.

In March 1819, the elegant steamship left New York for Savannah. The log, preserved in the Smithsonian Institution in Washington, DC, indicates that seamen were as superstitious then as now. It began by noting that 'the steam ship was bound toward Savannah.' To have said 'to' Savannah would have been presuming too much on good fortune—bad luck in other words.

Captain Rogers was hailed as a hero when he reached Savannah and advertisements were put into the local newspapers announcing a voyage to Europe. But, sad to say, no cargo and no passengers were forthcoming. The idea of sailing on a ship with a fire in her was just too much in that day. It was decided that a great publicity effort must be made to show that the ship was safe. She was sent up to Charleston with the hope that she might bring President Monroe down to Savannah since he was making a good will tour of the young nation. The President, however, was too wise a politician to leave the famed South Carolina port on a Georgian ship. Rivalry between the two states was keen. He came by coach and Captain Rogers brought his *Savannah* back empty. However, the President did agree to make a one-day excursion trip down the Savannah River on the revolutionary new ship. He brought with him Secretary of War,

John C. Calhoun, five Generals, two judges and other dignitaries.

Sails were 'partly used,' one report of the trip stated, 'although the paddle wheels were the essential powers that forced her through the water—and with the utmost majesty she proceeded down the sound.' Monroe was said to have promised to purchase the steamship for use as a cruiser off Cuba. Captain Rogers was determined, however, to prove her on a transatlantic crossing. More advertisements were published but still no passengers signed up. Although the principal stockholders of the Savannah Steam Ship Co were cotton merchants, none were bold enough to entrust even one bale to the ship. Company President Scarbrough tried to persuade his wife to go on the trip with him and she ended up by keeping him from going. The brave little vessel sailed empty on May 22, a day now observed in the United States as National Maritime Day.

Off Liverpool a revenue cutter spotted the *Savannah* with a column of smoke pouring from her bent smokestack. Naturally the cutter's captain assumed that the ship was on fire and went to her aid. This was exactly what Captain Rogers hoped would happen, and he sped off with paddle wheels churning in a direction against the wind, leaving the fast sailing craft astern. It created a sensation but the one month stay at Liverpool was not entirely a happy one, as the authorities were highly suspicious of the *Savannah*. Somehow the rumour had gone around that she had come over to rescue Napoleon from St Helena.

On her transatlantic crossing the *Savannah* had used her steam engines 16 per cent of the time, not counting the period she lay at anchor at the ocean outlet of the Savannah River. On her run from Liverpool to Copenhagen she used steam considerably more. Between Copenhagen and Stockholm she used her paddles 28 per cent of the time. On her last leg, from Stockholm to St Petersburg she would use the power plant just under 30 per cent of the time.

A heart-warming event took place in Stockholm. The *Savannah* got a passenger, two in fact! They were famed British General, Lord Lynedoch and his nephew Robert Graham. The British Lord left a diary of the voyage describing how enthusiastic he was about the ship's engines and Captain

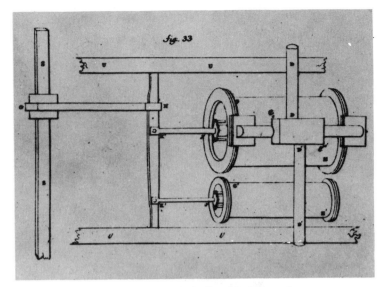

Above *This diagram of the inclined cylinder of the* Savannah *was drawn by Jean Baptiste Marestier, the French Naval Officer who saw the* Savannah *in Washington. The diagram is reproduced from Marestier's book on American steam vessels which was published in Paris in 1824 (courtesy of C. Bradford Mitchell).*

Below *A miniature of Captain Moses Rogers. On the front a painting on ivory set in red gold, on the back a wisp of Rogers' hair set into the glass (courtesy of Miss Mary Seely).*

STEAM SHIP "SAVANNAH" CAPT. MOSES RODGERS.
THE FIRST STEAMSHIP THAT CROSSED THE ATLANTIC OCEAN

Above Hayward print of Savannah. *This is typical of the inaccurate portrayals of steamships common in the 1850s (courtesy of Alexander Crosby Brown).*

Below Frank Braynard (right) with Lieutenant Commander Myron C. Thomas in the US Navy blimp during the 1958 search for the wreck of Savannah *off Fire Island, New York (courtesy of US Navy).*

Rogers. He said that were he younger he would go to live in America, so impressed was he with the mechanical inventiveness of the ship's Master. Also in Stockholm the King of Sweden offered to buy the *Savannah*, but having recently acquired Norway he was short of ready cash, the story went, and offered to exchange coal for the vessel. Captain Rogers declined, hoping that he would be able to sell the ship to Czar Alexander of Russia, who was known for his fondness for 'nicknacks'.

The Czar did make an offer to Captain Rogers. He tried to persuade him to remain in Russia, promising to give him a monopoly on all steamboating. But Rogers was a family man and determined to head for home. His last hope was President Monroe. The trip back to America included a stop at Arundel, Norway. It is quite likely that the engines were used at times on the return crossing since the *Savannah* had taken on a full supply of wood and coal in Russia.

President Monroe did not buy the vessel and, as a last resort, an advertisement was placed in a Washington paper saying that for $300 her engines could be removed and then she 'would be just as good as any other ship'. This is just what happened and the vessel was used for a brief period as a sailing packet between Savannah and New York. She was lost off Fire Island, New York on November 5 1821. Ten days later, never having heard of the ship's loss, Captain Rogers died of malaria at Georgetown, South Carolina. He had been serving on a steamer sailing up and down the Pee Dee River. He was buried without even a tombstone in Cheraw, South Carolina, a sad ending for such a far-sighted and able seaman.

Gross tonnage: 319
Length overall: 151 feet
Length between perpendiculars (bp): 99 feet
Width: 25 feet 10 inches
Machinery: One cylinder, inclined
Speed: 5 knots without sail
Capacity: 32 passengers
Built: Crocket & Fickett, New York, 1819
Demise: Grounded 1821 off Fire Island

Sirius

Directly under her long, traditional bowsprit was a handsomely-carved figure of a dog. He held between his paws the carving of a star. It was the dog star 'Sirius' and the ship was named *Sirius*. She would be a ship of many honours, a very special ship. The contemporary authority on early paddle steamers, H. Philip Spratt, of the Science Museum, London, states that without question she was the first vessel to cross the Atlantic under sustained steam power. She used sails as well, as all steamers did for many years, but she was the first steamship to use the surface condenser and was therefore able to have fresh water in her boilers instead of salt. This meant she did not have to stop repeatedly to let her engines cool and permit her engineers to go into her boilers and chop out the caked salt—a tremendous technological advance. But an even greater honour belongs to *Sirius*. Although built as a coastwise packet, she was selected to race Isambard Kingdom Brunel's new monster steamship, the *Great Western*, across the Atlantic to New York. What's more, she won! She is by all rights the first to hold the coveted Blue Riband—emblem of speed supremacy on the Atlantic. The year was 1838.

Only three years before this historic first Atlantic race by steamships, a Dr Lardner, lecturing at Liverpool, had ridiculed the claims being made that steamships would be built to cross the Western Ocean. His talk was revived by the *Liverpool Albion* as follows: 'As to the project announced in the newspapers of making the voyage directly from New York to Liverpool, it was, he had no hesitation in saying, perfectly chimerical, and they might as well talk of making a voyage from New York or Liverpool to the moon.'

The *Sirius* was built in 1837 for the St George Steam Packet Co, later to become the City of Cork Steam Packet Co, for service between London and Cork. She was constructed by Messrs Robert Menzies and Son, at Leith, Scotland. Her engines were of the side-lever type and could produce 320 nominal horsepower. They were built by Messrs Thomas Wingate and Co, of Whiteinch, near Glasgow. They had two cylinders of 60 inch diameter with a 6 foot stroke. The *Sirius* had a steam pressure of 5 lb per square inch. Her boilers consumed about 24 tons of coal a day. Her paddle wheels were 24 feet in diameter and could make 15 revolutions per minute at a speed of 9 knots.

Just how many passengers she could accommodate is not known, but an advertisement published in New York said this: 'This vessel has superior accommodations and is fitted with separate cabins for the accommodation of families, to which every possible attention will be given.' There were three classes of passengers carried, the advertisement noted. The price for passage in the cabin or top class was $140 and it included 'provisions, wines etc'. Second cabins cost $80 each,

and, while provisions were included, wines were not. Steerage passengers were also carried. The *Sirius* had a crew of 35 officers and men.

Five steamships had crossed the Atlantic between the time of the *Savannah* and the *Sirius*. They were the *Rising Star, Caroline, Curacao, Rhadamanthus* and *Royal William*. None of these repeated their voyages, but gradually the certainty that steam would come to the Atlantic came to be accepted. Famed railroad and bridge genius Brunel was also interested in the subject in the early 1830s. By 1836 the British Queen Steam Navigation Co was organised with the widely-publicised purpose of building a ship to be called the *British Queen* which would once and for all establish a steamship service linking the old world with the new. The company's shares were offered and quickly bought up by the public. In the stock proposal it was set forth that a 15-day passage was anticipated between London, Liverpool and New York. The keel of the *British Queen* was laid, but work did not progress as rapidly as had been hoped. The owners finally decided they had to charter another ship or all the honours would be taken by Brunel's *Great Western*. They picked *Sirius*.

She was a handsome craft. The surface condenser was not the only example of fresh, new thinking in her design. She only had two masts, a striking departure from the traditional three-mast profile of all major vessels of the day. A splendid model of the *Sirius* is in the Science Museum. It shows that her bow was of fine design. While her hull had the same beam as the *Savannah*, her paddle wheel boxes made her overall width 11 feet greater than the pioneer American craft. She was a third longer. She had a raised poop with skylights to the saloon below. Two lifeboats hung from davits on either side aft. Her steering wheel was in the traditional place at the stern. Her single, very tall smokestack was black at the top and supported by guy wires all around. Five bands gave the stack strength and a steam pipe rising just forward of the funnel gave added strength to it. A circular decoration was painted on the upper part of the paddle box and double bands of white paint added a decorative touch to the hull. A contemporary lithograph in the Stokes Collection of the New York Public Library offers a fine rendering of what she looked like. Another excellent picture of her was published in 1910 in H. R. A. Fletcher's *Steamships and Their Story*. The *Sirius* had foresails. Her foremast was fitted for three square sails and one large fore-and-aft sail. Her mainmast supported another large fore-and-aft sail. The Fletcher picture has a shield and other decorative designs on her paddle box. She had a row of ports aft and protruding windows with some gilded scroll work at the far aft and across the stern. The dog figurehead is clearly shown in both the Stokes and the Fletcher pictures.

The *Sirius* sailed from Blackwall, London, on March 28 1838. She was under the command of Lieutenant R. Roberts, a 35-year-old Royal Navy officer hired especially for the Atlantic crossing. He would soon prove his value to the British and American Steam Navigation Co, the new name of the original *British Queen* company. A dramatic moment took place on the passage down the Thames. Off Gravesend the *Sirius* overtook the *Great Western*, undergoing her trials. Apparently the two steamships sailed side by side for a time, and noted author Frank Bowen wrote that the smaller craft 'lengthened the distance between them to a mile'. Just astern was the American Line sailing packet *Quebec*, mastered by Captain Herbert, and there were many wagers passed aboard her. Most old salts bet that the sailing craft would arrive in New York first. The *Sirius* arrived at Cork and picked up passengers. She had a total of 40 aboard on the trip. She also loaded 450 more tons of coal and additional stores. Bowen noted that 'she certainly would not have been allowed to sail nowadays and must inevitably have foundered had she met bad weather'. It was April 4 when she departed and the *Great Western*, which had left London March 31, was racing to get ready to sail as well.

Above right Broadside view of Sirius *from a lithograph in the Stokes Collection, New York Public Library. The* Sirius *is arriving in New York, commencing regular steamship service between the Old World and the New. Note the 1838 American flag at her foremast.*
Right Sirius *under sail, a drawing used in H. R. A. Fletcher's* Steamships and their story, *published in 1910.*

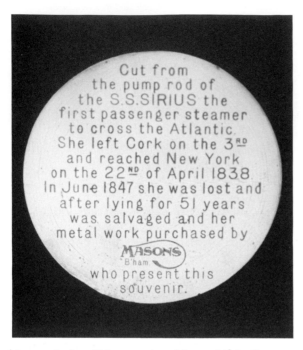

A souvenir from Sirius—*a piece of brass of 3½ in diameter. It was part of the ship's pump rod and was salvaged in 1898 (Wayne G. La Poe collection).*

The voyage started badly. There were strong head winds and the crew became mutinous, protesting that it was madness to proceed in so small a vessel. Like Columbus before him, Lieutenant Roberts got them back under control and the voyage continued. News about the projected voyages of the *Sirius* and the *Great Western* had gone on ahead to New York and their arrival was anticipated with much interest. Crowds assembled at the Battery each day and 'gazed wistfully in the direction of the Narrows,' wrote A. Fraser-Macdonald in his *Our Ocean Railways*. He continued: 'For several days their vigilance was unrewarded, but at last the enthusiastic watchers saw what appeared to be a streak of smoke on the horizon. At first it was scarcely perceptible. The faint sign, however, became steadily and rapidly intensified, and at length developed into the hull of a steamship, the revolving wheels of which were soon discernable. Then the cry of "Here she is!" was heard. ... The news now spread quickly

through the city and thousands hastened to the Battery in order to welcome the arrival of the expected nautical novelty.'

The *Sirius* reached New York on April 22, 18 days and 10 hours out of Cork. Her average speed was 6.7 knots. She had beaten the *Great Western* and all New York turned out to welcome her. The *Herald* for April 24 had this to say: 'Nothing is talked of but about the *Sirius*. She is the first steam vessel that has arrived here from England, and a glorious boat she is. Every merchant in New York went on board her yesterday. Lieutenant Roberts is the first man that ever navigated a steamship from Europe to America.' How fast the *Savannah* had been forgotten.

When she departed May 1 for her return passage thousands were assembled on the wharfs to cheer her. The Battery saluted her with 17 guns, a mark of respect seldom, or perhaps never before shown to any merchant vessel, according to Philip Spratt. She made one more transatlantic crossing and then was returned to her cross-Channel services. In January 1847, she ran onto a reef off Ballycotton Bay, near Cork, and became a total loss. Portions of her were raised 51 years later. Again in 1984, pieces of her engine framework, pump and much of her engine were located and brought up. Her fame is well established and she will live on in maritime history.

As a quaint postscript with the past the co-author Braynard's files contained a yellowed 1922 newspaper clipping. It described how the Reverend Vincent F. Ransome had been helped up into the pulpit of St Paul's Church, Weymouth, in January of that year. Although he was 90 years old at that point, it was said that his sermon was given in a voice 'still strong and clear'. 84 years before, as a boy of six, young Ransome had been one of the passengers on the historic first crossing of the *Sirius*.

Gross tonnage: 703
Length overall: 208 feet
Width: 25.8 feet
Machinery: Side-lever steam
Speed: 9 knots
Capacity: 40 plus
Built: Messrs Robert Menzies, Leith, 1837
Demise: Wrecked off Cork, 1847

Great Western

Among the great crowd watching the launching was a young lad from Canada, Henry Fry, later to become one of the best known chroniclers of steamships and author of the book *History of North Atlantic Steam Navigation*. He never forgot the moment, for he knew that history was being made. He was witnessing the birth of the first British steamship specifically built for transatlantic service—the *Great Western*. She was the first of three extraordinary steam vessels designed by that remarkable man famed for so many things—Isambard Kingdom Brunel. He was only 31 when she was launched. The *Great Western* was built for the Great Western Steamship Co by William Patterson at Bristol. The swift progress of her construction is what had led the rival British and American Steamship Co to charter *Sirius* to make their first Atlantic passage. Thus not only was regular transatlantic steamship service begun but the custom of racing for what became known as the Blue Riband of the Atlantic was inaugurated. Through some error the Hales Trophy, now owned by the American Merchant Marine Museum, Kings Point, New York, lists on its gilded base the *Great Western* as the first holder of the Blue Riband, whereas it was the *Sirius* which won that dramatic first race across the Atlantic.

Nevertheless the *Great Western* was an amazing vessel, a great step forward in naval architecture and a highly-successful steamship. After her there was no let down in the frantic race for bigger, faster, more luxurious liners on what would soon be recognised as the world's premier liner route.

Over twice as long as the *Savannah* and one third wider, the *Great Western* was designed by Brunel to have great longitudinal strength. Her ribs were of oak, and as thick as 'ships of the line'. They were bolted in pairs, and at the ship's bottom were reinforced with iron bolts, according to Henry Fry. Both the *Great Western* and the *British Queen*, her rival, were looked upon as wonderful achievements of British engineering, skill and enterprise'. The Brunel design called for four masts, all rigged with fore-and-aft sail. The foremast also had square sails. The paddle boxes were made to look much larger than in other steamers by a bulwark that stretched fore and aft far beyond the wheel area, forming a sheltered amidships deck that must have been quite appealing to her passengers. Two ovals formed the decoration on the outer side of the paddle boxes. A decidedly ornate gilded arrangement of carving and scroll work surrounded the windows at the stern. The single stack was shorter and thicker than on *Sirius*, and was supported not only by guy wires but also by two steam pipes, fore and aft. Excellent colour prints of the ship leaving England and New York have survived. The hull was sailed around from Bristol to London where the new ship's engines were installed by Messrs Maudslay, Sons and Field. Steam pressure remained at only 5 lb per square inch but a total of 750 horsepower was provided. Fuel consumption was 30 tons per day and the ship's reputed top speed was 11 knots, two knots greater than the 9 knots of *Sirius*.

A huge leap forward was registered in passenger capacity, with space for 120 in first class, 20 in second and berths for 100 more if necessary. With a crew of 60 this meant that a total of 300 could be carried. The main saloon was the talk of the day,

being 75 feet in length, 21 feet wide and 9 feet high. Joshua Field, whose unpublished manuscript entitled *Glances at Atantic Steam Navigation* is in the Science Museum, wrote in 1841 that the saloon was the largest and most luxurious room in any vessel of the day.

The *Great Western* came very close to disaster on the first leg of her first crossing. Everything had started out well and Brunel's distinguished father, Sir Mark Brunel, was aboard for a short space of time. He was disembarked in a small boat at Chapman Sands. Five miles above the Nore a fire was discovered in the lagging of the ship's boilers. The coal passers were forced to flee to the safety of the deck because of the smoke. The ship was headed in toward shore and beached. So dense was the smoke that it was an hour before the engines could be stopped. The fire was put out and a survey showed only superficial damage to the lagging and the deck. Even more fortunate, the whole event had happened at low tide, and when the tide came in the ship floated free and was able to proceed to Bristol.

Including the time lost by the accident the new ship made the 670-mile voyage from Blackwall, on the Thames, to Bristol in 58½ hours. Her actual steaming time saw her average nearly 13 mph. The wind and weather must have been perfect.

Nevertheless the necessary repairs and other last minute problems delayed the sailings from Bristol of the *Great Western* from the scheduled date of April 7 to April 8. This was enough to make her lose the first Atlantic race by steamships. She did very well on the crossing, however. From noon on the 8th to noon on the 9th she made 240 miles. Her day's runs for the next 14 days were as follows: 213, 206, 231, 218, 218, 241, 243, 185, 169, 206, 183, 192, 198, 230. On the 15th day she steamed 50 more miles in five hours, arriving with an average speed for the trip of 8.8 knots. She had logged 3,125 nautical miles.

A. Fraser-Macdonald in his *Our Ocean Railways*, published in 1893, describes the arrival of the *Great Western* at New York with an unabashed enthusiasm typical of someone writing from the heart: 'Cheer after cheer arose as the gallant ship steamed slowly up alongside of her rival (the *Sirius*), and then, amidst the greatest enthusiasm,

with bells ringing, and men cheering—as only Anglo-Saxons can—and the thunder of cannon, the New Yorkers welcome the elated passengers as they landed from both steamers.' Fraser-Macdonald, like Henry Fry, was another Canadian to whom the study of early steam vessels had been a passion. He remembered seeing the huge letters of the name of the first *Royal William* spread across her paddle-wheel box. He had been taken as a boy in May 1833, to see that ship being fitted with her engines at the St Mary's Foundry, Montreal, Canada.

Henry Fry dug up another significant passage from a New York newspaper commenting on the arrival of the *Great Western*: 'What may be the ultimate fate of this excitement—whether or not the expenses of equipment and fuel will admit of the employment of these vessels in the ordinary packet service—we cannot pretend to form an opinion; but of the entire feasibility of the passage of the Atlantic by steam, as far as regards safety, comfort, and dispatch, even in the roughest and most boisterous weather, the most sceptical must now cease to doubt.'

After being roundly feted in New York the *Great Western* prepared to sail for home on May 7. She took aboard 20,000 letters and 68 cabin passengers, the greatest number ever to be carried across on a single ship at that point, according to Frank Bowen in his book, *A Century of Atlantic Travel.*

Another published report put the imprint of finality on transatlantic travel by steamship at about this time. Writing as if there was nothing at all unusual in what it reported, the May 16 1838 *Lloyd's List* described news that was almost a month old in this fashion: 'The *Sirius* ('s) from Cork, was spoken with 22nd ult. about six hours sail from New York; and the *Great Western* ('s) from Bristol to New York, same day, lat. 40, lon. 67½ by the *Westminster*, Moore, arrived off Plymouth.'

The *Great Western* made 70 transatlantic passages from 1838 to 1844, carrying an average of 80 passengers. In 1839, for example, her longest eastward passage was 15 days and her shortest 12½. Her average eastward passage was 13.9 days. Westward, with the winds much less favourable, she averaged 16.12 days. But the immense advantage of steam over sail can be seen by com-

Above *A Samuel Walters painting of* Great Western *leaving New York with sails furled and entirely under steam power.*
Right *With two paddle wheel tugs in the foreground, the* Great Western *is shown leaving England on her historic first transatlantic crossing* (I. N. Phelps Stokes collection, courtesy of New York Public Library).
Below right *Passing Portishead Point on her first voyage to New York. An old print from a Samuel Walters painting.*

parison with the 33.17-day average westward passage of the Black Ball Line sailing packets.

The heroic *Great Western* was sold in 1847 to the Royal Mail Steam Packet Co Ltd. She was operated successfully for ten more years on their service to the West Indies, with Southampton as her home port. She was finally scrapped in 1857 at Vauxhall.

Gross tonnage: 1,320
Length overall: 236 feet
Width: 35.3 feet
Machinery: Side-lever steam
Speed: 9–11 knots
Capacity: 240
Built: William Patterson, Bristol, 1837
Demise: Scrapped at Vauxhall, 1857

Great Western

Great Britain

The human spirit soars when it comes in contact with great engineering feats that promise good things for mankind. No ship has ever brought a greater soaring of spirits and been more worthy of such excitement than the *Great Britain*. She was with every right considered one of the 'most gigantic achievements of the day,' when on July 19 1839, her keel was laid at Bristol. Even at this point she had already had two earlier names (*City of New York* and *Mammoth*) and one major change in design—from wood to iron.

Before she was finished another major change in plans would see her half-finished paddle-wheel engines abandoned in favour of a single huge propeller. She was the largest ship of her day, the first major Atlantic liner built of iron and the first to use a propeller! What a masterful mind it was that set all this in motion! What a genius was Isambard Kingdom Brunel. And yet even he could not have dreamed that his ship would survive grounding on an exposed and rocky Irish coast, bankruptcy of her owners, complete rebuilding and use on a service different from that intended, conversion into a sailing ship and finally in 1886 abandonment as beyond repair on the Falkland Islands. Yet she did survive all these. All was not lost even after this. More soaring spirits came into the scene and the *Great Britain* was salvaged and brought back on a barge to Bristol, where at this writing she is being slowly but superbly restored to her original grandeur and design.

Books have already been written on this wonderful steamship. Like the *Vasa* she is still with us and will remain one of the great illustrations of man's progress. While life remains on this planet, the *Great Britain* will stand along with the great cathedrals as one of man's truly genuine mechanical achievements. To get some perspective on what she meant a century and a half ago, let us look at her through the eyes of a visitor to Bristol in 1844—the King of Saxony. His name is of no importance, but a book about his impressions was written by his physician, a Dr C. G. Carus, and published in 1846 in London:

'The morning in Bristol was employed in visiting the docks and particularly that greatest of all steamers, the *Great Britain*. . . . The engineer who has directed the building, and who speaks German very tolerably, conducted the king through the whole labyrinth of the interior. . . . The vessel is entirely built of iron, and the material alone, exclusive of the iron-work contained in the machinery, weighs 1,800 tons. . . . She is not impelled through the water like other steamers by paddle wheels at each side but by means of an Archimedean screw introduced in the keel and under the rudder. The force of this fragment of a spiral when acting on water I have long understood, and that this form of wheel, instead of that of paddle wheels was not immediately adopted for steamboats, only proves how difficult it is for the human intellect to seize the easiest and best means

Fifty Famous Liners 2

at once. The iron thread of the screw is to revolve 50 times in the minute, with a diameter of 16 feet, and it is expected that this pressure will be powerful enough to propel the vessel with sufficient speed. She does not, however, entirely depend upon the propeller, but is furnished with six small masts, to which sails can be attached to drive on the colossus in a favourable wind. The internal arrangements are very elegant and comfortable.

'Two decks contain large saloons surrounded by smaller cabins so that several hundred passengers can easily be accommodated; the greatest care has been taken to ensure a good kitchen and every comfort for the passengers: the two steam engines are each of 500 horsepower, and 150 men are to serve as crew, machinists, stokers, etc. So far everything seems to be as it should be. There are only two small points to be mentioned: first, it appears doubtful whether the vessel, when completed, can ever be got out of the narrow dock and along the Avon into the sea; and this appears doubtful even to those who understand the matter; and, secondly, whether a ship of such dimensions is fit for sea-service at all. It is feared, and as it appears not entirely without reason, that if the vessel were to be raised at once under the bows and under the stern by two waves, the weight of the machinery in the centre might possibly break her in two; and it is, indeed, believed that the *President*, though not so large as the *Great Britain*, must have been lost in this manner. At any rate, it would appear necessary to be particularly cautious in the first few trips.'

Dr Carus was not without reason in his first worry. The ship was successfully launched in her specially-built drydock, but when she was finished, a year later, it took an additional six months and much money to widen the entrance to the Floating Harbour so that she could get out. The lock into the Cumberland Basin was 44 feet wide, and the ship's maximum beam was 51 feet. Brunel had planned to float her out at high water and knew that it would be necessary to remove the coping stones around the top edge of the lock. But the installing of her heavy engines had made her sit deeper in the water than even he had anticipated. No doubt it was a most embarrassing dilemma, one that has given cause for many chuckles over the years.

Queen Victoria toured the *Great Britain* when the monster vessel tied up at London in the summer of 1845. As described by the *Illustrated London News*, the Queen and Prince Albert were 'quite amazed at the enormous length of the ship'. The royal couple went down into the engine-room where the Queen was again prompted to comments of wonder. She was interested 'in the immense chain which turns the screw shaft'. After that the tour took them to the after promenade saloon and staterooms. Again there were expressions of astonishment at the vastness of the dining saloon. Her Majesty sat in one of the chairs which had been positioned so as to permit her to see the many mirrors and experience the 'almost boundless' sensation of the cabin's size.

A splendid booklet produced by the SS *Great Britain* Project and for sale in their gift shop provides a good review of several features of the famous ship not so well known as her iron hull and her propeller. Her masts were unique. All but one were hinged on the weather deck, to facilitate the revolutionary wire rope rigging that was used instead of hemp. The rigging could be made taut whatever the weather and would hold the masts at whatever angle was desired. The masts were made with very short topmasts so that most of the sail handling could be done from deck, a feature that permitted a smaller crew than would normally be needed. The hull was made of iron plates riveted to iron frames. The plates were overlapping, like clinker-built wooden vessels. The ship had watertight bulkheads, five athwartships and two longitudinally. They could be sealed with watertight doors, another revolutionary feature that added much to the vessel's safety.

On July 19 1970, the anniversary of her keel laying and of her launching, the still-sturdy hull of *Great Britain* was eased into the same graving dock in which she had been built so long before. It was a successful end to a salvage job of heroic proportions. Prince Philip was aboard and lent the SS *Great Britain* Project his warm support. A letter signed by the Prince is carried on the opening page of the project's 32-page booklet about their efforts. It concludes: 'Bringing this great ship back to Britain was in itself a remarkable achievement and it also proved her basic structural soundness. The next job is to restore her to her former condition.

Every person who visits the vessel is making a useful contribution to this exacting and fascinating work. I wish the Project Committee every success in this ambitious and exciting venture which will provide a living record of a great British engineering triumph by one of history's most original engineers.'

Since that date work on the preservation and gradual restoration of the *Great Britain* has gone forward in the hands of the group responsible for her salvage. Chairman of the project when it got underway was Richard Goold-Adams, an expert on international affairs. The project's naval architect was Ewan Corlett, who had been interested in the *Great Britain* since 1952. The large initial financing had come through the good will of Jack Hayward, to whom the saving of the historic ship became a 'romantic challenge'. In the first 15

months after the ship returned to Bristol more than a quarter of a million visitors toured her, showing that she could be made to support herself. The SS *Great Britain* Project, however, is well aware that more and more funds are necessary to properly restore the interior and maintain this forerunner of all modern liners. (Readers are urged to send donations to the SS *Great Britain* Project. It is registered as a charity, number 262158. Do your bit!)

Gross tonnage: 3,443
Length overall: 322 feet (excluding bowsprit)
Width: 51 feet
Machinery: 4 inclined cylinders
Speed: 10 knots
Capacity: 252
Built: Wm Patterson, Bristol, 1842–44
Demise: Museum ship at Bristol

Launching the Great Britain (courtesy of Oceanic Navigation Research Society).

Above Great Britain *had a triumphant reception in London and was visited by Queen Victoria. Here she is seen leaving Blackwall for her maiden voyage* (courtesy of Oceanic Navigation Research Society).

Above right *Aground off Iceland* (courtesy of Oceanic Navigation Research Society).

Below *After a career as both a steamer and a sailing ship Great Britain was wrecked on the Falkland Islands. This picture shows her lying in Sparrows Cove.*

Below right *The original ship's bell which was retrieved from an outlying sheep station on the Falklands* (courtesy of R. J. Bradbury).

Baltic

The *Baltic* became famous for her sea-green, shell-shaped spittoons! She was the only American steamship to break the Atlantic speed record for one century, doing it exactly 100 years to the month before it was broken again by the SS *United States* in 1952. She lived to see active service on the Union side in the American Civil War. She was an interesting and historic liner.

Edward Knight Collins was in many ways the American Samuel Cunard. He was a man with long experience in maritime affairs when he started his steamship company. His famous Dramatic Line operated transatlantic sailing packets for many years before he turned to steam. He was a man with great ambition and strong character. He fitted into the hurley-burley American scene in the days before the Civil War like hand to glove. His extraordinary successes in the early days of the Collins Line shook the staid British shipping scene to its roots.

But the tides of history were running against him. From the onset the climate in which he operated made Collins entirely dependent upon government subsidies. The vast, open American western frontier not only meant a floodgate of opportunity for labour but virtually ensured high wages and a higher standard of living than had ever been known anywhere before. To expect American seamen to work at wage levels in effect in the old world was unrealistic. With sailing packets, America briefly had the edge over British packet lines because the whole concept of the packet of sailing on a certain day, cargo or not, was pioneered by Americans. But the lesson that the future was in steam shown by the *Savannah* of 1819 was rejected by American shipowners. One New York shipping leader, whose unusual name makes him hard to forget—Preserved Fish—had ordered six steam vessels at the time of the *Savannah*. When he saw her poor reception by shippers and the travelling public he cancelled the order and built six sailing packets. He was the founder of the highly successful Swallow Tail Line.

Two major American transatlantic steamship lines preceeded the Collins Line. They were the Bremen Line and the Havre Line, but neither of them had the glamour of the Collins effort. Neither of these initial American efforts competed directly with Cunard, which was very well established on the Atlantic when Collins took up the challenge. His first four liners were named *Atlantic*, *Pacific*, *Arctic* and *Baltic*. The first two were built in 1849 and the latter pair the next year. All four were virtually identical. These and the other early American Atlantic steamships were the first Atlantic liners to have plum stems, a style change that was to be universally adopted by all ship designers not only on the Atlantic but on every ocean. The return of the 'clipper bow' style would not happen until the innovative *Normandie* brought it back in 1932. The elimination of the traditional bowsprit must have made these early American steamships seem shockingly new and may well have contributed to their fame. Their sterns were also different. They were rounded instead of square.

The new Collins ships boasted many other features which became the talk of the trade such as staterooms with double beds for newly-married couples. There was a barbershop on each new Collins Line ship, with glass cases containing perfume and featuring a well-stuffed barber chair with an inclined back. Rose, satin and olive woods were used in the two largest saloons. Some of the tables were of 'beautifully variegated marble' with metal supports. Rich carpets and seat covers were everywhere. The public rooms had painted glass windows. Mirrors were used in abundance. Each of the 150 staterooms had a novel bell system with a bell-rope near each berth communicating with the new 'Annunciator', a patented machine consisting of a circular plate covered with numbers corresponding to the staterooms.

The immediate success of the Collins ships brought loud huzzahs from the American public. Two Collins ships were the first to cross the Atlantic in under ten days. Between January and November 1852 the Collins vessels carried 4,306 passengers compared to 2,969 carried by Cunarders. The competition from America also brought freight rates down from £7 per ton to £4. These were later to be seen as the halcyon days of

American steam on the oceans of the world. Never before, or never afterward, would the American flag fly so proudly.

The construction of the four Collins liners was made possible by a large subsidy from Congress, substantially increased after early operating experience showed that costs were higher than anticipated. The situation was summarised by Cunard Director Charles McIver in a letter to Samuel Cunard: 'The Collins Company are pretty much in the situation of finding that breaking our windows with sovereigns, though very fine fun, is too costly to keep up'.

While they were not as large as the *Great Britain*, the four Collins Line steamships were the largest in regular service on the Atlantic. They also carried considerably more passengers than their Cunard competitors. In addition they had substantially larger crews, 140 persons compared with 89 for Cunard's *Britannia*. Their boilers consumed 87 tons of coal per day to give them the speeds that made them famous. This was in contrast to only 37 tons a day for the much slower *Britannia*. Cunard built a new vessel to compete with Collins and named her *Asia*. To her owners' disappointment she consumed about 100 tons of coal a day but could not equal the American quartet in speed.

Many other features in addition to speed and luxury distinguished the four Collins ships. They had steam heated staterooms and their lifeboats were made of galvanised iron—the beginning of the end for wooden boats. They could accommodate 1,000 tons of coal in their bunkers. Their tall single smokestacks were black with a red band at the top, and their black wooden hulls had a deep red band around them.

Much has been made by maritime historians of the fact that two of the four new Collins Line steamships were lost, but this sad fact was not at all unusual in that day. Many lines were subject to such disasters and remained in the competitive picture, building replacements as soon as the losses happened. This could not happen with Collins, because of his almost total dependence on Congressional subsidies. The weak link in the whole Collins picture was this fact. Even when the first subsidy was being debated, Congressmen and Senators from the Southern states were hesitant about building a fleet of fast vessels that could be used as troopships against them should they ever leave the Union. By 1858 when a renewal of the ten-year subsidy was called for, this opposition was rampant. The legislation was killed. Outside political influences and the growth of the West thus put an early end to the strong effort made on the Atlantic by Collins. So final was this end that it was not until 1895 that two more major liners were built in an American yard for service under the Stars and Stripes on the North Atlantic.

The twin disasters that struck Collins took place in 1854 and 1856. The first was on September 27 when the *Arctic*, bound for New York with 233 passengers (including 150 in first class) was struck by a small French steamship the *Vesta*. The *Vesta* called for help and a boat was put out from *Arctic* to go to her aid. But, by strange fate, the French ship was built of iron. A gale was blowing and when it was discovered that the *Arctic* was actually sinking, several of her boats were lost due to high seas. Only two boats survived, saving 31 of the passengers and 14 crew. Some 72 men and 4 women had sought brief safety on a large wooden raft built at

the last minute while the ship was sinking. All but one of these were swept into the sea and drowned.

Mrs E. K. Collins and her only son and daughter were among those lost. Still another famous name was headlined in stories about this tragedy. George Washington Rogers, son of Captain Moses Rogers, master of the *Savannah*, was Chief Engineer aboard the *Arctic*. He was lost. Alexander Crosby Brown has written a fine book about the *Arctic*'s sinking entitled *Women and Children Last*.

The *Pacific*, with 45 passengers and a crew of 141, left Liverpool on January 23 1856. Cunard's new *Persia*, their first iron paddle wheeler, was in service and the two palatial steamers left at the same time. The *Persia* struck an iceberg and survived to tell her tale. The *Pacific* was never heard from again.

A new ship was built by Collins and entered service in 1857, the two-stacked *Adriatic*. She would prove to be the last wooden paddle steamer constructed for the Atlantic. After the 1858 failure of Collins she was sold to the Galway Line. The *Atlantic*, first of the four Collins steamers, and the *Baltic*, fastest of the four, were laid up after the failure and eventually sold to the US Navy for service in the US Civil War. They were used briefly after the conflict by the North American Lloyd but this company did not last very long. The *Baltic* was converted into a sailing ship and eventually scrapped in 1880—a long and somewhat chequered life for a fine ship.

Gross tonnage: 2,860
Length overall: 300 feet
Width: 45 feet
Machinery: Side-lever steam
Speed: 11.75 knots
Capacity: 250
Built: W. H. Brown, New York, 1850
Demise: Scrapped in Boston, 1880

Left *The* Atlantic, *one of Baltic's sister ships, at her New York pier. From the book* Rollo's Tour on the Atlantic, *written in 1853 and published in 1883.*

Below *The pilot on the* Atlantic, *atop the starboard paddle box. Another illustration from* Rollo's Tour on the Atlantic.

THE STEAMER AT THE WHARF.

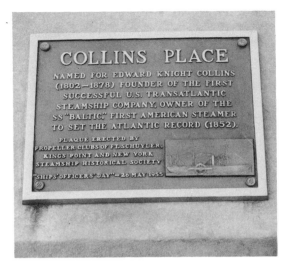

SPEAKING A COLLINS STEAMER.

Above *A bronze plaque honouring E. K. Collins and the* Baltic *at the US Merchant Marine Academy. Kings Point, New York (courtesy of US Merchant Marine Academy).*

Above right *'Speaking a Collins Steamer.' A print carried in the March 10 1855 issue of* Ballou's Pictorial Drawing Room Companion.

Right *The Collins Line speed queen* Baltic—*a contemporary print by N. Currier.*

Below *An excellent painting of the* Baltic *from the Whiteball Club, 17 Battery Place, New York.*

Scotia

Few ocean liners have ever seemed so perfect in outline and style as the sleek, the graceful, the handsome Cunarder *Scotia*, completed in 1862. Perhaps since she represented the end of an era, she approached perfection because her designers had the benefit of all the earlier design errors. Possibly her naval architects, sensing that there would be no more paddle wheelers after her, went all out to design the ship of beauty, the ideally-proportioned liner. Philip Spratt called her 'the last and finest paddle-driven vessel of the Cunard Steamship Co'. Henry Fry was even more expansive, describing the *Scotia* as 'the finest, fastest and strongest ship of her day'. Her lines were so clean and uncluttered and her proportions so good that she actually looked smaller than she really was. The author (FOB) is preparing a book on the Cunard paddle steamers and will end this study with the *Scotia*.

A beautifully-shaped, somewhat more delicate and refined bowsprit rose at a very modest angle with a figurehead below it at *Scotia*'s stem. Two tall masts hinted at the standard silhouette of all future steamships. The masts were unusual in that they combined three masts in one—the mast proper, the top-mast and an upper top-mast. The masts proper measured 30 inches diameter. Two square yards were fitted on each mast, as were fore-and-aft sail yards. The foredeck swept aft to the gracefully-low paddle boxes and on toward the stern, forming a continuous line bow to stern. The *Scotia*'s after body featured a highly-refined counter design which was to remain standard on Atlantic liners until the development of the cruiser stern just before World War I. Some Atlantic liners would be built with the counter stern like *Scotia*'s as late as 1951—notably the *Independence* and the *Constitution*.

The *Scotia*'s most striking feature were her two tall red and black smokestacks. A steam pipe was afixed aft of the forward stack and a similar pipe was tied in to the forward edge of the second stack. Each funnel had the traditional black top with three thin black bands dividing the red-painted remainder in equal divisions.

The paddle boxes were decorated with four half circles over a mass of gilded filigree. They gave the

ship an overall width of 76.5 feet, compared to her width of hull of 47.8 feet. A narrow, railed walkway, or bridge, connected the tops of the two paddle boxes, but the steering wheel remained at the far stern. It would not be long, however, with ships getting longer and longer, that the wheel would have to be moved forward. The *Scotia* had class and no other design feature showed this better than her tall flagstaff at the very stern. It rose at a dramatic rake and was almost as tall as the twin smokestacks. A fine model of the *Scotia* at the Science Museum, London, shows seven lifeboats fitted on deck, aft of the forward stack. Just forward of this stack was a tall air funnel.

The *Scotia*'s hull was divided into seven watertight bulkheads, port to starboard. She had a double bottom and lengthwise her hull was divided into four compartments. There were five keelsons in her flat bottom to give longitudinal strength. Her bow was framed diagonally for the danger of collision at sea with icebergs or other ships was all too common.

Launched on June 25 1861, the *Scotia* did not make her maiden voyage until 1862. She broke all records on her return passage with a time of 8 days, 3 hours. She held the Blue Riband from 1862 to 1867, a long time in that day of rapid steamship evolution. She averaged 13½ knots in service. On her trials she was said to have made 16½ knots. Her 975 horsepower engine burned about 180 tons of coal per day. She had a capacity of 1,800 tons. She used her sails as well as her power plant in

A superb painting of Scotia *by Samuel Walters, with the US flag at her foremast she is clearly en route to New York. A sailing packet may be made out to the stern in the distance.*

regular service, as did all steamships in that day. Her paddle wheels were 40 feet in diameter, the largest on the Atlantic except for the huge *Great Eastern*, built three years before.

The regularity and steadiness of the *Scotia* won her a fine reputation among travellers. During one terrible storm she met Brunel's huge *Great Eastern* at sea. The monster ship was nearly six times larger in tonnage than the Cunard flyer and had been banged about terribly by the storm. Her two oversized paddle wheels had both been smashed, her rudder had been broken and some passengers had been injured by flying debris. To make matters more horrible, one of the cows from the ship's cowhouse, had been flung right through a skylight and into the main saloon. While all this was happening, the *Scotia* hove into sight, from New York. According to a *Great Eastern* passenger, writing some time later, the famous Cunarder looked stately and magnificent, 'and as she gracefully rode over the big seas without any effort, simply playing with them, she told us what design, knowledge and equipment could do'.

Perhaps the most important thing about the *Scotia* was that she served as a yardstick to finally convince Cunard management that the screw propeller was superior to the paddle wheel. Cunard built the iron screw *China* the same year that they introduced the *Scotia*. The comparisons all favoured the screw vessel. Their normal speed at sea was about the same, 14 knots, but the *China* did it with only 2,250 horsepower and with a consumption of 82 tons of coal a day. The *Scotia*, which was of 3,871 tons, had to produce 4,900

horsepower to make this same speed, and used 164 tons of coal per day to do it. The *Scotia* held a clear lead in cargo capacity, being able to carry 1,400 tons compared to the 1,050 tons the *China* could carry. But the much smaller area needed for the *China*'s engines allowed her to carry 160 in first and 771 in third class, compared to the 300 first class carried by *Scotia*.

The *Scotia* was built by Robert Napier & Sons, of Glasgow, who had built the slightly smaller *Persia* six years before, another Cunard beauty and their first iron steamship. The public loved both these handsome ships. The *Scotia* served a remarkable 13 years under the golden lion house-flag of Cunard. Laid up in 1875, the gallant lady, already old in point of design, was sold in 1879 to the Telegraph Construction and Maintenance Co, for use as a cable laying ship. She was rebuilt, with her huge paddle wheels being removed and a new twin-screw drive installed. She got new engines in the process.

She was still laying cables 18 years later when a tremendous explosion at sea blew her bow off. Her forward collision bulkhead was destroyed but she survived. She was rebuilt and put back into service as a cable layer, lasting until 1904. In that year the historic ship was wrecked off Guam where another and equally famous Cunarder would be wrecked seven decades later—the lovely *Caronia*. The *Scotia*'s 43-year life was something of a record for ships of that period. She deserves to be remembered.

Gross tonnage: 3,871
Length overall: 400 feet
Width: 47.8 feet
Machinery: Side-lever steam
Speed: 13.5 knots
Capacity: 300
Built: Robert Napier & Sons, Glasgow, 1862
Demise: Wrecked off Guam, Pacific, 1904

Above *An engraving, probably copied from Walters' painting, showing* Scotia *approaching America. For some reason the stacks are shown as being shorter than in the painting, probably an error.* **Below** *A paddle wheel tender going out to meet* Scotia *off Queenstown as the Cunarder pauses to drop mail.*

St Louis

A lad of 18 leaned over the rail and looked down at the bald head of President Grover Cleveland. At least 50,000 Americans were on hand that November day in 1884 at the Cramp Yard in Philadelphia to watch the launch of the greatest American liner of her era, the first really fast, really first class liner ordered for American flag service on the North Atlantic since the last Collins liner *Adriatic*. Mrs Cleveland christened the new ship. The boy, who later went on to become one of his country's most famous ship captains, was Herbert Hartley. The ship being launched was the *St Louis*, who with her sister, the *St Paul*, was being built by special arrangement with the American Congress. The American Line had stunned the shipping world by buying two of the Atlantic's most famous vessels, the Inman Line's record breakers *City of Paris* and *City of New York*. The sale and transfer from British to American flag was conditional upon American Line's promise to build, in the United States, two even larger liners. The *St Louis*, always the more fortunate of the two, would do heroic service in two wars. She did much to restore American maritime prestige on the Atlantic, although the Blue Riband eluded her. She was fast, very fast for her day, but could not break the record. When new, she was one of the world's largest liners with a gross tonnage of 11,629. If her tonnage had been measured by British/European standards it would have been around 15,000 gross. American tonnage measurement then, as at this writing, did not include the cubic measurement of spaces in the superstructure.

Although at the time of the *St Louis* there were no other American liners on the North Atlantic, there was a strong and healthy coastal shipping industry. Sea routes between US ports were protected from competition from abroad and a number of well-established lines ran large fleets of small and medium sized liners. The *St Louis* and *St Paul* were much like the most modern of these, only larger and somewhat more elegant. They were 554 feet overall, twin screw vessels and each could make 20 knots. Their outline was simplicity in itself, with a straight prow and full counter stern. Two masts, not rigged for sail, and two tall smokestacks, widely spaced, gave them a graceful and sturdy look.

They were in sharp contrast to the Inman Line pair that they joined to establish the American Line's service between New York and Southampton. The former British-flag vessels had been strikingly fine looking craft with clipper bows, bowsprits, three masts and three closely-spaced smokestacks. The middle stack was removed when they came under the American flag to make them look more like their American running mates. This change spoiled their design completely. As originally built the *St Louis* had heavy cowls on her stacks. The *St Paul* never had them and they were removed from her sister after six months of service.

The *St Louis* was the heroine in one of the Atlantic's most famous rescues in the worst of the winter of 1898. It was February 5 and the liner was two days out of Southampton, about 500 miles west of the Scilly Islands. Shortly after 1am the sound of distant cannon had been heard and rocket flashes were seen against a dark horizon. Captain William G. Randle, on the bridge of the *St Louis*, turned his ship toward the distress signals and soon saw a single-stacked passenger liner, down by the stern and wallowing in high seas. She was the Holland America Line's *Veendam* and she had sailed from Rotterdam two days earlier with 212 aboard,

St Louis

including 118 Russian, German and Polish immigrants. There were nine in cabin class. The evening of February 4 had seen the beginning of the end for the little vessel. A pounding crash felt throughout the ship was the signal of disaster. Water began pouring into a huge hole in the stern where the propeller had been. The ship had struck something, perhaps a submerged derelict, no one will ever know, and every man aboard was ordered to operate the hand pumps and work the bucket lines. An auxiliary donkey engine kept the automatic pumps working when the main engines were swamped as the 420-foot ship slowly began to sink.

When the *St Louis* was sighted, the men on the *Veendam* had been bailing for eight hours and were stiff with exhaustion and chill. By then, only one of the Dutch liner's boats was still intact. Despite the terrible seas, the cold and the risk, volunteer boat crews were quickly mustered on the *St Louis* and three of her clinker-built boats were lowered away. The first brought back 90 persons, and the first passenger helped up the side was a tiny baby who promptly seized hold of Captain Randle's beard. All 212 were saved and only minutes afterwards the Dutch ship disappeared below the waves.

War with Spain loomed on the American horizon early in this same year over the question of 'freedom' for Cuba. In April the *St Louis* and the *New York* were ordered to rush for home without picking up any passengers or cargo. They sped together back across the Atlantic and with two other American Line express steamers were pressed into immediate US Navy service. The two newer ships retained their own names but the *New York* became the *Harvard* and the *Paris* became the *Yale*.

The *St Louis* sailed April 30 1898 with 27 officers and 350 naval ratings for war duty. Her assignment was to search out the Spanish fleet and destroy all enemy communications. Early in May she severed the cable linking the Virgin Islands and Puerto Rico. On May 16 she was under fire off Santiago de Cuba. She was grappling for a cable, steaming back and forth across the harbour and getting closer and closer to the forts on shore. One of the ship's officers told the story like this:

'About noon when the *St Louis* had reached a position about a mile from Morro Castle, our grapnel caught the cable. The Spaniards discovered our object and a battery to the east of Morro opened fire with a six-inch gun, the first shot falling about 200 yards short of the *St Louis*. Captain (Caspar F.) Goodrich thereupon ordered the fire to be returned by the two six-pounders mounted on the starboard side, which were the only guns that could be brought to bear on the shore battery. Ensign Payne quickly fired the forward gun and Lieutenant Catlin fired the aft gun, the shots falling thick and fast on shore. Another shell from the six-inch gun of the shore battery whistled over the *St Louis* and struck the water only a few yards beyond us. That was the last shot fired from that gun as the next moment it was destroyed by one of the six-pounders from *St Louis*. Another mortar battery next opened fire from the brow of a hill on Caspas Point some distance back in the bay and the shells began to descend dangerously near. The fusillade was made more irritating because the mortar was far beyond the range of the small guns with which *St Louis* was armed. The guns of our ship were then turned upon the signal station to the east of Morro, where the Spaniards had been signalling. A few shots tore away the roof and the men bolted without waiting to haul down their last signal. The *St Louis* moved out of range of the mortars and then stopped to finish heaving up the grapnel. The cable was brought up and severed.'

The engagement had lasted 52 minutes. All the time the liner had been motionless in the water, broadside to the forts, just a mile and a tenth out from shore. One of the shells from a Santiago fort passed so close overhead that it cut away some of the mast stays. In all the liner's starboard forward gun fired 66 shots. The aft gun fired 106 shots. Three hours after the *St Louis* had left Santiago the Spanish fleet under Admiral Cervera arrived, only to find themselves cut off from communications with Madrid. The *St Louis* then cut cables between Guantanamo and Haiti and between Cienfuegos and the Spanish forces in Cuba. She was ordered back to New York where two additional guns were mounted forward and 3,500 tons of coal taken on, a job done in 24 hours. She was present at the battle of Santiago when Cervera tried to force his way to sea and got his fleet destroyed in the attempt. He was among the many Spaniards taken

Launching the St Louis *in 1894 at Philadelphia.*

aboard the *St Louis* as prisoners. The war ended, and on September 3 1898 the *St Louis* was returned to service as an Atlantic liner.

Between the Spanish–American War and World War I, the *St Louis* continued without new sisters, becoming older and more out of date as each foreign line added newer, faster and much larger vessels. In World War I she was again taken by the US Navy, this time being renamed *Louisville* and assigned to the transport service. She carried 2,000 troops and sometimes even more. Some say she sank a German U-boat but this was never confirmed. On her final wartime crossing many of those aboard died from Spanish influenza. The liner at that time was under the command of Captain Herbert Hartley, who had ridden her down the ways at her launching. The story of her World War I experiences is told in full in a cloth-bound book put out by the US Navy's Transport Corps.

In January 1920, a careless worker's blow torch set fire to the grand old *St Louis* in a Hoboken, New Jersey shipyard. The fire was so serious that the liner had to be scuttled. As she went down she listed against the *Kroonland*, another two-stacked American Line steamer also built by Cramps at Philadelphia. The *St Louis* was declared a total loss

and turned over to the underwriters. She was refloated and the insurance people, heartless souls, made known that she might be good enough 'to use under half boiler power to bring bananas from the West Indies to New York for two or three years'.

In October 1921 major news stories told how 500 men were hard at work reconditioning the *St Louis* so that she could make a round the world cruise to carry exhibits of 300 to 350 American manufacturers 'to the four points of the compass'. She was to be converted to burn oil fuel at the same time. The scheme failed and for three more years the liner lay idle at Hoboken. In the summer of 1924 she was towed by a Dutch tug to Italy and scrapped, following by a year the last voyage of the *St Paul*, which went to Germany, under tow, for demolition.

Gross tonnage: 11,629 (later 10,230)
Length overall: 554 feet
Width: 63 feet
Machinery: Quadruple expansion, twin screw
Speed: 20 knots
Capacity: 1,320
Built: William Cramp & Sons, Ship and Engine Building Co, Philadelphia, Pennsylvania, 1884
Demise: Scrapped in Italy, 1924

Above *The* St Louis *in the Delaware river in 1895.* **Below** *Cowls removed, she looks much more attractive in this well-remembered Currier & Ives print.*

PUBLISHED BY CURRIER & IVES

The Magnificent Steamship "ST. LOUIS" *of the American Line*

LENGTH OVER ALL 554 FT.   DEPTH FROM UPPER DECK CABINS TO KEEL 42 FT.   BREADTH 63 FT.

TONNAGE 11,600   HORSE POWER 20,000

Above St Louis *leaving the dock at New York.* **Below** St Louis *approaching England, back in transatlantic service after the Spanish–American War.*

Kaiser Wilhelm Der Grosse

When Kaiser Wilhelm II attended the Spithead Naval Review of 1889, he was most impressed with Britain's mighty fleet of warships. Grouped in orderly formation, they sparked the Imperial ego and imagination. However, another floating marvel also caught the German Emperor's discriminating eye, the White Star passenger liner *Teutonic*, the biggest ship then afloat. She was 9,900 gross tons and 582 feet long.

When the Kaiser and his party returned to Berlin, word spread immediately that both the Imperial Navy and Merchant Marine must grow and reach out for distinction and power. More specifically, for the commercial fleet, Germany must have the largest liner afloat. She must also be the fastest, taking the prized Blue Riband from a contented Victorian Britain. It would be the supreme rivalry, a competition that must end with a Teutonic victory. In quick time, the directors of the highly successful North German Lloyd were made aware of the Kaiser's ambitious plans. Designers were set to work, to create the most novel and outstanding German ship to date. It would take, however, nearly eight years for her to become a reality.

Ordered from the expert yards of the Vulcan Works at Stettin, this new flagship was revolutionary in almost every way. Planned to reach over 14,000 tons and 650 feet, no ship—passenger or otherwise—could surpass her dimensions at the time. (The 18,900-ton *Great Eastern* of 1859, which was 689 feet in length, was scrapped in 1891. This unique, eccentric, highly unprofitable ship has retained her own, quite separate place in maritime history (see *Fifty Famous Liners, volume one*).) The German liner would be, in fact, the first of the large ocean liners, the so-called 'superliners'. Fitted with powerful triple-expansion engines that were intended to produce a service speed of nearly 22 knots, her machinery was linked to no less than four rather thin funnels. Being the first of the 14 liners to have as many stacks, she immediately prompted rumours of larger five- and even six-funnel ships. Her four stacks sparked further notoriety and popularity, especially among passengers who delighted in travelling in the world's largest liner with the greatest number of smokestacks. In short time, size, speed and even safety would be equated with the number of stacks found aboard a liner. The highly sought emigrants were especially fascinated with a ship's funnels and often selected the ship with the highest number. Until the First Great War, the four-stackers were the most popular liners on the North Atlantic.

The new liner's four stacks, while made deliberately tall so as to clear thick coal smoke and hot cinders, rested on a long, very slender hull. Even the superstructure was especially long and low. Two tall masts balanced the overall design. Being the first of the big 'ocean greyhounds', she was noticeably lengthy, sleek and certainly racy. Speeding across the North Atlantic in subsequent years, she resembled something of a man-made serpent. Launched on May 4 1897, in the presence of the Kaiser, she was aptly given a royal name: *Kaiser Wilhelm Der Grosse*, honouring the Kaiser's grandfather, Kaiser Wilhelm I. As she hit the waters of Stettin for the first time, it was also the beginning of a sparkling 'German decade', of brilliant maritime craftsmanship and technology. It was the first time that Britain had been so seriously outstepped.

In that late summer, the new ship ran her trials and proved to be a most impressive performer. On September 9 1897, she left Bremerhaven for New York on her eight-day maiden voyage. Thousands gathered to see her, to marvel at the biggest ship in the world and possibly even to tour her luxurious innards. She was, of course, the first of the so-called 'floating palaces' as well. It was a gilded age on the high seas of carved woods, crystal, overhead skylights, magnificently woven carpets and enormous marble baths. In first class, there was yet another novelty: all of the 558 passengers could be seated at one time in the restaurant.

In November of her maiden season, the *Kaiser Wilhelm Der Grosse* swept the Atlantic. She bluntly grabbed the Blue Riband from the British *Lucania*, a 12,900-ton Cunarder. The German ship's record stood at 22.35 knots while her predecessor was placed at 21.81 knots. For the first time in passenger ship history, the speed pennant flew from the mast of a German liner. The biggest ship in the world was now the fastest as well—and she was German. The Kaiser was thrilled.

The North German Lloyd's arch rival, the Hamburg America Line, took very serious notice of this new ship. Naturally, they wanted a record-breaker of their own. They too went to the Vulcan Shipyards and commissioned a larger ship, at 16,500 tons, with even more powerful engines. Named *Deutschland*, she was first introduced nearly three years later, in the summer of 1900. On her maiden crossing that July, she took the Riband with a recorded average speed of 22.42 knots. Then, a year later, she improved on her own record with 23.51 knots on an eastbound passage. In firm determination, the North German Lloyd responded with three additional four-stackers as well as several other major ships. All looked similar to the *Kaiser Wilhelm Der Grosse*, and the first of this new tonnage, the *Kronprinz Wilhelm*, was delivered in August 1901. She was 9 feet longer and 600 tons larger than the earlier ship. Her design then led to the *Kaiser Wilhelm II*, which jumped to 707 feet in length and 19,300 tons. Added to the Lloyd fleet in April 1903, she was the next contender for the Blue Riband.

However, setting records is not an easy accomplishment. It took three years before she could outrun the *Deutschland*, but with only the slightest improvement of 23.58 knots (against the earlier 23.51 knots). The *Kaiser Wilhelm II* returned the prized Riband to the North German Lloyd. Britain was sorely envious. 'These German monsters must be challenged and beaten', was the comment of one Member of Parliament. The response was a liberal construction loan and subsequent operating subsidy to the Cunard Company to build the superb *Lusitania* and *Mauretania* of 1907. The latter ship would secure the Riband for Britain for 22 years. Her record speeds were over 26 knots.

The Germans completed their quartet of four-stackers in that same summer of 1907 with the *Kronprinzessin Cecilie* (see *Fifty Famous Liners, volume one*). Although something of a duplicate to the earlier, record-breaking *Kaiser Wilhelm II*, she could not muster the additional speed to surpass the new British twins. Her best speed was 23.6 knots, a full three knots less than the Cunarders. Germany would not regain the Blue Riband until 1929, when the *Bremen* ushered in a new generation of superships and succeeded the veteran *Mauretania*.

The *Kaiser Wilhelm Der Grosse* was nearly lost on the afternoon of June 30 1900. While docked at North German Lloyd's terminal at Hoboken, just across from New York City, fire broke out on the piers and, fed by a strong southerly breeze, spread quickly. The docks and several ships were ablaze in a matter of minutes. The famed four-stacker was berthed in company with three other Lloyd liners, the *Bremen* (of 1897), *Main* and *Saale*. In Jeanette Edwards Rattray's *The Perils of the Port of New York* (Dodd, Mead & Company, 1973), she gave a detailed account of the huge inferno. 'At that time of the fire, the New York City Fire Department, including its fireboats, had no jurisdiction in the state of New Jersey. It was unable to give aid to vessels in distress until they were in the open stream and neutral waters [of the Hudson River]. Then, it did heroic work.

'Sightseers on the *Kaiser Wilhelm Der Grosse* heard hundreds of barrels of pitch exploding from the heat like gunfire. They made a wild rush for the gangways. Panic was averted by the ship's officers, who announced immediately that the vessel would proceed quickly into midstream. A stern hawser was already glowing from the heat. With decks ablaze, woodwork crackling and clouds of steam roaring through her exhaust pipes, the ship made a terrifying spectacle as she slowly made her way to safety. The 'KWDG' [*Kaiser Wilhelm Der Grosse*] was damaged but not seriously. Tugs went to her aid and the guests were transferred. The fire just spoiled her looks.'

While the three other liners were either seriously damaged or destroyed totally, the Lloyd's Hoboken dockland was in ruins. It was the worst fire that New York Harbor had yet known. Years later, in an equally dangerous incident, on November 21 1906, the *Kaiser Wilhelm Der Grosse* was rammed by the British freighter *Orinoco* off Cherbourg. Five passengers on the German liner were killed.

In 1913, over 15 years since her glorious, triumphant maiden season, the *Kaiser Wilhelm Der Grosse* was demoted. She was then the oldest of the big liners in the North German Lloyd fleet. Her first and second class accommodations were eliminated as the ship was converted for the booming low-fare emigrant trade, carrying third class and steerage passengers only. Her transatlantic fares began at $15. Westbound, she sailed full; homewards, she went practically empty.

A postcard view of the Kaiser Wilhelm Der Grosse *arriving at her Hoboken pier with the Manhattan skyline in the background.*

The veteran liner was at her Bremerhaven berth when the First Great War was declared in August 1914. Immediately, she was given to the Imperial Navy and hurriedly outfitted as an armed merchant cruiser. Sent to sea, she broke through the Allied blockade by cautiously sailing northward to the Norwegian coast and then turning westwards when well north of Scotland. Once in the open Atlantic, this ship of joy and luxury became a sinister menace. She sank two Allied vessels, one of them being the British freighter *Hyades*. She also held-up two British passenger ships, the 15,000-ton *Arlanza* and the 6,500-ton *Galician*. Fortunately, they were later allowed to continue on their voyages as they were fully booked with innocent, unarmed passengers. Then, as the *Kaiser Wilhelm Der Grosse*'s coal supplies were running low, she made a dash for Rio de Oro, a Spanish colony along the West African coast. Once there, three colliers went alongside the former liner and, even as Spanish authorities requested that she leave immediately, the refuelling continued. This delay was to spell the end for the great ship.

The British cadet training ship *Highflyer*, an obsolete cruiser, mounting eleven six-inch guns, arrived on August 26 and ordered the German ship to leave port. The order was refused. The *Highflyer* opened fire and, after a short, but fierce battle, the four-stacker—with armament of only ten four-inch guns—was defeated. With little ammunition and hope left, the Captain ordered that the illustrious *Kaiser Wilhelm Der Grosse* be scuttled to avoid the inevitable capture. It was a sorry ending to the first of the world's superliners.

Gross tonnage: 14,349 (1897); 13,952 (1913)
Length overall: 655 feet
Width: 66 feet
Machinery: Steam triple expansion engines, twin screw
Speed: 22 knots
Capacity: 558 first class, 338 second class and 1,074 steerage (1897); reduced to third class and steerage only (1913)
Built: Vulcan Shipyards, Stettin, Germany, 1897
Demise: Deliberately scuttled off Rio de Oro, West Africa, August 26 1914

Top and above *Two views of* Kaiser Wilhelm Der Grosse *under way* (courtesy of Arnold Kludas).

Right *A silver napkin ring from the* Kaiser Wilhelm Der Grosse.

The lovely four-stacker Kaiser Wilhelm Der Grosse.

Republic

'We could tell it was coming', Captain Sealby remembered. He was master of the White Star Line's *Republic*, which was sinking in the Atlantic. He and Second Officer Williams were alone on the bridge of the stricken vessel. All her passengers and other crew members had been safely rescued and the mortally-wounded White Star ship was under tow. Her life was ebbing.

'When we realised that at last the time to desert the *Republic* was close at hand Williams and I just stood there and waited. Suddenly we heard a rumbling and then a cracking sound aft and the stern of the *Republic* began to go down rapidly. I turned to Williams and said, "Well, old man, what do you think about it?".'

Fortunately both were saved, but despite the bravery of Captain Sealby and Second Officer Williams in going down with their ship on a cold January night in the North Atlantic they were forgotten and the hero of the whole affair was a 25 year old lad aboard named John Robinson Binns. Jack Binns was the ship's radio operator and the sinking was the occasion of the first sending out of a radio distress signal that resulted in a rescue at sea. The year was 1909 and the distress signal was CQD. It was not until later in that year that the now-famous SOS was chosen as the signal for ships needing help.

The *Republic* had started out in life as the *Columbus*, proud new flagship of the Dominion Line. She had made only two voyages under Dominion's house-flag when White Star Line assumed control of the Dominion Line and the *Columbus* was renamed *Republic*. She was put on White Star's Mediterranean–New York service. A fine vessel, she built up a good following of loyal passengers. Among these were three relatives of co-author Braynard, who sailed February 20 1908, from Naples. Great-uncle the Reverend Edwin N. Crasto wrote in his trip diary on *Republic* letterhead that the liner was a 'remarkably fine steady ship'.

Among the many letters brought aboard when the *Republic* made her brief early morning stop at the Azores was one from Carrie Upham, my (FOB's) mother-to-be. There were only 40 passengers in first class on this westbound crossing.

Although the first several days were rough and my two great-aunts Sue and Margaret were both seasick, the weather got better and great-Uncle Edwin's diary records how he played shuffleboard. On March 4 the ship reached New York after a leisurely passage of 14 days.

Real fame came to the *Republic* on a Mediterranean cruise the following year. She left New York on January 22 with 250 in first class, 200 third class passengers and a crew of 300. At 5 am the next morning the great liner was hit by a westbound Italian immigrant vessel named the *Florida*. The collision took place about nine miles south-by-east of Nantucket and 70 miles due east of Montauk Point. It resembled the *Stockholm–Andrea Doria* collision in that the smaller craft *Florida* slammed into the larger *Republic*, doing great damage to her own prow but remaining watertight. At first there was panic among the immigrants who thought their ship would sink. Captain Sealby realized how severely his ship had been injured and began preparations to abandon ship. He ordered Radio Operator Binns to send out his distress call. His passengers and many of his crew then began to change ships. The *Florida*, in due course, took most of them aboard without incident.

The dramatic 'CQD' fingered out over the airwaves by Jack Binns, was picked up by the American radio station at Siasconsett, Massachu-

setts, which relayed it to a number of liners in the area. One of these was the *New York* of the American Line, originally the Inmann *City of New York*. Others to get the relay were the Cunarder *Lucania*, the *Furnesia*, of Furness Witney & Co, the French Line's *La Lorraine* and the *Baltic* of White Star. The *Baltic* was the closest and arrived early the next day, February 24, followed by the *New York* and the *Lucania*. The scene was set for one of the great rescues in maritime history, and the first in which the relatively new invention of radio would prove its great worth. The *Baltic* took aboard both the *Republic*'s and the *Florida*'s passengers as night fell. As a principle of honour Captain Sealby remained aboard the *Republic* until the very last.

As a postscript to this widely-known story, there is an account in manuscript form in my files describing how the *Republic* could have been saved. The American steamer *City of Everett*, Captain Thomas Fenlon commanding, was towing the barge *Standard Oil Co 95* from Boston to Philadelphia. Her radio picked up the *Republic*'s signal at 6.30 am on January 23. Captain Fenlon determined to offer his ship and barge to the vessels in distress. The barge could assist in pumping out water from either vessel or with steam to activate their pumps or both. The *City of Everett* could tow the ship that needed towing the most. The sea was smooth and there was thick fog. Knowing that the *Baltic*, closest of the rescue liners, was still many hours off, Captain Fenlon headed for the scene of the crash. At 2.45 pm, about eight hours after the collision, he heard a fog horn ahead. Slowing down he sighted the *Republic* 15 minutes later, drifting very slowly alongside.

'We offered to tow him to shoal water. He said he was in communication with his New York office and that they were sending Chapman and Merrit's wrecking fleet. We then went to the *Florida* and offered the Captain our assistance. He said he was waiting for the *Baltic* to arrive to take off the passengers of the *Republic* who had been transferred to the *Florida*. Most all [*sic*] of the *Florida*'s boats were tied alongside her. The sea was so smooth that they were laying very comfortably alongside with no danger of damage whatever.

'At 6 pm we launched our number one lifeboat and crew in charge of the First Officer and instruc-

ted him to make it clear, to both the Captain of the *Florida* and the Captain of the *Republic*, that our ship and barge were entirely equipped for wrecking and towing. We had all modern machinery for a job of this particular type. . . . Our offer to tow was made the second time and was again refused. The fog continued very dense. Visibility was not over 300 feet and remained that way all night. It commenced to clear a little about 9 am on January 24. The *Baltic* showed up about 9.30 am. It might have been later. About 10 am I could hear the fog horns of other ships blowing, and, all of my offers of assistance having been refused, I decided to leave the scene and continue my voyage to Philadelphia via Sandy Hook Pilot Boat, where I gave my sealed report to the Captain of the Pilot Boat to deliver to 26 Broadway.

'In my own mind I feel assured that had the Master of the *Republic* engaged the *City of Everett* and Barge *Standard Oil Co 95* on their arrival at the scene at 3 pm January 23 1909, we would have had the *Republic* anchored in the Vineyard by noon January 24. Of course, this is only one man's opinion.'

This record comes from an undated letter written to Eugene F. Moran by Captain Fenlon from Deer Creek Ranch, Hunt, Texas, and was found in the files of the Moran Towing Co when I served there as Director of Public Relations between 1960 and 1970.

Shortly before the *Republic* made her final plunge, 30 of her crew returned to assist in an effort to have the *Baltic* tow the mortally-wounded 15,000-ton liner. They were rescued when she went down. The accident was not without loss of life, however, as six were lost at the moment of impact. Two of the dead were passengers aboard the *Republic*. The four others were black seamen in the bow of the *Florida*. When the Italian liner crept into New York her flags were at half mast indicating that 'death stalked on board', according to a January 22 1933 story in the *New York Times*.

Captain Sealby and Second Officer Williams and Jack Binns were among the last to be picked up, being rescued from the sea by smaller craft that had come on the scene.

The *Republic*'s beautiful Harland & Wolff-designed hull rose slowly into the air in her last moments and then slipped into the whirling suction of the Atlantic toward the bottom, roughly 240 to 280 feet below the surface. At this writing several groups of divers are planning efforts to recover gold from the *Republic*. The story held currently is that $115 million (1984 value) in $10 US gold pieces is still entombed in the sunken hull of the White Star Line steamer.

Gross tonnage: 15,378
Length overall: 570 feet
Width: 67.8 feet
Machinery: Quadruple expansion engines
Speed: 16 knots
Capacity: Figures not available
Built: Harland & Wolff, Belfast, 1903
Demise: Sunk, January 23/24 1909

Above Republic *entering New York Harbor.* **Below** *A very rare and somewhat faint photograph of the sinking of the* Republic *which appeared in the* New York Tribune. *The* Republic *is listing and already down by the stern. The America Line's* New York *and the Cunarder* Lucania *are standing by.*

SS. "REPUBLIC," WHITE STAR LINE

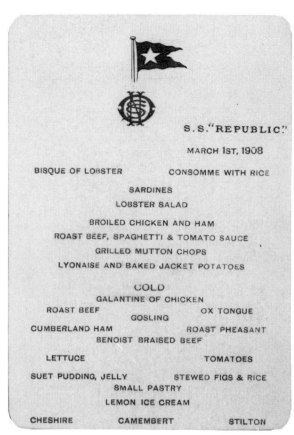

S.S. "REPUBLIC."

MARCH 1ST, 1908

BISQUE OF LOBSTER   CONSOMME WITH RICE

SARDINES

LOBSTER SALAD

BROILED CHICKEN AND HAM

ROAST BEEF, SPAGHETTI & TOMATO SAUCE

GRILLED MUTTON CHOPS

LYONAISE AND BAKED JACKET POTATOES

COLD

GALANTINE OF CHICKEN

ROAST BEEF   OX TONGUE

GOSLING

CUMBERLAND HAM   ROAST PHEASANT

BENOIST BRAISED BEEF

LETTUCE   TOMATOES

SUET PUDDING, JELLY   STEWED FIGS & RICE

SMALL PASTRY

LEMON ICE CREAM

CHESHIRE   CAMEMBERT   STILTON

Above left *Postcard artist's impression of the* Republic *with the size of her smokestack somewhat exaggerated.* **Above right** *Souvenirs of a voyage on the* Republic *in 1908—a menu and* (**Below**) *'Abstract of log'.*

ABSTRACT OF LOG

S.S. 'REPUBLIC   COMMANDER: JAS McAULEY

... ...

LEFT PONTA DELGADA FEBRUARY 26TH. 1908, AT 11-8 A.M.

DATE	MILES	LAT	LONG	REMARKS
Feb. 26	13	37.45	25.56	mod. breeze, fine, light swell
27	390	38.12	34.10	gentle breeze, showery, smooth sea
28	387	38.38	42.22	„ fine „
29	375	39.04	50.22	moderate to fresh breeze, squally, slight sea
Mar. 1	281	39.20	56.24	fresh breeze to mod. gale, rough sea
2	282	39.37	62.29	mod gale to strong breeze, rough sea
3	317	39.58	69.20	strong to mod breeze, moderate sea
	208	to Sandy Hook L.V.		Arrived Mar. 4th, at 3-0 a.m.
Total 2253		Passage 6 days	19 hours	9 minutes

Manchuria

When she was launched in the autumn of 1903, at the New York Shipbuilding Corporation yards at Camden, New Jersey, just across from Philadelphia, few of those present could have imagined that this ship's career would span nearly half a century. Assuredly, she was among the most successful of all American passenger ships.

She was the second of a pair of identical sister-ships, both ordered by the Atlantic Transport Company of West Virginia. Evidently, there was some rethinking and then ownership changes during the early stages of construction. The first ship, thought to be named *Minnelora*, was launched as the *Mongolia*. The second ship was to become the *Minnekahda*. Both were intended for North Atlantic service. However, being bought by the Pacific Mail Line as well, this second vessel was also renamed. Christened as the *Manchuria*, it was a choice far more fitting to their intended trans-pacific service.

Set to be launched on October 31, the *Manchuria* was embarrassingly 'stuck' when just halfway out of her building slip. She could not be freed for 48 hours, until November 2. Months later, in the spring of 1904, the new ship was duly sent from New York, around the South American continent and then northward to her base at California. That June she set out on her maiden voyage, from San Francisco and Los Angeles to Honolulu, Yokohama, Kobe, Manila and Hong Kong. Her passenger quarters were appropriately arranged between 350 in a high standard, spacious first class, a modest 68 in second class and then, the most lucrative of all, 1,300 in steerage. Primarily used by Asian migrants bound for America, this latter space was usually filled to the very last dormitory berth on her eastward passages. A three-week voyage from Hong Kong to San Francisco could cost as little as $12 in 1905. Being among the largest liners then in regular Pacific service, the *Manchuria* (and *Mongolia*) enjoyed considerable success for over a decade.

In 1915, a year or so after the outbreak of World War I, the *Manchuria* was shifted to other American owners, in fact her intended operators, the Atlantic Transport Company. She was reas-signed to the Atlantic Transport Line's special wartime neutrality service between New York and London. Huge American flags were painted along her sides and bold white letters read 'AMERICAN S.S. MONGOLIA.' Most fortunately, she sailed unharmed. Then, soon after the USA entered that conflict, in 1917, the ship was again transferred. Given over to the American Army, she was armed and outfitted as the transport USS *Manchuria* for vital troop service to western Europe.

Again, sailing undamaged, she was hastily restored in 1919 and placed under the house-flag of the American Line, which was soon to be merged into the United States Lines, for 'austerity service' between New York and Hamburg. With almost all of the prewar German liners lost or seized, her work was most important. She brought countless immigrants in an opposite direction, on westward voyages. However, within a few years, by the early '20s, this lucrative third-class steerage trade had all but vanished. Because of US government quotas, immigration on the North Atlantic slumped from 1 million in 1914 to a mere 150,000 a decade later.

Seeking alternative employment, the *Manchuria* went to her fourth owners, the Panama Pacific Line, another American shipper, in 1923. Sailing on a tropical service, between New York, Havana, the Panama Canal, Los Angeles and San Francisco, she was especially refitted and modernised. Her sailings were often booked as two-week cruises or for the full month roundtrip. Her berthing was reduced to two classes: 256 in first class and 1,350 in third. Her tonnage increased, however, by nearly 2,000 tons, to 15,445. Her primary fleet-mates were two similarly-sized ships, the former Red Star liners *Kroonland* and *Lapland*, and her sister-ship, the *Mongolia*. In 1926, there was yet another refit for the *Manchuria*. This time, her accommodation was reduced further still, to 240 in first class and 834 in the former third class section, which was renamed as cabin class.

When new liner tonnage came onto the American intercoastal trade in 1928–29, namely Panama Pacific's *California*, *Pennsylvania* and *Virginia*, the *Manchuria* was again put on the block. She was sold to the Dollar Line, the San Francisco-based forerunner to the present-day American President Lines, who renamed her as their *President Johnson*. The *Mongolia* was included in the purchase and became the *President Fillmore*. Once more refitted, their passenger spaces were reduced to 300 all-first class berths. They were placed on Dollar's 105-day around-the-world service, sailing from New York to Havana, the Panama Canal, Los Angeles, San Francisco, Honolulu, Kobe, Shanghai, Hong Kong, Manila, Singapore, Penang, Colombo, Suez, Alexandria, Naples, Genoa, Marseilles and then across the Atlantic to Boston before concluding at New York. Unfortunately, the *President Fillmore* was not successful and was laid-up after only five voyages.

The former *Manchuria* continued in regular service until 1932, when she was sent to drydock for more alterations. Her first class berths were increased to 450. However, due to the vastly decreasing passenger and cargo demands caused by the Depression, she was sent on two 'bargain' cruises to the Mediterranean. Soon afterward, she was laid-up to await better times. Briefly reactivated for further world voyages, she was more permanently laid-up in December 1935. She would not resume sailing until called to duty for her second world conflict, in late 1941. She passed over to American President ownership in 1938 without even having left her moorings.

The *President Johnson* was, despite her age of nearly 40 years, assigned to the War Shipping Administration soon after the Japanese attack on Pearl Harbor. Painted over in tones of grey, she once again gave valiant, accident-free service. The *President Fillmore*, laid-up for nearly a decade, from 1931, was sold in 1940 to Mr Arnold Bernstein's Compania Transatlantica Centroamericana for refugee and evacuation service. Renamed *Pana-manian*, she too survived the hostilities and was finally scrapped at Hong Kong in 1946.

The *President Johnson* was decommissioned in early 1946 and thought to be an unlikely candidate for any further service. However, with the very urgent passenger needs (for refugees and migrants especially) and the complication of a vastly reduced European liner fleet, she was sold to the Tagus Navigation Company of Lisbon. Rechristened as the *Santa Cruz*, she carried third class passengers only between Lisbon, Rio de Janeiro, Santos, Montevideo and Buenos Aires. A year or so later, in 1948, changing from Portuguese to Panamanian registry, she was time-chartered to the greatly diminished Italian Line. She continued in low-fare South American service, but her voyages originated at Naples and Genoa. She gave four more years of valuable and profitable service. When, in 1952, the brand new Italian liners *Augustus* and *Giulio Cesare* were commissioned, she was finally relieved. Nearly exhausted and close to her fiftieth year, the old *Manchuria* was sent to Savona and broken-up. It was a remarkable career for an otherwise quite ordinary ship.

Gross tonnage: 13,639 (1904); 15,543 (1929); 16,111 (1947)
Length overall: 616 feet
Width: 65 feet
Machinery: Steam quadruple expansion engines, twin screw
Speed: 16 knots
Capacity: 350 first class, 68 second class, 1,300 steerage (1904); 265 first class and 1,350 third class (1924); 240 first class and 834 cabin class (1926); 300 first class (1928); 450 first class (1932); approximately 1,200 third class (1947)
Built: New York Shipping Co, Camden, New Jersey, 1904
Demise: Scrapped at Savona, Italy, 1952

PACIFIC MAIL STEAMSHIP COMPANY'S TRANS-PACIFIC FLEET
S.S. "MONGOLIA," 27,000 TONS   S.S. "MANCHURIA," 27,000 TONS
S.S. "KOREA,"   18,000 TONS   S.S. "SIBERIA,"   18,000 TONS
S.S. "CHINA," 10,200 TONS

Above *A postcard of* Manchuria *with an all black stack and Pacific Mail colours.*

Left *A gun being loaded aboard when the* Manchuria *was pressed into service on the Atlantic after America entered World War 1. She fired the first shot fired by an American vessel in that conflict.*

Above right *American Line passenger list dated May 13 1922.*

Right *The third class dining saloon on* Manchuria *after she was acquired by the American Line for transatlantic service after the First World War.*

Fifty Famous Liners 2

CABIN PASSENGERS
AMERICAN LINE
S. S. MANCHURIA
FROM HAMBURG TO NEW YORK
SATURDAY, MAI 13th 1922

Commander: A. Zeeder, Commander U. S. N. R. F.
Chief Engineer: W. Forsyth, Lieut. U. S. N. R. F.
Surgeon: E. H. Earl   Purser: A. J. Fitzgerald
Asst. Purser: W. J. MacIntyre Chief Steward: P. Rosling

CABIN PASSENGERS TO NEW YORK:

Amthor, Miss Anna
          Katharina
Atkinson, Mr. C.

Baehren, Mr. Otto
Bayer, Mr. Andrew
Becher, Mr. Eugen
Beier, Mrs. Aug.
Biehl, Miss Frieda
Bormann, Miss Guta
Bormann, Miss Elise

Dasek, Miss Susanna
Diestel, Mr. John

Falkenstein, Mr. H.
Frankl, Mr. Georg
Frankl, Miss Juliana
Frohboese, Mr. Hans

Goldberg, Mr. J.
Golding, Mrs. Zipa
Gonsas, Miss Elijosius
Grimm, Miss Lena

Groeller, Mr. Johann
Grolmann, Miss Bluna

Haller, Mrs. Marie E.
Hanish, Mrs. Isabella
Hanish, Miss Claire
Harrendorf, Mr. William
Harrison, Mrs. Rosalie
Harrison, Master Caspar
Hoehn, Mr. August
Hoelzl, Miss Rosa

Jurkschelsky, Mrs. Sore
Jurkschelsky, Miss Beile
Jurkschelsky, Miss Zina

Kelemen, Miss Tereze
Keller, Mr. Herbert
Kleinermann, Mrs. Hava
Kleinermann, Miss Krenna
Kling, Mr. Alois
Kling, Mrs. Rosa
Kling, Master William
Koenig, Mr. Alwin

Kratzer, Mr. Caspar
Kratzer, Mrs. Anna
Krebs, Miss Marie
Krieger, Mr. Ed.
Krieger, Mrs. Anne

Lison, Mrs. Perlia
Lison, Mr. Janchel
Lison, Mrs. Mindlea
    and child Sime

Mattescheck, Miss E.
Melia, Miss Rose
Milch, Mr.
Miles, Mrs. Feighe
Mitchell, Miss Blanche
Mueller, Mr. Hugo

Nachmann, Mrs. Elisabeth

Patzwald, Mr. Johan
Patzwald, Mrs. Caroline
Planzer, Mr. Paul
Potent, Miss Maria
Premister, Mrs. Rosa
Premister, Miss Maria

Reichl, Mr. Franz
Reichl, Miss Anna
Rheinthaler, Miss Hilda
Rogers, Mr. Will.
Rogers, Mrs. Will.

Ruedenauer, Mr. Joh.
Ruedenauer, Mrs. Stefanie
Ruggles, Miss Edith

Schatz, Mr. L. A.
Schulte, Mr. Fritz
Schutt, Mr. Fritz
Schwendener, Mr. Georges
Siegle, Miss Else
Stogsdal, Col. R. R.

Tittmann, Mr. Alfred
Treiger, Mrs. Schewa

Ulz, Miss Amalie
Unger, Miss Theresia
Unger, Master Josef
Unger, Miss Angela

Vitolo, Mrs. Rich.

Wedel, Mrs. Hedwig
Weishaupt, Mr. Karl
Weiss, Miss Mina
Wendt, Miss Elsa
Windisch, Miss Marie
Wunderlich, Mrs.
Wurm, Mr. Alex
Wurm, Mrs. Rosalie

Zimmer, Miss Kath.

PANAMA PACIFIC LINER "MANCHURIA"

Above *Transferred to the Panama Pacific Line the* Manchuria *was given a white hull, as shown in this postcard.* **Below** *Taken over by the Army in World War 2, she became the US Army Transport* President Johnson.

Minnesota

As a saga of human initiative, high goals and achievement, the life of the liner *Minnesota* and her short-lived sister-ship *Dakota* needs telling. In many ways the story is much like that of Brunel and his giant failure, the *Great Eastern.* But that tale has been told and retold. The remarkable historical episode of William A. Fairburn and his *Minnesota*, sad to say, has almost been forgotten. Up to a point it represents one of the most extraordinary examples of designing talent ever, a *tour-de-force* of naval architecture and marine engineering. The sister-ships involved were the largest ships ever built in America, and, very briefly, the world's largest ships. The stakes were high—the development of trade with China. The prime mover was one of America's most impressive railroad moguls, James J. Hill. The denouement—after a few brief bright moments—an almost complete failure. And there is a decidedly unusual postscript to it all, as well.

Two men were the principal actors in this story—James J. Hill and young William Fairburn. Hill was a Canadian by birth. He began his career in railroading in the State of Minnesota. As he rose to higher and higher positions he learned that to fill freight cars he would need ships. In 1870 he acquired the flat-bottomed steamer *Selkirk* and he used her to bring wheat from Winnipeg via the Red River. After the Spanish-American War, many in America saw visions of grandeur in the Pacific. Hill had pushed his railroad ventures all the way to Seattle. He wanted to extend his system across the Pacific to the Orient. Ships could do it and he would need huge ships, the largest cargo carriers ever built in the world. And he would build them to carry passengers as well. From the mechanical and design standpoint his dream would come true. The ships would be most successful, but from the business standpoint he was far ahead of his time. James J. Hill had always been a most optimistic person. He figured that if every resident of only one Chinese province would eat just one ounce of flour a day, he could sell 60,000,000 bushels every year as a starter. But where would the Chinese get the money to buy his wheat? He had not considered things like that.

The second chief character in the *Minnesota* story was only 23 years old in the winter of 1899–1900 when he worked out the designs for a pair of monster ships to serve James J. Hill. A genius from the start, William Fairburn was out of high school and working in the Bath Iron Works at the age of 14. Recognised by all who came in contact with him as amazing with figures, he was guided with care by friendly superiors who saw to it that he got experience in every shop in the yard. As time passed he decided that he needed expert training in design theory and engineering, even more than practical experience. He went to Scotland and enrolled at Glasgow University under J.

Minnesota

49

Havard Biles, known then by many as the world's foremost naval architect. Returning home he leaped into the contest to win the most coveted American ship design plum of the era. Many of the world's leading naval architects including Professor Biles of Glasgow were in the competition. Hill liked what Fairburn showed him and he got the assignment. Quite something, for even then the new Hill ships were being called 'the world's largest'. They would be over 20,000 gross tons, and, at that point, the largest ship ever built in the United States was the 13,639-ton *Manchuria*.

Hill was sure that young Fairburn could deliver —so sure that he agreed to the young genius' first drastic suggestion. There was no yard in the area suitable to build the giant vessels projected, said Fairburn, speaking of the New England area. So he proposed to build a brand new yard. No sooner said than done. In March 1900, the 'ideal place' to build the new sea queens was found. It was a 40-acre shorefront property with a solid rock foundation and running down to deep water at Groton, Connecticut. The Eastern Shipbuilding Co was formed and a plant created. An example of the quality of work Fairburn could demand may be seen in the man he picked as his chief draftsman for the new yard. He brought him over from Glasgow. Among the many famous ships he would design later in life would be the world's first nuclear passenger/cargo liner *Savannah*. He was George Gillis Sharp, whose name would become far more famous than Fairburn's in the marine field. Fairburn brought fresh thinking into all phases of his assignment. For example he chose boilers for his two new monster vessels from the Stirling Co, an unknown firm in Barberton, Ohio. He did this over the furious protests of leading boiler makers. His choice would later have a profound effect on his career.

The *Minnesota* was described in publicity as 'six times the size of the usual Pacific vessels and twice as large as a modern battleship. All this was true. The six-volume work called *Merchant Sail*, published many years later by the Fairburn Historical Foundation, claimed that the two Hill vessels were the largest ships in the world when they were originally laid down, or 'in frame' in shipyard parlance. The White Star Line's *Celtic*, launched in 1902, quite definitely had a greater gross tonnage (20,904) and was longer and wider by a fraction than the *Minnesota* but Fairburn claimed in an address given in 1903 before the Massachusetts Institute of Technology that his new liners would be heavier than any other vessels in the world. He was referring to their anticipated 45,000 ton displacement at load draft, expected to be 42 feet. And he was correct in this respect.

The two new ships would be huge by any standards, and they would cost an astounding (in that day) $5 million each. They would measure 630 feet in length and would be able to carry over 30,000 tons of cargo in addition to 8,000 tons of water and 5,000 tons of coal. Fairburn listed the breakdown of their passenger accommodations as follows: 200 in first class; 100 in second, 100 in third, 1,200 in steerage or 2,000 troops. Each ship would have a crew of 250, but in service this figure increased substantially.

Passenger spaces were on the bridge deck, boat deck, promenade deck, upper deck and main deck. Aft on the boat deck was a 'fan-ventilated, Flemish oak' smoking room, large for the day. Forward on the promenade deck was a library and what was called a 'Ladies' Boudoir' with piano. The upper deck featured a covered promenade on which passengers could completely circle the superstructure. This deck also was the location of the mahogany-lined dining saloon for first class which could seat 350. It extended from one side to the other and faced the forward end of the superstructure. It had windows on all three sides, something very few other liners in the world had at that time. Just aft of the saloon a grand panelled stair led up to the library and ladies' boudoir. The first class cabins, all of which were outside and electrically heated, were on the upper deck and the promenade deck. Eight suites each with a large bath tub were on the boat deck.

Because the two new ships would often have Asiatic passengers a space was set aside to be used as an 'opium den' on the main deck far aft. It was actually labelled this way in the deck plan. A second passenger dining room was on the same deck, starboard side, just aft of the boiler hatch. The ships would attract good passenger lists and were much appreciated for their elegance. President Taft and party sailed aboard the *Minnesota* on a visit to the Philippines.

50

One of the era's most revolutionary design developments in cargo handling was introduced on the two great Hill liners. It was the electric winch. Each would have 37 of them, built by the Lidgerwood Manufacturing Co, which boasted as its corporate ancestor none other than Stephen Vale, who had built the engines for the elegant steam ship, the *Savannah*, of 1819. The electric winch would not find general acceptance until World War I.

The *Minnesota* was launched on April 16 1903. The christening was to be done by Clara Hill, daughter of the railroad magnate. She came early, dressed in dark blue *crepe de chine*, maroon coat, sable boa and flower-trimmed hat. Offshore, thousands watched on excursion boats. Thousands more were on the land points around the yard, including every member of the Connecticut State Senate, which had abandoned its deliberations to come in a body. The appointed hour came, Miss Hill prepared to swing—and nothing happened. A frantic message from the yard superintendent asked James J. Hill to confer beneath the ship's hull. He found 100 workmen battering the timbers holding the ship. They were swinging huge wooden rams, but the timbers would not budge. The crowd stood by, glued by curiosity. Miss Hill stuck it out for an hour on the cold platform before joining the other guests in the shelter of a shipyard fence. Porters from Hill's private railroad parlour car supplied a continuous stream of hot coffee and 'spirits'. Another hour passed and then the word came. Miss Hill rushed back, smashed her bottle and the *Minnesota* slid gracefully down the ways.

A much worse thing was to happen with the launch of the *Dakota*. The event became enmeshed in the growing battle throughout America for a constitutional amendment barring the use of liquor. Such an amendment was passed eventually and led to the period known as 'Prohibition'. Several groups of women reformers from North and South Dakota objected to the use of wine at the christening and urged that something else be used. Hill refused. His attitude provoked a violent 'bad fairy' response. The women started an action that led to the passage of several resolutions stating that it was hoped that no money would ever be made by the vessel and that no good luck would attend her.

The actual launching ceremonies were seriously tarred with this unfortunate publicity.

On August 21 1904, the *Minnesota* had her triumphal entry into New York on her delivery cruise to Seattle. She had to go around South America to reach Seattle but she left that city for Japan on her maiden voyage on January 2 1905, and broke all speed records with a passage of 13 days. She had a large passenger list on this first trip and carried in excess of 28,000 tons of paying freight. The *Dakota* also shone at first. On her delivery trip to Seattle she eclipsed the feat of the battleship *Oregon* during the Spanish-American War, when that warship had raced from west to east coast to protect America from the Spanish fleet. On her maiden voyage she set another new speed record, making it in 9 days and 11 hours. Unfortunately the *Dakota* was not long for this world. In September 1905 she ran aground near Tokyo and was a total loss.

Back at Groton the great shipyard met a somewhat similar fate. After the two huge Hill ships, only two small railroad car floats were built and the yard just died. For some reason, never explained, Mr Fairburn left the maritime industry shortly after the completion of *Dakota*. He went to work for the Diamond Match Co, owned by the same group that owned the Stirling Co, makers of the boilers for his two huge ships. He rapidly became president of the match company and by the end of his life was a millionaire many times over.

The *Minnesota* performed well, but a drastic drop in freight rates showed how unrealistic Hill's hopes had been. The ship began to loose money but was kept in service nonetheless for the next 11 years. Finally in October, 1915, the great old lady was withdrawn from service. A group of companies, greedy to make war profits out of England's food crisis, chartered her for a voyage to London. Boiler trouble, attributed to sabotage at the time, brought her to a stop off San Francisco. It took over a year to repair her and while still at San Francisco she was sold by the Great Northern Steamship Co, which Hill had created to operate her, to the International Mercantile Marine (IMM) for $2,690,000. Part of her vast cargo of wheat was removed to enable her to get through the new Panama Canal and she arrived at New York on February 14 1917.

During World War I the ship was renamed *Troy* and operated across the Atlantic carrying cargo after cargo of record proportions. On her last trip she carried 32,000 measurement tons. After the war, the IMM converted the *Minnesota* to burn oil, expecting to put her into the third class trade on the Atlantic. The new legislation limiting immigration killed this plan. She lay idle for three years until in November 1923 she left New York under tow for a scrap yard in Germany.

Gross tonnage: 20,718
Length overall: 630 feet
Width: 73.5 feet
Machinery: Twin screw, steam
Speed: 14 knots
Capacity: 200 first, 100 second, 100 third, 1,200 steerage or 2,000 troops.
Built: Eastern Shipbuilding Co, Groton, Connecticut, 1904
Demise: Scrapped in Germany, 1924

Above *Loading coal in Japan. The* Minnesota, *'the world's largest and fastest freighter at the time she was launched', could also carry a large passenger list.*

Left *How the coal was handled—coal was brought alongside in sailing barges and loaded by hand by women 'longshoremen'.*

Above *Artist's impression of the* Minnesota, *probably done in 1903 or 1904.*

Below left *With World War 1 dazzle camouflage,* Minnesota *has been given the name* Troy *and is shown here with a gun replacing her old 'bow house'. She served gallantly throughout the war* (courtesy of Steamship Historical Society of America).

Below right *Being drydocked in the Orient, the* Minnesota *at Kolwoon with Oriental labourers in the foreground. Note the little 'bow house' for the lookout.*

Amerika

While the North German Lloyd had built three large and powerful four-stackers by 1905 and then had a fourth on order for delivery in 1907, their rival Hamburg–America Line planned a pair of equally large near-sisters that would emphasize size and luxury. Hamburg–America was not as interested in high speed. Their one successful bid for the Blue Riband, with their sole four-stacker, the *Deutschland* of 1900, was made at the expense of passenger comfort. The ship always suffered from excessive mechanical noises and rattling. Consequently, she was never the comfortable or highly popular ship that her Hamburg-based owners would have liked. The company never seriously sought the Riband again. Instead, they would build successively larger liners with exceptionally high standard accommodations that included special, publicity-gaining novelties in first class.

Hapag directors and designers were much impressed with the largest quartet of ships then afloat, the White Star Line's sisters *Cedric* and *Celtic* of 20,900 tons and their larger offspring, the sisters *Adriatic* and *Baltic* of 23,800 tons. Instead of using a three- or four-funnel design, they reverted to an earlier standard of four masts and two very tall, very thin stacks. It was a more traditional appearance, one that often reminded

passengers and crewmembers of the vanishing sail-ship era. Hapag even went to White Star's long-time friend and partner, the Harland & Wolff Company at Belfast in Northern Ireland. They were then the premier ocean liner designers and builders in the world. Hapag wanted the very best. Rumour was, however, that the new liner was actually planned for some British owners, possibly even White Star itself, and then secretly sold, before construction began, to the Germans. Most importantly, she was to be a Hapag liner from the laying of the first keel plates.

While the new ship was intended, at least to some extent, for the finest in first class travel, her biggest profits and greatest number of passengers would come from the very lowest shipboard class, those souls in below-deck steerage. When she was commissioned, in the autumn of 1905, emigrants from Europe were arriving in New York Harbor at an average rate of 12,000 a day. Hapag wanted a larger share of this lucrative trade and therefore needed larger ships. Furthermore, it was a common belief that many emigrants preferred ships with American names, or at least American-sounding names. Consequently, the name *Amerika* was selected. At a projected 22,200 tons and 700 feet, she would be the largest ship in the world.

Launched on April 20 1905, she was ready for her maiden voyage from Hamburg to New York via Southampton and Cherbourg in October. She was immediately and happily accepted as the superb new Hapag flagship. Her accommodation included the distinction of the first elevator aboard a liner. Company literature further described her, 'This vessel is planned to be the highest type of passenger and freight ship ever built—having great promenade decks, large cabins with lower berths only, grand combinations of first class suites and, in addition to a luxurious dining saloon, a perfectly equipped restaurant à la carte, the latter being under the supervision of the famous Ritz–Carlton Hotel of London. In the dining room, small party tables have been provided in place of long tables, and an à la carte service has been added. There is also a gymnasium, Turkish and electric baths and last, but not least, the first passenger ship elevator, running through five decks.'

The *Amerika*'s design and general concept was repeated in a slightly larger successor. However, this new ship was ordered from a German ship-builder, the Vulcan Works at Stettin. She would be over 2,000 tons larger, at 24,581 tons. Her length would be placed at 705 feet. She would outstep the *Amerika* as the world's largest ship, but then only to be displaced, in 1907, by Cunard's new 31,900-ton, 790-foot long speed queens *Lusitania* and *Mauretania*. Thought to be called *Europa*, the perfect complimentary name to *Amerika*, she was instead given the name of her launching sponsor, the Empress of Germany. She entered service in May 1906, as the *Kaiserin Auguste Victoria*. The two new ships made an attractive and highly profitable team.

The *Amerika* was not without her opportunities for headline news, however. In 1907, she went aground twice, once in the Elbe and then off Altonburgh. In January 1909, she rescued the crew from the Italian passenger steamer *Florida*, which was thought to be sinking after a collision with White Star's *Republic*. In 1910, some £8,000 in jewels were stolen from the German liner's first class quarters. On October 4 1912, she rammed and sank the British submarine *B2* off Dover. Fifteen of the sub's crew were lost; only one survived. A year later, she was aground once again, this time in New York Harbor, off Staten Island.

In June 1914, with the arrival of Hapag's first of a trio of superliners, the 52,100-ton *Imperator* and the 54,200-ton *Vaterland* (the latter then being the largest ship afloat and over twice the size of the *Amerika*), the older ship was transferred to a more secondary service, between Hamburg and Boston. Two months later, as the First World War erupted, she was laid-up at that New England port. Two other exiled German liners were berthed nearby, Hapag's *Cincinnati* and North German Lloyd's *Kronprinzessin Cecilie*. They were manned by skeleton crews and received only minimum maintenance.

Three years later, in April 1917, as the United States entered the War, the *Amerika* and all other laid-up German ships were seized officially. Sympathetic, loyalist crews set about to sabotage or even partially destroy these ships, but with less

than great success. Instead, they did destroy plans and other vital ingredients so necessary to their revitalisation. As in the case with the giant *Vaterland*, which was laid-up at Hoboken and which later became the USS *Leviathan*, plans had to be redrawn and needed parts had to be manu-factured specially, often even handmade.

The *Amerika* was recommissioned as the USS *America* on the following August 6. Repaired, cleaned and improved, she set out on her first mission, as part of the Allied Cruiser and Trans-port Force, in October. Between that date and October 1918, she made nine round voyages to Brest in France and carried 39,768 eastbound passengers. In heavy rains, on July 14 1918, she rammed and sank the British freighter *Instructor* of the Harrison Line. All of that ship's crew were rescued by the *America*.

Usually, the *America* sailed in the so-called '17 knot convoy', that comprised mostly of former German liners: the *George Washington*, *Von Steuben* (ex-*Kronprinz Wilhelm*), *Agamemnon* (ex-*Kaiser Wilhelm II*) and the *Mount Vernon* (ex-*Kronprinzessin Cecilie*). One other member was the French Line's

The Amerika *in drydock before World War 1.*

flagship *France*. The *America* generally berthed at the former Hamburg–America terminal at Hoboken, just across from New York City, but anchored about a half-mile offshore in the harbour at Brest. A squadron of destroyers escorted her (and the other troopers in the group) for the first 24 hours of the eastward voyage. Another squadron of small warships from Brest or St Nazaire met the group some 36 hours out on the edge of the Bay of Biscay to provide escort for that perilous last day. A roundtrip averaged a month, allowing for time spent in port at both ends.

During the early morning of October 15 1918, the *America* met with an unexplained disaster. She quite suddenly sank at her Hoboken pier, with the loss of 6 lives and $1 million in cargo and with damages that placed her out of service for four months. A subsequent inquiry offered a possible reason. It was the time of the maximum and minimum spring tides, during which it appeared that the vessel rested on the bottom on low tide. Coaling the ship proceeded all the night before in anticipation of sailing on the following day. All portholes on F deck, which was only 18 inches above the normal waterline, were open to air the ship and drive away the anti-influenza fumigants sprayed into the troop areas the day before. Coal was loaded in the bunkers, but was not trimmed as was customary, being piled heavily to port. The coaling ports, also close to the waterline, were not closed as well. Thus, around the entire ship, the F deck ports were open. Since the *America* was then resting on the bottom, naturally no list was observed when the coaling detail was secured. Then, as the flood tide set in during the early morning hours, the vessel became slightly water-borne again and took a severe list to port, pivoting on her port bilge. Soon, the coaling ports and the lower troop compartment ports were submerged. The rest of the story seems to have been a rather simple matter of hydraulics and fluid flow.

Only the *America's* forecastle, superstructure and fantail remained above the water. All of her lower decks, cargo and troop spaces were flooded. The famed Merritt & Chapman Salvage Company was called in and began emergency pumping. On December 12, she was finally raised and moved to the Brooklyn Navy Yard for full repairs. She resumed troop service in February and, in eight

roundtrips, brought over 50,000 troops home. She was returned to the Army Transport Service that September and laid-up pending disposal.

In the spring of 1920, it was decided that the *Amerika*, along with several other ex-German liners, would be given over to the United States Shipping Board (later to become the United States Lines) for transatlantic service, particularly to the Channel ports and hard-pressed Germany. The ship was sent to the Morse Drydock & Repair Company in Brooklyn and thoroughly restored. Thereafter, beginning that June, she sailed between New York, Southampton, Le Havre and Bremerhaven. Two large refits followed. In 1923, she was improved further at the Brooklyn Navy Yard. In March 1926, while undergoing her next major overhaul, she was badly damaged in a $1 million fire at the Newport News Shipyards. In view of her 21 years, it was thought that she would be broken-up. Instead, however, she underwent a year's worth of extensive repairs before resuming United States Lines' luxury service. An early victim of the Depression and then soon to be replaced by the new sister-ships *Washington* and *Manhattan*, the *Amerika* was laid-up in Chesapeake Bay in 1931. She sat in lonely, silent company with three of her onetime German fleetmates, the *George Washington* and the former *Kaiser Wilhelm II* and *Kronprinzessin Cecilie*. She might well have finally gone for scrap if the Second World War had not started.

Selected to become an accommodation ship, she was sent to the Bethlehem Steel Shipyards at Baltimore in October 1940. Renamed *Edmund B. Alexander*, she left New York in the following January, under the escort of the Coast Guard cutter *Duane*, to serve as barracks for 1,200 troops at St Johns, Newfoundland. Mechanically exhausted, she could barely muster 10 knots. As built, she was still a coal burner. She returned to New York in June.

There was much faith in the merits of this old ship. After another major refit, this time at the Atlantic Basin Iron Works at Brooklyn, she was placed on the short-haul New Orleans–Panama Canal run. A year later, in May 1942, with America now at war herself, she was returned to the Bethlehem Yards at Baltimore and thoroughly converted and modernised. New oil-burning machinery was fitted, which gave a service speed of 17 knots, and berthing was provided for some 5,000 troops. In April 1943, she returned to the North Atlantic and remained on military service, both with troops, the wounded and later war brides, children and refugees, until May 1949. Although briefly laid-up at Hawkins Point in Maryland, she was moved to the Federal Defense Fleet in the Hudson River, at Jones Point, New York. She sat in company of over two-hundred wartime ships, from Liberty and Victory Class freighters to her United States Lines' successors, the former *Washington* and *Manhattan*. Few of these ships would ever see service again. In January 1957, in one of the first 'ship clearing' efforts, the fifty-two-year-old *Amerika* was released for sale. Her obvious destination was the scrapheap. She arrived at Baltimore under tow, on January 27,

and was promptly demolished by the Bethlehem Steel Corporation. She was then the last remainder of that big pre-First War German liner fleet.

Gross tonnage: 22,225 (1905); 22,622 (1907); 21,114 (1923); 21,329 (1927)
Length overall: 700 feet
Width: 74 feet
Machinery: Steam quadruple expansion engines, twin screw
Speed: 17.5 knots
Capacity: 420 first class, 254 second class, 223 third class and 1,765 steerage (1905); 225 first class, 425 second class and 1,500 third class (1920); 692 cabin class and 1,056 third class (1923)
Built: Harland & Wolff Ltd, Belfast, Northern Ireland, 1905
Demise: Scrapped at Baltimore, 1957–58

The Amerika *was seized by the USA in 1917. This rare photograph shows her evacuating the 'Czecho-Slovak forces' from Siberia at the end of the First World War.*

Left America *helps at the rescue of the crew from the British cargo ship* Ovida *in mid-Atlantic in 1930. The photograph was taken from* Mauretania.

Below left America *going up the East River under Brooklyn Bridge to the Navy yard for repairs. Note how her four masts have been 'topped' so that she could get under the bridge.*

Right *Bringing troops home from the Second World War, she docks in Manhattan.*

Below *Being towed to the scrap yard on January 16 1957—a sad sight! Note the large single stack that had replaced her two tall stacks during her last restoration in World War 2.*

Amerika

Presidente Wilson

Although the historic Austro-Hungarian Empire was on its last legs in 1911, and although their tottering old Emperor Franz Josef would clearly have no male successor, it was strange, almost sad, that the handsome new flagship of the Austro–American Line was christened *Kaiser Franz Josef I*. The Roman numeral 'I' was always used in her name and appeared on her shiny black hull with its thin gold line just below the white superstructure. It would have seemed even stranger in 1911 to that tall, quiet history professor at a New Jersey college to predict that his name would grace those same bows and that good-looking counter stern before too many years had passed. Had a fortune teller hinted at such a development to Woodrow Wilson, he would have chuckled quietly, but such was to be the case, and it is under the name *Presidente Wilson* that most maritime historians remember this fine liner.

The Austrian Shipping Union (Societa Anonima Unione Austriaca Di Navigazione) was founded in 1903. Behind it were the famous Cosulich brothers of Trieste. They had been in shipping since 1857. The company entered 'big time' Atlantic competition in 1908 when they added a fine new liner to their fleet. They named her *Martha Washington*, in line with the custom of using names designed to appeal to immigrants. Built by Russell & Co, of Scotland, she was a vessel of 8,145 gross tons, and one of the best looking of pre World War I Atlantic liners. Her two tall stacks were unusually close together giving her a unique silhouette. As was done with a number of passenger ships, her original pilot house was found to be too low and a second bridge and pilot house was added atop it. The combination never looked just right, but it did make her forward superstructure impressive.

The Cosulich family at this point decided to enter the shipbuilding field and created the Cantiere Navale Triestino yard at Monfalcone, Trieste. Their first steamer was a little 800-tonner built in 1910. By the next year they leaped into prominence by launching in September what would become the spectacular beauty—the *Kaiser Franz Josef I*. In American advertisements and company folders the name was usually written as *Kaiser Franz Joseph I*. She was completed with very tall stacks (later cut down, I believe) which had cowls on their tops. The colouring of the stacks was black at the top, then red, then white, then red. One special feature which lent a regal feeling to her appearance were her windows. They had gently rounded tops and dark curtains, with lace tie-backs, could be seen within each window. She was a proud and beautiful liner.

The *Kaiser Franz Josef I* made her maiden voyage in February 1912, to Buenos Aires. She was then put on the New York run. With two sets of quadruple-expansion engines supplied by D. Rowan & Co, of Glasgow, she could make close to 18 knots. She had elegant accommodation in first class for 125, could take 550 in second and 1,230 in steerage. In 1913 the company had an outstanding year. It had 37 sailings to New York, landing 1,228, 7,465 and 33,895 passengers in first, second and steerage class, respectively. Austro–American owned 29 ocean-going steamers and had five more building. It also operated a fortnightly service to South America.

A folder published in mid-1913 by this line had many quaint tidbits for today's historian. At the top of one page it listed the fleet as follows:

'Fleet—
Regularly employed in passenger (cabin and steerage) service consists of the six new twin-screw steamers. Twin-screw 3-funnel Oil Burner (Building):

Kaiser Franz Josef I	
Martha Washington	
Laura	*Alice*
Argentina	*Oceania*

Also, if required, the single-screw steamers:

Sofia Hohenberg	*Atlanta*
Francesca	*Columbia*
Eugenia	*Georgia*
Belvedere (new)	

All twin-screw steamers are equipped with wireless system and passengers can make use of same for private communication at regular rates. The latest inventions for hygiene and sanitary comforts are installed on board as well as the submarine telephone, automatic electric sounder and the thermotank system for heating and ventilating third class sleeping quarters. Special attention is called to the innovations on the Express SS *Kaiser Franz Josef I* (new).

So proud were the Austro–American people of their new three-funnelled liner that she was mentioned in three different places on this folder. She was to be named *Kaiserin Elizabeth* and was built at Monfalcone. In addition to three stacks she would have had a length of 540 feet and a beam of 69 feet. She would be placed in service 'as early in 1914 as possible'.

Sad to say World War I intervened and the *Kaiserin Elizabeth*, ready for launching, was severely damaged by fire. When Italy entered the conflict she became a target for Italian guns. Later she was used as an observation post by the Italians and became a target for German guns. She was never launched, being scrapped on the ways in 1920, according to material uncovered by Mark Goldberg and used in his new book *A Brief History of Navigazione Libera Triestina*. When the war ended the company became Cosulich Societa Triestina di Navigazione, coming to be known as the Cosulich Line. For a time the line planned to rename the *Kaiser Franz Josef I* the *General Diaz*, but instead selected 'the hero' of Versailles. By good fortune she had not been damaged in the war. On May 5 1919, the *Presidente Wilson* made her first postwar voyage, departing Genoa for Marseilles and New York.

Globe Tours in New York ran an announcement of a 64-day cruise to the Mediterranean leaving January 24 1922, aboard 'the sumptuous twin screw SS *Presidente Wilson*'. The cruise included a four-week tour of Italy and France. Passengers would return on the 'floating palace SS *Rotterdam*'. Cosulich advertisements that year introduced a new slogan: 'Every Trip a Tour'. New ports were added to the *Wilson*'s itinerary in 1923. She stopped at the Azores, Gibraltar, Algiers, Naples, Ragusa, Messina, Patris (Athens) and Trieste. The minimum first class fare in 1923 eastbound was shown as $235. For the first time since the war the *Martha Washington* was listed. She had been returned to Italy by the United States, having been seized in New York when World War I began for

America and was used as an American troopship.

In 1925–6 the *Presidente Wilson* was converted to burn oil. She was averaging six to seven trips to New York a year. One of her best known masters was Captain Robert Stuparich. In 1927 one of the most elegant steamship brochures ever put out was produced for the Cosulich Line. Its cover was a gem being made of yellow–white paper, almost as heavy as cardboard. A golden cord emerged at the left from two holes, holding the pages together. The cord theme was reproduced in the centre of the cover entwining a large Roman-style blue letter 'C' for Cosulich. Above this, in distinctive lettering, were the words 'Cosulich', on the left, and 'Line Trieste' on the right. In the middle was an embossed reproduction of a crown, in gold, red and blue. Inside, after three blank pages, was the second title page, also featuring the crown and yellow cord entwined over the large 'C'. A full-page photo of the *Presidente Wilson* followed, edged in a gold border made up of a thick inner line and four delicate outer lines. Thirteen full-page interior photos followed, each with the same golden border. Elegant features were highlighted such as rounded mahogany joiner work, potted palms, wicker furniture, ornately-decorated metallic stair railings, tasseled lamp shades, wooden bulkhead panels with gold filigree, tall leather-backed chairs edged with gilt hobnails, ornate (imitation) fireplaces, decorative domes, Oriental carpets, fluted columns and the like. Five more pages were given to the *Martha Washington*. A final illustration showed an artist's conception of the *Vulcania*, then building for the company.

Presidente Wilson

The artist could not refrain from having huge billows of smoke coming from her single stack, even though she was a motor-ship and not supposed to smoke at all. At least he made it white smoke! A 1927 cabin rates flyer showed that Cosulich literature was still using the identical smokestack design it used in 1913 folders. More than that, the same oval insert in the white band of the stack showed the identical artist's conception of the flagship, but now she was identified as the *Presidente Wilson*. The ship's speed was given as 20 knots and her displacement tonnage of 22,000 was used to make her seem larger than she was. The finest cabin on the ship cost $350 each for two in off season and $385 in season. Inside cabins could be had on D deck for $253. Second cabin fares ranged from $115 to $180. Intermediate second cabin rates began at $105 per berth in an inside cabin. This flyer also publicised the *Vulcania*, calling her 'the World's Largest Motor Vessel and Most Luxurious Ship Afloat'. Her maiden voyage was listed as being set for February 18 1928.

A 1927 deck plan for *Presidente Wilson*, today a priceless artifact, showed decks B, C, D, E and F. Cabins 1 and 8 had private toilet and tub bath. They were on the promenade deck (deck B) and passengers could make a complete circuit of the superstructure on this deck. A smoking room was forward and the 'Verandah Cafe' aft. Deck C featured a music room forward with windows on three sides. Then came the lounge-foyer and the 'Grand Stairwell'. Ten more cabins with toilet and tub bath were among the staterooms on this deck. The first class dining saloon was forward on deck D, and had windows on three sides, real windows with curtains. A larger dining room for second

class was aft of the casing for the second smoke-stack. It had long tables with fixed swivel chairs. A small second class music room and a small smoking room were next, with a chapel, using the space from a cargo hatch. Next on D deck were five-berth cabins and a very small steerage smoking room far aft. With tufted couches on three sides, it must have been permanently crowded. Deck E had a large steerage dining saloon far aft, right over the twin screws. A small music room was forward of the dining saloon on the starboard side, seating 25 at the most. Then a stretch of four-berth cabins. More four-berth staterooms were on deck F, aft.

By 1929 the *Presidente Wilson* was averaging less than 100 passengers on westbound crossings, and about 200 on eastbound trips. On her April 18 eastbound crossing she had only three passengers. She was, by now, outmoded, and, in 1930, was sold to Lloyd Triestino and renamed *Gange*. Five years later she was again renamed, becoming the *Marco Polo*. She was turned over to the Adriatica Co and sailed between Italy and Greece, Crete, Turkey, the Dodecanese, Cyprus, Syria, Palestine and Egypt. When war came she was pressed into trooping service. In 1944 she was scuttled by the retreating Germans at La Spezia. Five years later, with peace, she was raised and scrapped.

Gross tonnage: 12,577
Length overall: 500 feet
Width: 60 feet
Machinery: Reciprocating, twin screw
Speed: 18 knots
Capacity: 125 in first; 550 in second and 1,230 in steerage
Built: Cantiere Navale Triestino, Monfalcone, 1911
Demise: Scrapped in Italy, 1950

A sailing schedule cancellation card using the Anglicised ship's name.

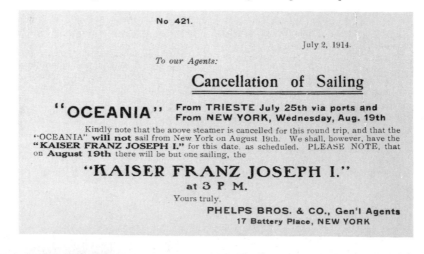

Above *A pre-World War 1 photograph of the liner.* **Below** *In her prime as* Presidente Wilson. *Note the cowls on both stacks (courtesy of Cosulich Line).* **Bottom** *The ship was turned over to Lloyd Triestone and given the name* Marco Polo. *Note the 'Lion of St Mark' design on her two shortened smokestacks.*

Bergensfjord (1913)

In Noel Bonsor's excellent *North Atlantic Seaway* Volume 4), he wrote that the pioneer North Atlantic passenger service under the Norwegian flag started in 1871. Within a year or two, a severe slump set-in and the service closed down. Over 30 years passed before a serious attempt was made to establish a successor. This was the Norwegian America Line, created in August 1910. They hoped to open a service to New York by chartering the faulty North German Lloyd liner *Kaiser Friedrich*, a 12,400-tonner that dated from 1898. The charter agreement never materialised and instead, with sufficient financing in hand, the new company asked for bids for as many as four 11,000-ton passenger ships. Two of these were realised. The second of the pair, the *Bergensfjord*, has had a most diverse career.

The new ships were designed primarily for Norwegian emigrant service to North America, trading between Christiania (now Oslo), Christiansand, Stavanger, Bergen, Halifax and New York. The *Kristianiafjord* was the pioneer ship and was commissioned in June 1913; the *Bergensfjord* followed in September. Like all subsequent Norwegian liners, they came from foreign shipyards that had both the experience and adequate slipways for such tonnage. Their accommodation reflected the trade requirements of the time: a mere 100 in first class, 250 in second class and then 850 in steerage.

Soon after the First World War began in the summer of 1914, the ships were routed via the north of Scotland and later began making periodic calls at Kirkwall in the Orkney Islands. In such tense times, they were filled to capacity, often with worried westbound escapists and evacuees, and soon prompted their owners to think of a third, larger version. Named *Stavangerfjord*, she did not appear, however, until 1918. Although her building order was briefly cancelled by the British government (she was ordered from the Cammell Laird Yards at Birkenhead) for more pressing military work, she was abruptly needed as a replacement when the *Kristianiafjord* was wrecked near Cape Race in July 1917. When the hostilities ended, the surviving *Bergensfjord* was thereafter paired with the brand new *Stavangerfjord* and so remained for some 20 years thereafter.

Like so many other Atlantic passenger ships, the *Bergensfjord* was converted from the less efficient, often dirty coal burning system to an oil-fired vessel. This change took place in 1920. Four years later, however, she was nearly lost. While outbound from Bergen, in July 1924, she was badly damaged following an engine room explosion. She had to be beached and her passengers evacuated. into rescue ships. In the weeks that followed, she was gently refloated and then towed to drydock for full repairs. Thereafter, her berthing configurations were revised on several occasions and she underwent a large refit at the A. G. Weser Yards at Bremen in 1931. New turbines were fitted and once again her accommodation was altered and improved. Her passenger quarters included two fine suites, located on A deck which each consisted of a bedroom, sitting room and full bathroom. The public rooms were of an especially high standard. The main lounge was located on A deck. The smoking room was forward and included alcove seats. The deck around these rooms was glass enclosed. B deck included the music room, a ladies room and the writing room. The first class dining saloon, located on C deck, could seat 97 persons. Another amenity was a fully-equipped gymnasium.

The *Bergensfjord* was detained at New York in April 1940 for safety. She would never again return to her homeland. Several months later, she was seized by the Allies and allocated to the British. Although she retained her Norwegian officers and crew, she was placed under the management of Furness, Withy & Co. Thereafter, she made continuous military sailings and, most fortunately, without serious incident. She was released in February 1946 and returned to the Norwegian America Line.

Despite the very apparent postwar passenger needs, her Norwegian owners decided not to reactivate the 34-year-old ship. Instead, in the following November, she was sold to a brand new firm, the Home Lines of Genoa. These new owners, with a diverse background that included not only Italian, but American, Swiss, Swedish and Greek financial links, was created purposely in 1946 for the booming low-fare tourist and emigrant trades, especially to Latin America. The *Bergensfjord* was an ideal conversion, having been a high-capacity wartime troopship. Renamed *Argentina* and refitted at Genoa, her revised accommodation again reflected her new service: only 32 in first class and 969 in tourist class. As the first of a succession of Home Lines passenger ships, she was sent initially to South America, being routed from Naples and Genoa to Rio de Janeiro, Santos, Montevideo and Buenos Aires. Two years later, in 1949, she was shifted to the Caribbean run, to the West Indian islands and La Guaira in Venezuela. Once again, emigrants were her mainstay.

In 1951, the *Argentina* was temporarily placed on the North Atlantic run to America, to Halifax and New York. Her scheduled partner was another elderly ship, the *Homeland*, the former *Virginian* of 1905. This team lasted but a year. The *Argentina* was no longer a comparable ship to the improved calibre of the Home Lines. She was better suited to low-fare sailings or even charter work, which included a voyage for the French government with members of the French Foreign Legion that were bound from Algeria to Indo-China. At the end of 1952, with no further Home Lines' work in sight, she went to the auction block.

She was also the first major passenger ship for her next owners, the Zim Israel Navigation Company of Haifa. Formed in 1945, they were now interested in forming a direct passenger ship link to North America. With little alteration other than some repainting, the ship was renamed *Jerusalem* and sent to Halifax and New York from Haifa, Limassol, Malta and Cannes. Subsequent ports of call included Piraeus and Genoa. Despite her 40 odd years, she made a fine introduction for this relatively new Israeli firm. Then, in the late summer of 1955, as they commissioned the first of their new West German-built passenger tonnage, the sluggish and tired *Jerusalem* was withdrawn from full Atlantic service. Thereafter, she was kept within the Mediterranean, working the busy run between Marseilles and Haifa with both emigrants, students and tourists. Two years later, in 1957, she was renamed *Aliya* in preparation for a brand new *Jerusalem* to come into service. Little time remained, however. In 1958, as she was

finally laid-up, it was reported that she would go to Brussels for use as a hotel-ship during the World's Fair exposition. The project never materialised. A year later, this veteran ship—the second Norwegian America liner and the first for both the Home and Zim lines—was scrapped. She met her end at La Spezia in Italy.

Gross tonnage: 10,666 (1913); 11,015 (1931)
Length overall: 530 feet
Width: 61 feet
Machinery: Steam quadruple-expansion engines, twin screw (1913); Steam turbines, twin screw (1931)
Speed: 15 knots (1913); 16 knots (1931); 15 knots (1953)
Capacity: 100 first class, 250 second class and 850 third class (1913); 367 cabin class and 572 third class (1925); 90 cabin class, 155 tourist class and 500 third class (1927); 32 first class and 969 tourist class (1946); 33 first class and 741 tourist class (1953)
Built: Cammell, Laird & Co Ltd, Birkenhead, England, 1913
Demise: Scrapped at La Spezia, Italy, 1959

Bergensfjord (1913)

Left *In March 1924* Bergensfjord *had a bad fire aboard after leaving Christiana for New York. Passengers were sent ashore in her own boats. She was quickly repaired and put back into service.*

Below left *March 17 1940.* Bergensfjord *is held in New York because she would not carry US mail to Europe.*

Above right *She was operated by the British Government during World War 2 (courtesy of Victor Scrivens Collection).*

Right *Sold to Home Lines, she became the* Argentina *and served between Mediterranean ports and South America (courtesy of Home Lines).*

Right *Sold once again she became Zim Line's* Jerusalem, *the first major passenger ship in the Israeli fleet. She made transatlantic crossings and also ran within the Mediterranean (courtesy of Antonio Scrimali).*

Frederik VIII

The Skandinavien–Amerika Linien (Scandinavian –American Line) was founded on October 1 1898, succeeding the old Thingvalla Line, which had been serving between Copenhagen and New York since 1880. The parent company—Det Forenede Dampskibs-Selskab, can trace its origin back to 1866. A new building programme began immediately with the 9,946-ton twin-screw *Oscar II*, launched in Glasgow by A. Stephen & Sons on November 14 1901, a vessel famous in her own right. She would be followed in 1903 by the *Hellig Olav*, of 10,185 gross tons and later in the same year by the 10,095-ton *United States*.

The programme was completed by the addition of a still-larger vessel (11,850 tons) distinguished by having two instead of one smokestacks, the *Frederik VIII*. Launched in 1913, she was named in honour of the late King of Denmark who had reigned from 1906 to 1912. The new beauty was delivered early in 1914 and immediately provisioned and sent on her maiden voyage. She sailed February 5 1914, for New York. Almost a month later, on March 2, to be exact, the *New York Tribune* carried a picture of the ship under a three-column headline that read: 'Liner *Frederik VIII*, Which Had Novel Maiden Trip'. Sad to say my files (FOB) only contain the clipping of the picture. Someday a study of old newspapers will disclose what was so 'novel' about that crossing.

All through World War I these four Danish ships maintained water communication between the United States and Scandinavia. The *Oscar II* was selected by Henry Ford for his heroic attempt to stop the fighting in that asinine and pointless bloodletting. He assembled a large group of anti-war leaders and led them on a peace crusade to Scandinavia. There were so many who wanted to go that several dozen were booked to sail aboard the *Frederik VIII*, which sailed some days later, after *Oscar II* had been filled up. Unfortunately the press and public had been so brainwashed as to the nobility of their respective causes on both sides of the conflict that the venture was a dismal failure. One of the few happy moments took place when the *Oscar II* sailed out of Kirkwall, Norway, for Christiansand. As she left the harbour the *Frederik VIII* entered and both groups 'rushed to the rails and cheered and sang to each other as they passed', wrote Barbara S. Kraft, in her splendid book *The Peace Ship*.

Three years later the *Frederik VIII* had a decidedly 'novel' crossing. In February 1917, she took back to Germany Count Johann von Bernstorff, former German Ambassador to the United States, his Countess and their party of 155 German consuls and officials. America was about to succumb to war fever led by a President elected because he had 'kept us out of the war'. The *Frederik VIII* was pictured in the world's press with her name painted in large white letters, along with the word 'Danmark' on both sides of her hull under her twin black, red and black stacks. She also had two large Danish flags, red with their white cross, painted near the bow and stern on either side, reaching down almost to the red waterline.

From its beginning the Scandinavian–American Line spent money to have fine brochures, even for third class. One of the most striking from the standpoint of colour reproduction was produced by the company for their 'superior 3rd Class' accommodation in 1914. It folded into a No 10 envelope mailer. The front two folds were identical except that on the right was a striking colour rendering of *Frederik VIII* and on the left an equally handsome one of three smaller, one-stackers. The ship paintings were framed with a thin gold double line frame and were placed on a mottled brownish background. As a result their colours stood out with a brilliance seldom seen in ship literature. The pale blue sky in the ship portraits made a strikingly good background for the slightly exaggerated but still reasonably accurate ship renderings. Below was the company emblem with the national flags of Sweden, the United States, Norway and Denmark sprouting from a circular design within whose border was the company's full name: Det Forenede Dampskibs-Selskab. Inside the circle was the company house-flag—a light blue background and white old-style cross.

The inside double-page spread was devoted to another grand coloured painting—this time the *Frederik VIII* in broadside, bow to the right. It was the same one that had been used by the *Tribune* in its 'novel' maiden voyage story. As printed in the 1914 folder the name of the artist could be seen. It was Fred Wrens, who had doubtless done the two bow-view paintings on the cover. The originals of these paintings were prominently displayed in the New York office of the line at 27 Whitehall Street. The name 'Scandinavian–American Line', cut in stone, was spread across the face of the eight-storey office building and remained there for all to see many years after the company had ceased its passenger service to New York. The author (FOB) tried unsuccessfully to save these paintings from destruction when the building was demolished.

The 1914 folder was produced when the *Titanic* disaster was very much in everyone's mind, leading to the emphasis on safety in its first sentence: 'These modern steamers are built with water-tight compartments, have double bottoms, bilge keels to insure steadiness, are equipped with wireless telegraphy, and carry boats and life saving apparatus in excess of possible requirements at any time for the total number of passengers and crew.' There followed another interesting sentence: 'The officers and crew are all SCANDINAVIANS [their own capital letters] and only SCANDINAVIAN and DANISH passengers are carried in third class.' The three menus shown inside the fold were all in Danish. Passage time was given as $9\frac{1}{2}$ days for the three older ships and $8\frac{1}{2}$ for *Frederik VIII*. Within the folder were coloured views of a two-berth and a four-berth stateroom and a 'corner of the Dining Room'. Another quote from the brochure's text: 'There is a doctor and trained nurses and a well-equipped hospital and dispensary on every steamer, and in case of sickness during the voyage medical attendance and medicine is furnished free. A matron and stewardess look after the welfare of women traveling alone. Each steamer carries an orchestra of skilled musicians and free concerts are given daily. . . .'

Art seemed to be important to the Scandinavian–American Line, fortunately for us today. Two *Frederik VIII* postcards in common use during her lifetime are worth mentioning for this reason. One, signed by a R. Greetelet (?) showed her with a large sailing sloop to her port and a smaller ketch crossing her bows. The painting was excellent. Kronborg Castle was in the distant left background. The other card was also superb. It was done by Chr Mølsted and is a very fine piece of real art! Showing the liner in about the same position in the Øresund as the other card, this view has a placid grandeur about it that is reminiscent of the works of Turner. The water is calm, permitting finely-executed shadows of the liner, of Kronborg Castle and of the other craft to the right. The big ship's hull is dark at the bow, but illuminated by a lovely slanting slash of sunlight where the lines of the ship assume their full width. But the crowning achievement was the pair of smokestacks, perhaps made a bit taller than they really were for artistic purposes. From each a full tower of dark smoke curls straight up, proof of how placid the air was. For the *piece de resistance*, the artist showed a blob of sheer white—steam—coming from the whistle on the forward stack and backgrounded with the dark smoke—the ship was announcing herself with a deep-throated blast. The painting lives!

In March 1921, the *Oscar II* started to carry cabin class passengers instead of first and second.

This trend was followed by the three other company ships in due course. The year 1921 was a grand year from the standpoint of passengers, the best the company ever had in the post-war period. On eight westbound crossings the *Frederik VIII* carried 6,029. She did even better on the seven eastbound trips—6,821 passengers. The company did not seem to suffer from the cut in quotas by the United States as much as did other lines. With from six to eight crossings each way each year passenger totals for *Frederik VIII* declined slowly to 2,886 westbound in 1926 and 2,494 eastbound. Then, slowly, business began to improve. A new post-war high was set in 1928 for *Frederik VIII* with nine crossings. She carried 5,150 westbound and 3,155 eastbound. It would never be so good again.

The *Frederik VIII* was painted by many artists. One of the most appealing pictures of her was a starboard three-quarters view showing her covered with flags. There were five signal flags from her bridge-top hoist, the Danish merchant ship flag at her prow and national ensign at the stern, the American flag was at the foremast top and the company house-flag at the mainmast. This view was reproduced on tin, frame and all, and widely circulated. It was used as the centre spread in a 16-page colour folder produced in 1927 in Denmark. Still another painting of the company flagship was used on the two outside covers of this lovely brochure, made to fold into a No 10 business envelope. In two different places artistic colour renderings of all four company ships are shown.

One painting of the *Oscar II* shown in this folder was particularly fine. It was painted by the noted American artist Fred Pansing and shows her being welcomed on her maiden voyage in New York Harbor. Many other bits of colourful art mark this brochure as especially appealing. One, for example, shows a lady passenger leaning against a rail near a life ring marked *United States* and gazing at the *Frederik VIII* passing on a blue sea dotted with gulls. She had a red and white scarf blowing in the breeze around her neck.

Although the passenger traffic was declining, more attractive folders continued to come out. A Cabin Class brochure published in 1930 opened into an 18 inch by 12 inch broadside featuring ten photographs of ship interiors. Real windows, with pull-back curtains gave an expansive feeling to the 'artistically decorated Music-saloon' and the 'festive Dining Saloon' on the *Frederik VIII*.

An eight-page tourist third cabin folder produced the next year had more fine interior shots. There was the 'elegant and cozy' ladies' room on the *Frederik VIII*, and 'one of the sunny staterooms on the same ship'. Just getting to Copenhagen on these liners was a cruise and their motto—'The Scenic Route to Europe' was a good one.

As the older liners were slowly dispensed with, the *Frederik VIII* sailed on right through the worst of the Depression. In 1930 on eight westbound trips she carried 4,221 passengers with 3,061 selecting her for eastbound crossings. The Depression was at its worst for the liner in 1934 when only seven crossings were made with 1,669 sailing eastbound and 1,016 westbound. The grand old lady averaged only 280 per eastbound crossing on the nine 1935 trips she made and 227 per trip westbound. In December 1935 her 1936 sailing schedule was cancelled. She was laid up and in late 1936 was sold for scrap. An outstanding and most successful ship she was.

Gross tonnage: 11,850
Length overall: 544 feet
Width: 62 feet
Machinery: Triple expansion
Speed: 17 knots
Capacity: 250 first, 300 second, 1,000 third
Built: A. G. Vulcan, Stettin, 1914
Demise: Scrapped by Hughes & Bolksom, Blyth, England, 1936

Right *View of the interior of* Frederik VIII *reproduced from a brochure of 1914.*

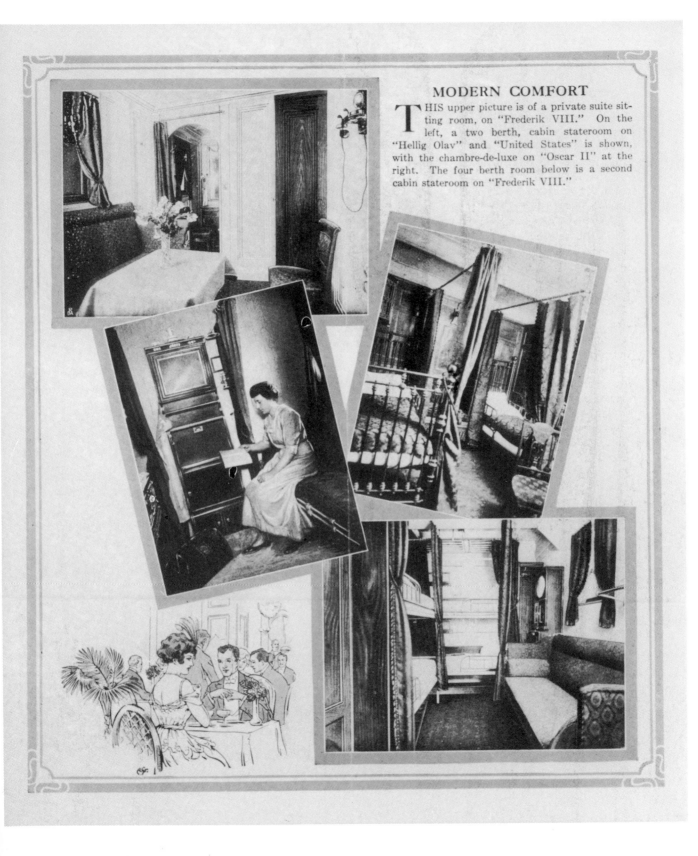

MODERN COMFORT

THIS upper picture is of a private suite sitting room, on "Frederik VIII." On the left, a two berth, cabin stateroom on "Hellig Olav" and "United States" is shown, with the chambre-de-luxe on "Oscar II" at the right. The four berth room below is a second cabin stateroom on "Frederik VIII."

Above Frederik VIII *in 1914 showing her name and the word 'Danmark' painted on her hull. She sailed throughout the war as a neutral ship.* **Below** *Postcard of a painting of* Frederik VIII *by Chr Mølsted.*

Providence

Cyprien Fabre & Co, of Marseilles, bought their first steamship in 1868. She was the *Phenicien*, of 461 tons. And so began one of the most successful of French shipping companies. It is not known exactly when this line adopted red, white and blue for their smokestack colourings, but they did and the custom was retained down to World War II when their passenger services came to a halt. The blue at the top of the stack was a slightly lighter shade than the blue chosen for ships of United States Lines after World War I, but otherwise the companies had similar stack markings. A third line also had red, white and blue funnel colours in the inter-war period. This was the Canadian National Line which operated ships from Canada to New York and the Caribbean. At one point there were in service three Canadian National liners, two Fabre Line steamships and the *Leviathan*, all boasting three red, white and blue stacks. Quite a class!

The *Providence* is the ship we will concentrate on in this chapter, although we will tell the story of her identical sister, the *Patria*, as well, since their lives were so intimately connected. The Fabre Line grew rapidly and established a transatlantic passenger and freight service that rivalled some of the major companies in number of voyages and passengers carried. By 1913 the line made 45 transatlantic voyages and carried westbound 54,434 passengers, about two-thirds landed at New York and the rest at Providence, Rhode Island. The port of Providence was picked because Fabre had won mail contracts from Portugal and there was a large Portuguese settlement in Rhode Island, principally fishermen and sons of fishermen from the Grand Banks areas and out of Cape Verde Islands. The name *Providence* was a natural for a ship in this service, and as World War I loomed nearer and nearer, the Fabre Line decided it would select the name for one of their two new liners ordered from the Forges & Chantiers de la Mediterranee, at La Seyne, near Marseilles.

Up until this point the company had operated small ships with one, or perhaps two funnels. The new ships would be close to 12,000 gross tons and would boast three perfectly proportioned stacks!

And the fact that they had three funnels would be used for their entire careers in virtually all newspaper and magazine advertisements to set them apart from other ships as something special! It was to be a major selling point for the two beautiful liners. The *Patria* was finished first. She saw brief service before World War I. The *Providence* was launched on August 4 1914, just four days after 'the lights went out all over Europe'. It would be six years before she would enter service.

We do not know what happened to *Patria* during the war although one post card was issued showing her at anchor and rusting all over with dark stacks and superstructure. The photograph is not dated but two pre-war style airplanes are shown flying overhead suggesting that it must have been made around 1914 or 1915. What may well be a small gun appears right at the bow atop the forecastle hinting at some kind of war use. When the war ended the *Patria* was cleaned up and quickly put on the New York run with the smaller Fabre Line steamers *Canada*, *Madonna*, *Roma* and *Britannia*.

The *Providence*, which fortunately survived the war in an unfinished state, was completed by Fabre and on June 2 1920, sailed from Marseilles for her first voyage to Providence and New York. Marseilles was home port for Fabre Line. Stops were made at Lisbon and the Azores. The new liner had a gross tonnage of 11,900. Fabre also added two former Austrian ships to their transatlantic service in 1920, the *Asia* and the *Braga*. Business was booming. The line carried 58,253 passengers westbound and brought home 32,709 others in 1920.

In 1921 business took a sharp decline. Restrictions on immigration to the United States and efforts by Italy to force Italians to sail on Italian ships cut drastically into Fabre's trade. The company reduced its Atlantic fleet to only four ships, the *Sinaia* and the *Alesia* (ex *Montreal*) and its two flagships *Patria* and *Providence*. In 1924 the line began to offer Mediterranean cruises to Americans and their popularity helped the company to remain afloat. A rather strange pattern evolved with the formal cruise starting at New York and ending at Marseilles, the Americans often going on to England and returning on a ship of another line.

A special minimum cruise rate for a 40-day cruise in 1927 New York or Boston to Marseilles was $545. If a Fabre ship was used the minimum round trip fare was $720. The cruise rate included all shore excursions and hotels in Palestine and Egypt. Twelve ports were visited with stops ranging from 12 hours to 3½ days. The cruise folder showed a fine photo of the *Providence* and *Patria* moored side by side, bow out. The company was careful to note under the rate listings for both flagships that they were 'twin screw—3 funnels.'

The *Providence* sailed January 12 1927, from New York for her first 40-day cruise of that year. At Naples passengers had to shift to the smaller, two-stacked *Canada* for the remainder of the trip, as the *Providence* was needed to make another westbound crossing to America. All this was planned in advance and the cruise passengers took it in their stride. Each Mediterranean cruise with Fabre was limited to 200 passengers. The 1927 brochure had this to say about the adventure ahead: 'A cruise along the Mediterranean—the sun-kissed azure sea—in a safe, comfortable,

luxurious vessel. . . . Can one picture a greater delight, a more glorious prospect, when shore excursions at the various ports of call add to the unique enjoyment of the voyage?'

Cruise business was booming in 1927 and for the winter of that year a large and well illustrated brochure was put out. Its cover had a fine painting by E. Richelet of the Colossuses of Memnon, and many shades of purple and red were used to give an exotic feeling. The opening page had comments from 1926 cruise passengers: 'The trip we have just made was a Dream!' It continued: 'Our 1927 Cruises offer you the same advantages, with a programme even more complete . . . no trouble, no worry about arrangements or anything whatever . . . the Fabre Line, by means of its minutely perfected organisation, offers you the means of realising all your desires. It undertakes to make life for you at once pleasant, amusing and instructive. Nothing is spared in order that you may carry away with you, after a trip on the Fabre vessels, the impression of a lovely dream, too soon ended. . . .' The text was put in a type that resembled handwriting, to make it more believable.

Then came a page of photos of *Patria* and *Providence* backed with a page of interiors . . . smoking room, promenade deck, glass-sheltered verandah. The interiors were less ornate, perhaps more modern than many vessels of the time. Another page of interiors showed a first class suite with bath. It featured two brass beds, a desk and chair and large easy chair. A dining saloon view showed real windows on three sides. Most ship dining saloons of the day were deep down in the hull and had portholes designed to look like windows from the inside looking out. The social room also had real windows with many easy chairs and panelled walls.

The back of the folder included a page of comments from 14 happy passengers from the year before: Mrs L. S. Sedburry, of Gallatin, Tennessee, said: 'The service is excellent and the comfort could not be better.' L. R. Crisp, of Decatur, Illinois, wrote: 'It is impossible to improve on perfection.'

The winter 1928 Mediterranean cruise folder issued by Fabre was done in France and filled with interesting wood cuts printed in an unusual red-orange colour. Improved economic conditions in the world led to the production of an elaborate 1928–29 cruise brochure for American tourists. The introductory paragraphs illustrate how the stock market was coming to have a hold on Americans no matter where they were:

'Just as in other places where happiness abounds, there are receptions and banquets on board, dances, card parties and afternoon teas, and often the friendships formed through these pleasant activities form one of the greatest pleasures of the trip. Besides, business men who cannot separate themselves completely from the exigencies of their work can find in the trip an invaluable kind of rest. The wireless is at their service to keep them in contact with any important business on land, yet the distance which separates the ship from port acts as a protection against the solicitation of their business acquaintances and against their own impulses to become engaged in some transaction or other, all of which results in a salutary mental repose. To these advantages there is added the incomparable air cure which a sea trip affords. Medical authorities are unanimous on the point that there is not only a complete change of air but a radical difference from one's daily habits on shore resulting in an almost miraculous therapeutic benefit.'

In 1930 the Fabre Line's motto was 'The Popular Route to the Mediterranean'. With the Depression it was changed, and in 1931 a new slogan appeared in Fabre advertisements: 'Travel in Luxury Without Extravagance'. Rates in the May 15 1931 'Sailings and Passenger Rates' folder varied from a minimum cabin class fare New York to Naples of $150 and roundtrip of $295 to a low of $90 one way in third class or $152 roundtrip.

On August 20 1931, Fabre newspaper advertisements hailed the new low rates on the 'twin-screw *Providence*—three funnels'. Still another motto appeared as the Depression worsened: 'Like Travelling In Your own Yacht'. The passenger business continued to decline, however, and finally in January 1932, the *Patria* and the *Providence* were chartered to the much larger Messageries Maritime, also of Marseilles. A history of that famous company shows that the old class categories were restored, with space for 168 being offered on each of the twins in first class, 216 in second, 316 in third and 88 in 'quatrimes'.

The *Providence* was requisitioned by the French government in 1939 to carry troops to Saigon. She continued trooping work for the next dozen years, but minus her white hull, and red, white and blue smokestacks. The *Patria*, also in war grey, was taken over for transport work but fate had an even sadder end in store for her. While at anchor in Haifa harbour on November 25 1940, she was rocked by a tremendous explosion. Her wreck remained visible for many years and was finally scrapped.

The *Providence*'s last voyage was under the command of a French naval officer named Captain Leduc. She dropped her anchor at Djeddah on November 6 1951, and was turned over to ship wreckers at La Spezia for demolition.

Gross tonnage: 11,900
Length overall: 512 feet
Length between perpendiculars (bp): 488.9 feet
Width: 59.8 feet
Machinery: Twin screw, steam
Speed: 17 knots
Capacity: 140 first, 250 second, 1,850 third
Built: Forges & Chantiers de la Med., La Seyne 1914
Demise: Scrapped December 1951, La Spezia

Providence *as shown on a Fabre Line postcard.*

PATRIA

Left *Postcard of* Patria, *sister-ship to* Providence, *laid up during World War 1.*

Below left Providence *at sea* (courtesy of W. B. Taylor Collection, Steamship Historical Society of America).

Right *A* Fabre Line *poster featuring* Providence (courtesy of Charles Sachs).

Below *Artist's impression of* Patria, *probably dating back to before 1914.*

Great Northern

'Her long and eventful life was so packed with spectacular and glamorous incidents that many . . . believed that "Hot Foot" was the greatest ship that ever sailed.'

So wrote former Chief Engineer John Carroll Carrothers about his favourite ship, the *Great Northern*. How she happened to be called 'Hot Foot' will be alluded to below. She was also known as the 'Palace of the Pacific'. Her career was indeed a brilliant and spectacular one. She was one of two fast sister-ships built by James J. Hill, who was known as the builder of the American Northwest. The sister was named *Northern Pacific*. Just as in the case of the two earlier Hill sister-ships—*Minnesota* and *Dakota*—the second one was the less fortunate, seemed accident prone and ended in disaster.

These two Hill ships were built in 1915 as part of his railroad dream. He had been barred from linking the Middle West with San Francisco by other rail interests and, thereupon, conceived the idea of building ships that would be fast enough to take freight or passengers from Minnesota to Portland, Oregon, and then down to San Francisco in competition with direct rail routes. He succeeded.

The two ships he built were named for his two rail systems. They could make 25 knots and were easily the fastest liners under the American flag. Each cost $1,945,000 and they were very expensive to operate. Each started her colourful career by making a highly-publicised voyage from New York to San Francisco via the Panama Canal.

From the start the *Great Northern* was 'special'. In December, 1915, after her delivery by Sun shipyard at Philadelphia, she steamed on a special cruise from Honolulu to San Francisco in a record time of 3 days, 18 hours and 51 minutes at an average of 23 knots, a mark that stood for 40 years. Her regular run was from Portland to San Francisco. She did it in 30½ hours. The two new sister-ships quickly established themselves on the route. The first class fare was $20 and 550 people could be carried in this top category. There was space for 110 in tourist and that cost $15. If you went third class the cost was only $8. An advertisement called the trip 'the ideal short sea voyage of a day and a night'. The advertisement pointed out that the ships had 'powerful wireless equipment and submarine signals'. The ships were run by Hill's Great Northern Pacific Steamship Co, but this phase of their careers was short lived.

America's entry into the war saw the Navy acquire these two lovely new liners, gut them and put them into transatlantic troopship service. Their high speed enabled them to travel alone. Small size, 8,255 gross tons, made going very rough in any kind of bad weather, but in smooth seas they could fly. The *Great Northern* set a round trip record from New York to Brest and return of 12 days, 1 hour and 35 minutes at an average speed of 21.3 knots. Her legion of loyal rooters claimed that she had beaten the *Leviathan* on the return leg of this voyage. For their war service both Hill liners were awarded 'Presidential Citations'.

Disaster overtook the *Northern Pacific* on a homeward crossing with a large list of wounded aboard. She ran aground at Saltaire on Fire Island, New York. Amazing good fortune and hard work saw every soul aboard transferred to other vessels and the ship pulled off, but not before her stern post had been cracked and other serious hull damage

Fifty Famous Liners 2

inflicted. This would be the beginning of the end for this lovely 'Palace of the Pacific'.

But for the *Great Northern* it was just one triumph after another. An honour awaited her that had never gone to any other Atlantic liner. Her great speed convinced the US Navy that she should be fitted out as flagship of the US Atlantic Fleet. She was renamed *Columbia* and assigned a cruiser destroyer to sail with her. She carried from her mainmast the four-star flag of Admiral Hilary P. Jones, Commander-in-Chief of the Fleet and America's senior Admiral afloat. She rated a formal salute from naval craft of all nations at this point, a distinction rarely accorded a passenger liner.

The Admiral Line, a booming coastal passenger service on the West Coast, bought the *Northern Pacific* from the government at this time. En route to this new peacetime assignment this handsome vessel burned, capsized and sank off the entrance to the Delaware River in 1922. The Admiral Line's energetic president, a man with great political power, was H. F. Alexander. He went directly to President Warren Harding to persuade the Navy to give up *Columbia*. He got his wish and promptly sent the liner to Philadelphia to be rebuilt for service under his houseflag from Seattle to San Francisco to Los Angeles. He spent nearly $500,000 on the job and he renamed her after himself—the SS *H. F. Alexander*.

'Here's a delightful, new and attractive trip to California that can be made in quick time on an exceptionally fine ship—formerly USS *Columbia*, Flagship of the Atlantic Fleet, US Navy', said a large advertisement in New York papers for May 9 1922. H. F. Alexander never missed a bet in promoting his ships. The fare was $250 on the 'Fastest Liner Flying the American Flag', the advertisement continued . . . 'Meals and berth included'. A brief brush with disaster occurred May 23 when the *H. F. Alexander* was leaving the shipyard for New York. With Mr Alexander and about 50 guests aboard she collided with the British freighter *Andrea*, which sank. Rescuing the cargo ship's crew of 35, the new Admiral Line steamer returned to the Cramp yard for a check up. Little damage had been done and she was soon back on the West Coast run for which she had been built.

Fares for the coastal trip from Seattle to Los Angeles ranged from $48 for a standard stateroom to $90 for a room with twin beds and private bath. A private telephone in every stateroom was one of the new features advertised. The ship also offered 'a splendid dance orchestra and dancing on deck'. It was advised that 'ordinary clothing is recommended as it is not customary to dress for dinner'. One company folder boasted that the *H. F. Alexander* was the 'largest, fastest and most luxurious coastwise liner in the world', and there was no exaggeration here. The 'Colonial Dining Saloon' sat 350 at tables of two, three, four and six.

Under the Admiral Line house-flag the liner had a dark green hull with a fine gold line from bow to stern. Her stacks were buff with the company's attractive insignia on either side and black tops. Her name—*H. F. Alexander*—was soon shortened to just 'H F' and that, in no time, became 'Hot Foot', because of her great speed. Two Captains relieved each other on alternating trips. The ship gained world-wide notice by being used for background shots in Hollywood movies. A number of films were shot on her attractive decks. The familiar smokestacks of the gallant old lady liner or an *H. F. Alexander* life-ring were constantly turning up in old TV moving pictures. She had glamour plus. One young chap who served as bellboy aboard would speak years later of his time aboard the famous ship—the youngster grew up to become the United Nation's famed Dr Ralph Bunche.

Old 'Hot Foot' had a close call in August 1922, but luck was with her. She smashed bow on, at top speed, into Cake Rock near the entrance to Puget Sound in bad fog. Her prow looked as bad as did that on the *Stockholm* after hitting the *Andrea Doria*. Towed stern first to a nearby Todd Shipyards drydock, she was repaired and back in service in 19 days—a good example of the old 'college try'.

During the autumn of 1925 she was tried on the New York to Miami run, but it really did not work out. The winter storms off Cape Hatteras played havoc with her schedule and she returned to service on the West Coast. This period in her life was remarkably happy and trouble free. She ran aground now and then but generally got off without much damage. After one grounding in 1933 on Point Wilson she had to be replaced for a brief period by the old *City of Los Angeles*, of Lassco Lines.

On July 29 1936, while making her customary 22 knots she struck something that her master, Captain Charles G. Hanson, thought might have been a log. He soon realised that she was not performing just right, but, as she was not taking any water, he continued on toward Seattle. The ship's knife-like bow had struck a whale and the force of her motion kept the poor thing hanging on the stem until she docked, when it fell loose. Captain Hansen was quoted as saying that the whale had died 'instantly'.

Bad times eventually forced the ship's retirement and when World War II began she was lying idle at San Francisco. In 1941 she was sold to the Canadian Pacific Steamship Co and converted again into a troopship. She was transferred to British registry but her name was retained. In due course she came back to the American flag. The old US Lines *America* had meanwhile been rebuilt as a troopship and renamed *Edmund B. Alexander*. To avoid confusion the *H.F. Alexander* was again renamed—becoming the *General George S. Simonds*. Her considerable period in lay up, however, and rough war service had damaged her machinery and she proved difficult to operate with high-speed convoys. She did serve, nevertheless, and participated in several key actions, most colourful of all being the taking of land reinforcements to Omaha Beach on the day after D-Day. She was second in line with destroyers on either side. The lead ship was the former Grace Line's *Santa Clara*, renamed the *Susan B. Anthony*. With

the old 'Palace of the Pacific' only moments behind her, the *Anthony* suddenly exploded and began to go down by the stern.

Old 'Hot Foot' speeded up and took the lead, safely disgorged her troops and headed back to England for more. She made several more trips to Normandy and then returned to the safety of the Caribbean for service with the Maritime Commission. The 'General' part of her name was dropped. When the war ended, the government restored her old name *H.F. Alexander* and she was anchored in the James River. Officially decommissioned on March 5 1946, she lay there with such veterans as the *President Warfield*, soon to become the *Exodus 1947*, and the *Naushon*, later named the *John A. Meseck*. This time no one wanted her. On January 15 1948, she was removed from the *Record* of the American Bureau of Shipping, she became a nonentity. The next month she was singled out from among the hundreds of dark hulks and taken in tow by two small tugs. They took her to the Sun Shipbuilding & Dry Dock Co yard at Chester, Pennsylvania, where she had been built, and she was scrapped.

Gross tonnage: 8,255
Length overall: 524 feet
Width: 63 feet
Machinery: Triple screw, turbine
Speed: 25 knots
Capacity: 550 first, 110 tourist, 200 third
Built: Sun Shipbuilding & Dry Dock Co, Chester, Pennsylvania, 1915
Demise: Scrapped at builders, 1948

Above Great Northern's *sister-ship*, Northern Pacific, *aground off Fire Island, New York.*

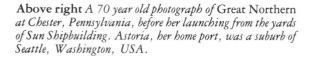

Above right *A 70 year old photograph of* Great Northern *at Chester, Pennsylvania, before her launching from the yards of Sun Shipbuilding. Astoria, her home port, was a suburb of Seattle, Washington, USA.*

Right *Navy flagship* Columbia, *ex-*Great Northern.

Left *USAT* Great Northern *in World War 1 colours.*

Right General George Simonds *as she looked when on active duty in World War 2.*

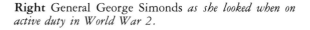

Resolute

The Germans have produced some of the world's greatest and most fascinating passenger ships. Particularly in the years prior to the two World Wars, German shippers seem to have built related series of liners—'strings' of similar ships, if you will. Beginning in 1897, the North German Lloyd became fascinated with long, very low and very powerful-looking four-stackers. Their rival, the Hamburg America Line, seemed to prefer a more traditional appearance: twin funnels set between four masts. The Germans assuredly reached for an ocean liner highpoint in 1912 when they commissioned the 52,100-ton *Imperator*, a three-stacker that resembled in every way Teutonic brilliance, might and splendour. She was followed, within two years, by the even bigger *Vaterland*, at 56,200 tons. These superships set a standard, and were duplicated albeit in somewhat smaller, less overwhelming triple-stackers.

These related ships began to steam out of German yards just before the outbreak of the First World War. The Hamburg South American Line had their 18,800-ton *Cap Trafalgar* and then the 20,500-ton *Cap Polonio*. Hamburg America created a very similar ship, the 21,400-ton *Admiral Von Tirpitz*, which was soon to be renamed more simply as the *Tirpitz*, but then only to be ceded to Britain and then more specifically to Canadian Pacific after the war years. She became their *Empress of Australia*. Two very similar Hamburg America liners were to follow. They were the near-sisters *William O'Swald* of 20,200 tons and the *Johann Heinrich Burchard* of 19,900 tons.

The *O'Swald* was ordered from the famed Weser Shipyards at Bremen; the *Burchard* from the Tecklenborg works at Geestemunde. Laid down and underway in that troubled summer of 1914, construction was soon halted. They sat out the war years untouched. However, secret negotiations were underway with a Dutch shipper, the Royal Holland Lloyd, to take the ships as reparation. Among others, the Germans had sunk the 14,000-ton *Tubantia* and the Dutch wanted replacement tonnage. Finally, with agreements in hand, the official sale took place in June 1916.

Construction and fitting-out, while delayed due to a shortage of labour and problems with available materials, was resumed in 1918. The ships were ready for service by early 1920. Thereafter, a sizeable controversy erupted. Although owned by the Dutch, the new ships were German-built and the Allies wanted them for their own reparations. In fact, the Allied shipping commissions even refused to acknowledge the sale to the Dutch. To them, they were still Hamburg America liners. The Dutch, in particular, remained adamant to the requests of the Allies, particularly the British. The new ships were given their Dutch names: the *O'Swald* became the *Brabantia* and the *Burchard* changed to *Limburgia*. Continual delays followed.

In February 1920, when the *Limburgia* was to be delivered to the Holland Lloyd, a British destroyer attempted to block her sailing. In deep fog, the liner was able to escape. To the utter frustration of the Allies, the ships were transferred and placed in Dutch passenger service. They traded from Amsterdam and Plymouth to Las Palmas in the Canaries and then across to Pernambuco, Bahia, Rio de Janeiro, Santos, Montevideo and finally a turnaround at Buenos Aires. The accommodation on both ships was arranged as 290 in first class, 320 in second and 400 in third class. Certainly, they were the biggest Dutch liners on the Latin American run.

Unfortunately, this Dutch-flag service was far less than successful. The Royal Holland Lloyd had overspent on these two ships and quickly fell onto financial hard times. They were quite close to collapse by 1922. Furthermore, those Allied arguments persisted about handing the two ships over to either American or British owners. The situation had now changed and such an alternative seemed far more possible. An agreeable sale price was arranged between the hard-pressed Royal Holland Lloyd and the United American Lines of New York. This latter firm wanted the two ships for their originally intended transatlantic run. They were the perfect medium-sized vessels for that service and particularly suitable for a growing medium in ocean travel, luxury one-class cruising. The *Brabantia* became the *Resolute* and set out on her first Atlantic crossing from New York in April 1922; the *Limburgia* switched to *Reliance* and transferred to her new route a month later, in May. Ironically, their sailings were timed to the ships of their initial owner, Hamburg America.

While both ships flew the American flag, they changed to Panamanian registry a year later, in one of the very early instances of passenger ships using a 'flag of convenience'. The US government had just started 'Prohibition', which would have kept such ships 'dry' and therefore less appealing to potential passengers. Three years later, in yet another change in plans, the ships were, in fact, cleared for resale to the Germans, who were already deeply engaged in rebuilding their depleted post-war fleet. The Hamburg America Line had four major passenger ships on the North Atlantic run to New York while the North German Lloyd was so pleased with their 32,300-ton *Columbus* that they were modifying her design into a pair of exceptionally powerful superliners, the 50,000-ton *Bremen* and *Europa* of 1929. The *Resolute* and *Reliance* were welcome additions, especially as they had been German built and then had established particularly high reputations, notably as cruise-ships.

While both briefly continued on the North Atlantic run, they were officially redesignated as full-time cruise-ships in 1928. Thereafter, they were sold as one-class ships. In 1934, they were thoroughly overhauled and converted, and their capacities were cut drastically to 500 first class berths only. The ships were described as having excellent accommodation with special attention being given to ventilation because of their frequent tropical voyages. Elevators were fitted wherever necessary. There were 280 staterooms, 28 of which were deluxe, which included a sitting room, bedroom, double bathrooms and a trunk room. The public rooms were equally luxurious. The dining room, located on B deck, could seat 350 persons at a single seating. It was two decks high and a gallery was placed along the sides. Tall glass windows gave it a very spacious feel. An orchestra balcony was positioned at the far end. Also on B deck was the shop, cruise office, an 'American Bar' and a very modern grill room, which included a central parquet dance floor and one wall which could be partially opened onto the deck.

The principal public spaces were on the promenade deck. The 'Verandah Cafe' connected with the smoking room. This latter lounge was done in fine wood panelling and supportive pillars. It included a marble mantle, a light frieze around the ceiling and a group of lights which formed an electrolier. The writing room and library were next and connected to the drawing room, which included a central skylight. One of the ship's finest spaces was the 'Winter Garden', which included a series of almost private alcoves of divans, tables and chairs, and which was made to appear especially spacious through the use of large mirrors. Also noteworthy were the flower shop, gymnasium and the large swimming pool, all placed on the boat deck. Not only was this pool most unusual in being positioned on a high, upper deck, but it was actually a full deck lower. Half of the ceiling on the boat deck could be pushed aside on wheels and thereby created a partially open-air setting. Otherwise, if closed, the pool area was well lighted by a series of small skylights.

The *Resolute* was always the slightly more popular for cruising of the two ships. An advertisement for her 1926 around-the-world cruise read: 'Westward via the Panama Canal, the *Resolute* offers a combination of features found on no other world cruising ship; an itinerary that will fascinate to the very end—an American management [cruise staff] fully conversant with the desires of American travellers, and European chefs and servants, trained in the continental way. These are the perfect appointments. The *Resolute* also offers all the privileges of foreign registry. Four months

perfect vacation on the "Queen of cruising steamships". Rates $1,500 and up including shore excursions.'

Two years later, in another stylised advertisement, the *Resolute*'s winter world cruise was promoted. 'Once aboard the "Queen of cruising steamships", remorseless winter is only a figment of a bad dream. Sun-painted hours pass in leisurely procession over cobalt or emerald seas. You visit far, strange lands in their gayest moods—Cairo, at the height of the social season; India, in February's May-like mildness; China in early springtime; and gorgeous Japan a-bloom with brilliant kimonos and cherry blossoms. And always, you return from exotic delight to home-like comfort—from the dynasty of Ramses II to the luxury of a Park Avenue hotel and the amenities of a Terrace Cafe. From the alabaster and ebony to the quiet peace of a spacious stateroom and the joys of a cuisine that brooks no rival. 30 countries, 63 cities, 140 days, 37,849 miles on land and sea, with rates from $2,000 including an extraordinary program of shore excursions.' Of course, both ships made more ordinary voyages as well. There were Bermuda and Nassau cruises for a week and 14–27 day Caribbean trips that were priced from $150 to $250.

The ships were, like almost all others, hard hit by the slump of the Depression. Regrettably, the Hamburg America Line was forced to re-evaluate the need for two deluxe cruise-ships. Consequently, the *Resolute* was offered for sale. However, in view of what was to happen to her sister-ship in less than two years, her German owners would have been more fortunate to have kept her in reserve. The Italians under Mussolini were then actively engaged in their East African campaign and desperately needed additional troopships. They even looked at White Star's giant *Olympic*, the sister-ship to the *Titanic*. The *Resolute* was sold and transferred in August 1935. Although owned by the Italian government's Directorate of Shipping, she was placed under the management of the Lloyd Triestino. She was renamed *Lombardia* and refitted to carry 103 first class passengers and 4,420 soldiers. It was a demoded, sorry last mission for such a glorious, happy ship.

Neither ship completely survived the Second World War. While the *Reliance* was more ex-tensively refitted in 1937 for further Hamburg America service (she became, in fact, a two-class ship), she caught fire while at Hamburg, on August 7 1938. Ablaze from end to end, she was so seriously damaged that the underwriters declared her as an economic loss. Her wrecked remains were laid-up, without any further intention. In 1940, as the Nazi war machine was well underway, she was sold to the immense Krupp Company, who wanted her steel for 'recycling'. Within a year, at Bremerhaven, she was dismantled totally.

The former *Resolute* as the Italian *Lombardia* saw little service after the war started. Among other Italian liners, she was hit during an Allied air raid on Naples harbour, on August 4 1943. Like her sister-ship, she burned out completely and was beyond any form of repair. Three years later, in 1946, her half-sunk hull was salvaged, brought into Naples for further inspection but then only to be sold to scrappers at La Spezia.

Gross tonnage: 20,200 (1920); 19,653 (1922); 17,258 (1923); 19,692 (1926); 20,006 (1935)
Length overall: 616 feet
Width: 72 feet
Machinery: Steam triple expansion engines, triple screw
Speed: 16 knots
Capacity: 335 first class, 284 second class, 469 third class and 857 steerage (as planned); 290 first class, 320 second class and 400 third class (1920); 497 all-first class (1934); 103 first class and 4,420 troops (1935)
Built: A. G. Weser Shipyards, Bremen, Germany, 1914–20
Demise: Bombed and sunk at Naples, on August 4 1943; scrapped at La Spezia in 1946

Above right Resolute's *stern in New York—this shows her flying the flag of Panama after it was found that having the US flag prevented her operators from selling liquor aboard because of Prohibition.*

Above far right The Resolute *listing badly when she arrived in Quanantine, New York, in 1924. Improper ballasting was blamed and the list quickly corrected.*

Right A *flag-bedecked* Resolute *outbound for yet another cruise* (courtesy of Fred Hawks).

American Banker

A major transfer of ships took place within the American Merchant Marine 1923–24. The United States Shipping Board, the owners of the United States Lines, sold five of their *President* passenger liners from their New York–London service to the Dollar Steamship Lines for their around-the-world trade. In return, the US Army cleared six 1920–21 built troop transports for sale to private owners and then rebuilding as transatlantic combination passenger-cargo ships. These latter vessels were given over to J. H. Winchester & Company of New York, who planned to sail them on that same London service under their subsidiary, the American Merchant Lines.

Built by the now long defunct American International Shipbuilding yards at Hog Island, Pennsylvania, the ships were delivered as the USS *Somme*, USS *Tours*, USS *Cantigny*, USS *Ourcq*, USS *Marne* and USS *Aisne*. Respectively, they became the *American Importer*, *American Shipper*, *American Banker*, *American Farmer*, *American Trader* and *American Merchant*. They were built as part of a class of freighters, known as the 'Hog Islanders'. Although otherwise unnoticed ships, the *Cantigny* had a special honour. While he was on an official visit to America, King Albert of the Belgians was asked if he would name the little transport. He accepted readily. Consequently, she became one of the very few American flag ships to have a European royal christening. The *Cantigny* was also the only member of this group to survive the Second World War and thereafter become a hardworking, worldwide passenger liner.

The ships were refitted in the winter and spring of 1924, in preparation for their introduction on the weekly London service. They were listed as having accommodation for 12 tourist class passengers. However, the American Merchant Lines at first refused to become a member of the established, all-powerful North Atlantic Passenger Ship Conference. In quick time, the conference directors asked recognised travel agents not to book passengers aboard these ships. The loss was immediate. Within two years, the Winchester Company owners reversed their decision and not only joined the Conference as a full member, but had each of the ships enlarged to carry 80 'tourist cabin' class passengers.

In 1929, when the mighty United States Shipping Board sold its United States Lines to P. W. Chapman & Company, this *American Merchant* class, as they were commonly known, was included in the transaction. They continued, however, to sail under their separate banner of the American Merchant Lines. Two years later, in the autumn of 1931, they were fully integrated into the United States Lines fleet, a decision prompted in no doubt by the sinister, slumping effects of the Depression. Soon afterward, a seventh ship, the *American Traveler*, joined this group.

In the mid-1930s, there were several changes in routing and frequent lay-ups for these ships, often at backwater berths in New York Harbor. Two of the ships ran an extended service, to Plymouth, Cherbourg and Hamburg. When this was dropped, an alternate run was created to Cobh, Liver-

pool and Manchester. Furthermore, a homeward call at Boston was also begun. However, all of these services ceased, including the direct run to London, in that frightening autumn of 1939. The ships were kept at New York for safety.

A year later, in 1940, because of American neutrality and her inability to openly transport war materials to Europe, these ships were, under emergency conditions, placed under the Belgian flag and assigned to the Societe Maritime Anveroise. All were given Belgian names. While some worked a service to Liverpool, others went to Le Havre or Cherbourg. Unfortunately, all but the *American Banker*, which had become the *Ville D'Anvers*, were sunk by German torpedoes within little more than ten months, between the late summer of 1940 and the spring of 1941. By that first peaceful summer, in 1945, the *American Banker* was quite incredibly the sole survivor of that original *American Merchant* class.

While the United States Lines saw the future of a London passenger service with nothing larger than their new class of 12-passenger C2 freighters, the *American Banker*—which reverted briefly to her original name—was left without a proper assignment. Consequently, she was given over to another American shipper, the Isbrandtsen Company, for further work. They placed her under the Honduran flag as the *City of Athens* and had 200 'austerity' berths fitted. Thereafter, she began a series of diverse passenger sailings, determined by charter, migrant demands and even the movement of refugees and prisoners. Managed by the T. J. Stevenson Company at New York, she began with three migrant trips from Istanbul to New York in the spring of 1947. Then, soon after a trip from Piraeus and Genoa to Baltimore, she was seized for debt by the local sheriffs. That August, she was sold at auction to another 'austerity passenger' firm, the Panamanian Lines. She was renamed *Protea*. Taken to Genoa, she was rebuilt with 965 third class berths. Her tonnage increased by nearly 1,500 tons, from 7,430 to 8,929. In the three years that followed, she sailed first for the Panamanian Lines and then another Panama-flag shipper, Compania Internacional Transportadora. In Noel Bonsor's *North Atlantic Seaway*, he gives the first full documentation of her movements during these years. She began with four roundtrips be-

tween Italy and Australia; a round voyage between Italy and Brazil; another trip to Central America; five sailings to Rio de Janeiro, Montevideo and Buenos Aires; two special refugee trips from Gdynia to Haifa; three more emigrant trips to Fremantle, Melbourne and Sydney from Genoa and Naples; and finally, in August 1951, a special troop charter for the French government from Marseilles to Indochina. That summer, she made three transatlantic trips for the newly established Incres Line, sailing between Antwerp, Plymouth and Montreal.

In early 1952, the Arosa Line had just been created by Swiss businessman Nicolo Rizzi. He had positive beliefs in the future of budget-tourist class service on the North Atlantic. His first purchase, in January 1952, was the *Protea*, the former *American Banker*. Renamed as *Arosa Kulm*, the ship's initial refit was the first of a series of modifications and improvements. Her quarters were always being modernised.

Arosa used the ship only during the peak passenger months, between April and November, on the St Lawrence route, between Bremerhaven, Zeebrugge, Southampton and Montreal. In winter, she was either laid-up, given out to charter or, in later years, sent on the occasional trip to Halifax. Staffed by a mix of German and Italian crewmembers, she became a popular ship. Within two years, Arosa was ready for their second liner, the laid-up American cruise-ship *Puerto Rico*, which became the *Arosa Star*. At its peak, in 1957–58, the Company was running four Atlantic liners, the other two being the *Arosa Sun* and *Arosa Sky*, both formerly with France's Messageries Maritimes.

Unfortunately, Mr Rizzi's earlier projections of low-fare transatlantic service were diminishing rapidly by 1958. That surge in post-war immigration to North America had eased, the student trade went to specially chartered tonnage and jet aircraft were about to make their first and startling appearance. The Arosa Line ships fell on hard times. There were less than pleasant news reports of small fires on the Arosa liners, poor shipboard conditions and even unpaid, disgruntled crewmembers. The company was losing money rapidly. In October, less than two years since she had been bought, the *Arosa Sky* had to be sold, an emergency bid to raise much needed capital. She went to Italy's Costa Line and became their *Bianca C.* However, two months later, the entire company collapsed. Creditors on both sides of the Atlantic requested that the three remaining Arosa passenger ships be seized for debt. The veteran *Arosa Kulm* was impounded, in December, at Plymouth. At 38 years old, there was little hope of a resale for further passenger service. Instead, she was auctioned to Belgian shipbreakers and was brought to Bruges, arriving on May 7 1959, to be broken-up. It was rather ironic that this little ship, which was launched by the Belgian king, should have concluded her long, very diverse career in his homeland.

Gross tonnage: 7,430 (1923); 8,929 (1947)
Length overall: 448 feet
Width: 58 feet
Machinery: Steam turbines, single screw
Speed: 14½ knots
Capacity: 12 tourist class (1923); 80 tourist cabin class (1926); 200 third class (1947); 965 third class (1948); 46 first class and 919 tourist class (1952); later changed to 20 first class and 945 tourist class, and then to 30 first class and 802 tourist class
Built: American International Shipbuilding Corporation, Hog Island, Pennsylvania, 1920
Demise: Scrapped at Bruges, Belgium, 1959

WAR PAINT
Old Glory Tells the Maritime
World That America Is at Peace

LONDON BOUND. The United States liner American Banker sails for London. She left yesterday without passengers. Ship will bring back about 150 Americans still in the war zone. —*Story on page 19.*

Left American Banker *bound for London during the early days of the war* (courtesy of New York Daily News).

Top right *The dining saloon on the little liner* (courtesy of US Lines).

Centre right *The sun deck aboard the* American Banker (courtesy of US Lines).

Below right *Lounge aboard* American Banker. *The simplicity of decor seemed to have added to the popularity of these vessels.*

Left *In the late 1940s the* American Banker *briefly sailed as the immigrant ship* City of Athens. *She is shown berthed at Pier 16 East River, New York* (courtesy of Vincent Messina collection).

Alfonso XIII

The Compania Trasatlantica was established in Barcelona on June 1 1881, but its earliest roots date back as far as 1856. The firm was commonly known as the Spanish Royal Mail Line. After the Civil War it became simply the Spanish Line. A major new building programme was begun when peace came after World War I. The company's first new ship was launched on September 14 1920, at Bilbao, at the yard of the Sociedad Espanola de Construccion Naval. She was christened *Alfonso XIII* after the reigning monarch of Spain. The new liner was badly damaged by a fire on October 26 1920, while fitting out and she had to be rebuilt. Trouble seemed to dog her. On her trials serious turbine malfunction developed leading to more work back at the yard. It was not until September 1923 that she was ready for her maiden voyage. She sailed from Bilbao for Santander, Coruna, Havana and Vera Cruz. Hers had not been a very promising beginning, but she was to prove a survivor. She would live through two other major fires and sail on over four decades and under three different names.

The *Alfonso XIII* was a good-looking ship, but not one with any particularly distinctive feature.

She had a straight stem and raised forecastle which was always painted black along with the rest of her hull. The forecastle on the *Cristobal Colon*, her sister-ship, was always done in white making her look not only larger but more like a major passenger ship. The *Alfonso XIII*'s bow anchors were placed unusually high up and quite far forward. Two tall pole masts and a large and well-proportioned single smokestack, equally placed between the masts, created the basic silhouette of this ship and her sister. As was true with many ship lines, they had a family look about them and could be spotted as a Spanish Royal Mail Line ship from far off. Four tall air funnels rose around the fore-mast. The forward face of the superstructure towered four decks high above the well deck. The lowest of these decks, the awning deck, had portholes facing forward, wise planning, as in bad weather this deck would often swirl with green water from the bow. The promenade and boat decks had large windows facing forward, with softly-slanted tops. The bridge on either side of the pilot house was stained dark mahogany, but, for some reason, the pilot house itself was painted all white. It was a small one with only five windows. Awnings offered shade on either side of the pilot house and on the deck above.

The superstructure proper was clean cut and modern looking, running two decks high for most of its length. Except for the forward portions, both of these decks featured open promenades, which could be closed in bad weather with canvas coverings. Six lifeboats were located on either side of the boat deck, the last four being pairs of two, nested. They were served by old-style radial davits. A dozen air funnels of various heights dotted the upper boat deck alongside the stack and aft. The after end of the superstructure was cut off abruptly, adding to the ship's relatively modern look. The main-mast rose in the 'well' aft of the superstructure, surrounded by more tall air funnels. Abaft of all this was a two-deck high after deck-house with a lifeboat atop on either side. The stern was of the modern-style cruiser type. The hull proper was black and there was a thin white boot topping above the red underwater portion of the hull, giving a finished look to the ship. The superstructure was white. The stack was all black with no identifying marks or stripes whatsoever, a tradition of the Spanish Royal Mail Line.

In outline the *Alfonso XIII* and *Cristobal Colon* were almost identical to the three slightly-larger companion liners that were built for the Spanish Line a few years later: *Marques de Comillas*, *Magallanes* and *Juan Sebastian Elcano*, with one major difference. That difference, and it did mean a lot, was the addition on the three newer ships of a second stack aft of the first. This was done without moving the mainmast, so there was more space between the foremast and the first stack than between the mainmast and the second stack. But with two stacks the ships looked much better in my opinion (FOB).

The *Cristobal Colon* sailed on her maiden voyage a month after the *Alfonso XIII* had begun her long-delayed debut. The two new liners were greeted with enthusiasm at each port they visited and were widely hailed in the marine press for their elegant Spanish-style interiors. Up to this point the Spanish Line had concentrated on its service to Havana and Vera Cruz, with an extraordinarily large fleet of good-sized passenger liners linking these ports with Bilbao, Santander, Gijon, Coruna, Vigo, Barcelona and Cadiz. By 1927 the company had 18 ships with a total tonnage of 111,593 gross. In that year it added New York to the route of its two newest liners, with the well-known firm of Garcia & Diaz as their agents in the United States.

A full-page oil company advertisement in *Marine Engineering and Shipping Age* magazine for March 1929 turned the spotlight briefly on a man whose face and name would otherwise have never been known in the maritime world. He was Chief Engineer Amador F. Lopez of the *Alfonso XIII*, a serious-looking gentleman with a kindly face. His picture was shown under a fine view of the liner being undocked at New York as a way of getting the company's message about its oils across. The text of the advertisement began: 'Another Royal Mail Liner and Gargoyle Marine Oils—Chief Engineer Amador Fernandez Lopez is responsible for efficient and economical operation in the engine room of the luxurious Spanish Royal Mail Liner *Alfonso XIII*. Maximum power, protection against costly break-downs, and the reduction of fuel and oil consumption are problems of prime importance. That is why Chief Engineer Lopez relies on Gargoyle Marine Oils for correct lubrication of the *Alfonso XIII*'s four steam turbines.'

A December 1930 Spanish Royal Mail Line brochure, appropriately done in golden-orange and black, featured the company's six newest ships: the *Manual Arnus*, which had come out before the *Alfonso XIII* and *Cristobal Colon* were described as the 'ever popular' and relegated to slightly smaller type, while the three new liners were highlighted. All six were listed under the heading: 'New Magnificent and Palatial Steamers.' These six ships still kept the categories of first, second, intermediate class and third. The *Manuel Calvo* was described as 'the popular Cabin Steamer', with rates one way transatlantic of $130 in cabin and $85.50 in third.

Even though the *Alfonso XIII* was at this point one of the smallest liners on the Atlantic, great emphasis was placed on suites and deluxe rooms. The 1930 rate sheet showed how this was done in a way unique to the Spanish Royal Mail Line.

'Promenade Deck
Suites A and B, each composed of sitting-room with Pullman sofa, cabin with brass bed and Pullman sofa, bathroom and baggage-room. (De Luxe)
For one person $630
For two persons $810
For three persons...................................$990... etc.

'Awning Deck
Suites C, D, E, each composed of a two-bed room with Pullman sofa and bathroom. (De Luxe)
For one person $490
For two persons $670
For three persons...................................$850... etc.'

And so on down more than two-thirds of the page, with a wide variety of combinations such as rooms with or the same rooms without baths, rooms for one, two or three persons etc. Main deck had two-berth rooms for $210 per person, while it offered four-berth cabins for $180 per person.

Only four lines were devoted to second class and only two prices were shown—$143 per person in two-berth rooms and $131 per person in four-berth rooms. Some 13 lines were given over to intermediate class with rates ranging from $105 to $100. For third class there was just one line: 'All cabins of 2, 4, 6 and 8 berths, per person . . . $85.50.'

The interiors of the *Alfonso XIII* and *Cristobal Colon* were described in glowing terms in this 1930 rate sheet. One picture of the 'Winter Garden' was provided: 'Our illustration shows the Winter Garden, which, like that of other Spanish liners, is a distinctive and unusual sort of rendezvous, typically Spanish. These boats, from stem to stern, exemplify the best modern practice in every detail of shipbuilding and equipment. However, the black and white views do not do justice to the vivid colours of the Spanish decoration. It is suggested that prospective travellers visit the ships and see their beauties for themselves. Any travel agent will gladly arrange for such a visit, whenever a Spanish Royal Mail liner is in port, in New York.'

The front cover of this brochure featured a good bow-on view of the *Juan Sebastian Elcano*, and the New York office at 25 Broadway, had a superb model of this beautiful liner in a large glass case along with models of several of the company's other ships. The folder was issued before the Civil War broke out in Spain and before the abdication of Alfonso XIII. It was still being given out after these events had happened, but the only change in the brochure was the pasting in of the name 'SS *Habana*' over *Alfonso XIII* inside above the rates for this liner. All through the brochure were other mentions of *Alfonso XIII*. One in particular must have been a problem. A fine painting of Alfonso XIII was described as hanging in the music room of the *Manuel Arnus*.

The abdication of King Alfonso XIII took place in 1931 and the new republican government in Spain brought many changes to the Spanish fleet. Three of its principal ships had to be renamed, the *Alfonso XIII* becoming the *Habana*; the *Reina Victoria Eugenia* being renamed the *Argentina*; and the *Infanta Isabel de Borbon* becoming *Uruguay*.

The Spanish Civil War began in July 1936 and the *Habana* was severely damaged by fire during the conflict. She survived and ran between Bordeaux and New York up until 1939 when she was laid up for a time. In 1943 she returned to service and suffered another serious fire, this time at New York. She was rebuilt as a passenger/cargo ship with elegant accommodation for 112 in first class. Her outline was completely changed with only the old forecastle resembling the original liner. Amidships a new superstructure, much shorter and more modern, rose with one tall mast atop a new pilot house. A single smokestack, considerably wider and slightly shorter replaced the old funnel. Everything was new and different and the ship lost most of her charm and appeal to ship lovers. She served from Barcelona to New Orleans and then between Coruna, Bilbao and New York. Menus from 1950 show that much of the pride in service and fine food was still alive in the ship's operation.

In 1960, when she was nearly 40 years old, the *Habana* was sold for scrap, but, for some reason, she was not scrapped. Two years later the scrapping company sold her for use as a floating fish factory ship. She was rebuilt and renamed *Galicia* and continued to serve for some years.

Gross tonnage: 14,130/10,551
Length overall: 500 feet
Width: 61 feet
Machinery: Four steam turbines
Speed: 17 knots
Capacity: 300 in first, 700 in three other classes/as rebuilt—112 in first
Built: Sociedad Espanola de Construccion Naval, Bilbao, 1920
Demise: Scrapped, 1978

Top right *As built in 1923 the Spanish Line's* Alfonso XIII *had a most distinguished profile with twin masts and a single all black stack* (courtesy of The Mariner's Museum).
Centre right Alfonso XIII *had a serious fire and emerged from repairs as the* Habana *with a much smaller superstructure and a new smokestack.*
Right Habana *arriving at New York in 1946* (courtesy of Victor Scrivens collection).

Paris

She was one of the finest and best decorated liners ever to sail the North Atlantic. She was a 'between the wars' ship, finished at the end of the first conflict and then destroyed before the onset of the second. She was a ship of enormous style. I (WHM) can readily recall a very special photograph. It was an evocative scene, clearly from the 1930s. The wooden planking of the ship's decks were heavily shadowed, either from a late afternoon sun or the photographer's outdoor lamps. A heavily-veiled, fur-wrapped, all-in-black Marlene Dietrich sat on at least a dozen polished steamer trunks, all of them appropriately stamped with steamer and hotel labels. That single photo spoke almost completely for the high glamour of the great ocean liners and the transatlantic trade in its prewar heyday. The setting was the *Paris*. Unfortunately, this fine ship—while part of a masterful four-vessel plan for the French line—has been largely forgotten, being so overshadowed by the magical memories of at least two French liners, the superb *Ile de France* and the immortal *Normandie*.

The *Paris* was an immediate follow-up to the high success of the 23,600-ton *France* of 1912. The French had, with that ship, just entered the large luxury ship class. They wanted more. Their concepts were fed by a very lucrative loan and subsidy agreement with the French government. Accordingly, at least four big liners would be needed to maintain a deluxe, high-speed service to New York. While passenger service was certainly a most important consideration, the efficient and prompt delivery of mails was equally important in those pre-aircraft days. The designs for the beautifully-appointed, four-funnel *France* were reworked at the Penhoet Shipyards at St Nazaire. The refinements and alterations included a larger three-funnel design that would reach forward decoratively rather than backward. The gilded Louis XIV of the earlier liner would become a more startling Art Nouveau, even primitive Art Deco, on the new vessel.

The *Paris* was intended to enter service in 1915, and was then to be followed by two additional liners by 1920. The war interrupted this grand plan. While she was launched in 1913, her construction was halted soon after the outbreak of war in the following year. She sat untouched for nearly two years. Then, in September 1916, she was launched on special orders from the French government. The slipway that she occupied was needed for far more urgent warship work. The brand new hull of the liner was then towed to Quiberon and laid-up for the duration of the war with Germany. At best, the French Line plan would have to be altered, in fact so substantially altered that the third liner (the *Ile de France*) would not arrive until 1927 and the fourth (the *Lafayette*) until 1930.

The new *Paris* was returned to her builder's yard and then completed in 1919–20. In June 1921, after a series of successful trials and glowing praises over her 'new generation' interiors, she was ready to begin her maiden crossing to New York. Based at Le Havre, she called at Southampton in both directions. She was the highly popular flagship of the entire French Merchant Marine until the first arrival of the larger, even more luxurious *Ile de France* in the spring of 1927.

In A. G. Norton's *Ships of the North Atlantic*, published in London in 1936, he wrote of the *Paris*, 'For the greater part, this ship is very modern, but in some of the rooms, the earlier styles persist, although all of them have very modern fittings. The cabins are very well arranged and ten of the suites have private verandahs. The Sun Deck has the Terrace Cafe, part of which is open to the outdoor deck, and forward of the Cafe is the Balcony of the Smoking Room from which stairs lead down to the Main Smoking Room on the Promenade Deck with its modern furniture and indirect lighting.

'The Promenade Deck is enclosed with glass screens for the whole of its length and is brought out slightly on each side. It is also rubber-tiled to deaden sound and to prevent slipping. Other rooms on this deck beside the Main Smoking Room are the "Salon de The", where "moderne" is the style and which is supplemented by light-coloured walls, indirect lighting and a large skylight. In the centre of this room is one of the finest achievements of the *Paris*' decorator, namely the illuminated dance floor, where frosted glass panels in the actual floor are illuminated from beneath by lights, giving a very pleasing effect. Next is the Balcony of the Main Foyer. Then, there is the Grand Salon in the style of the time of Marie Antoinette, yet in a modern way. It has a large dome, the topmost part of which is glass as well as large windows and mirrors. At one end is a stage. Forward of this is the panelled library, where books in both French and English can be found. The foremost room on the Promenade Deck is the gymnasium, which is well equipped and well lighted.'

Mr Norton's verbal tour of the *Paris* continued, 'The next deck down is A Deck where the Main Entrance is to be found. Here also is the Main Foyer where fine woods are cleverly introduced. Indirect lighting gives an admirable effect and the ironwork on the wide stairs is definitely the feature. On C Deck is the Main Dining Room from which a large stairway leads to the Balcony Dining Saloon, supported by square pillars, over which is a large dome of glass forming a central nave with an aisle on each side both upstairs and downstairs. Halfway up the staircase at one end of the Dining Saloon is an array of magnificent mirrors reflecting the light and colours of the room. There are 130 tables in the restaurant, most of which seat four persons each.'

The *Paris* did have an unusual share of mishaps, however. On October 15 1927, she rammed and sank the freighter *Bessengen* off New York Harbor's Robbins Reef Lighthouse. Six were dead. On April 6 1929, she went aground, again in New York's Lower Bay. Her French captain reported, 'After passing the Statue of Liberty, we encountered heavy fog, with visibility at a half mile or less, and then, quite suddenly, the pilot misjudged'. Less than two weeks later, on April 18, she was aground again, off Britain's Eddystone Light. But far worse problems were ahead. On August 20 of that same year, the *Paris* was almost completely destroyed by fire while at her Le Havre berth. The blaze began in the third class accommodation, spread to second class and then into the first class quarters. Initial reports were that she might have to be scrapped. However, within five months, at her builder's yard at St Nazaire, she was restored and even modernised. Her berthing plans were rearranged from 563 to 560 in first class, 460 to 530 in second class, and from 1,092 to 844 in third class.

The *Paris* was affected by the declining passenger demands of the early Depression. In a rather desperate search for alternative revenue, she was sent on one-class cruises. In the winter of 1931, she set off on her first Mediterranean trip, to Teneriffe, Casablanca, Gibraltar, Algiers, Naples, Corsica, Monte Carlo, Cannes, Majorca and the Azores. Priced at just over $16 a day, these fares included the option of leaving the ship on the French Riviera and then travelling by train for a stay in Paris and then to Le Havre for a return on the new and very noteworthy *Ile de France*. One advertisement for these *Paris* cruises included reference to the bleak economic times, 'Old General Depression will not be allowed up the gangplank: these cruises are planned to make Time (which all the economists say is the cure) really go to work for you!'

When the *Normandie* came into service in the spring of 1935, and as the veteran *France* was sold to the breakers, the *Paris* became the oldest big liner in the French Line fleet. Her need on the North Atlantic run had steadily declined. She turned more and more to cruising. That same year, there were rumours that she would be converted totally for cruise service and would even be redone in a heat-resistant white hull. In fact, she was never repainted although at least one large brochure showed her in this guise. Often leased to the big Raymond-Whitcomb travel firm of New York, one of the last cruises for the *Paris* was a five-week 'early summer' cruise that left New York in

June 1938, bound for Madeira, Lisbon, Santander, St Jean-de-Luz, Bordeaux, St Nazaire, Lorient, Brest, Cobh, Dublin, Greenock, Oslo, Gothenburg, Copenhagen and then return to Le Havre. Fares again included a first-class return to New York in any of the other French liners, including the *Normandie*. Full passage rates began at $550.

While the *Paris* was being loaded with French art treasures, that were to be displayed at the New York World's Fair of 1939–40, she again became yet another victim of that vulnerability so common to French and French-built ships: fire. The blaze broke out on April 19, as the ship was berthed at her Le Havre terminal, with the *Champlain* moored just ahead and the *Normandie* behind in the huge graving dock. Firefighters were immediately summoned and then committed another ill to burning ships: too much water. A day later, the *Paris* capsized, leaving less than a quarter of her starboard side poking above the local waters. She was lost completely. Immediately, her two masts had to be cut so that the *Normandie* could be moved out of her repair berth. However, little else was done to the burned-out *Paris*. When, in a matter of months, the Second World War started, her salvage became less and less of a concern.

During the thorough bombings on Le Havre in 1944, the wreck of the *Paris* was damaged further still. Clearing the harbour debris and ruined shipping terminals were a foremost post-war concern. Again, the *Paris* was left untouched. In November 1946, when the former German superliner *Europa* was about to begin her refit for the French as their *Liberte*, she was ripped by an Atlantic gale and slammed into the wreckage of the *Paris*. Most fortunately, while the big liner was holed badly, she settled in an upright position and could therefore be salvaged. As for the remains of the *Paris*, harbour authorities at Le Havre finally realised that she was a menace. She was dismantled where she lay during 1947.

Gross tonnage: 34,569
Length overall: 764 feet
Width: 85 feet
Machinery: Steam turbines, quadruple screw
Speed: 21 knots
Capacity: 563 first class, 460 second class and 1,092 third class (1921); 560 first class, 530 second class and 844 third class (1929)
Built: Penhoet Shipyards, St Nazaire, France, 1913–21
Demise: Burnt out and sunk at Le Havre, April 19–20 1939; wreck scrapped in 1947

Below left *Foyer and grand staircase, a French Line postcard view of the* Paris. **Below right** *In April 1929 the* Paris *grounded off Brooklyn while outward bound with over 1,000 passengers aboard. This bow view shows lighters removing fuel to lighten her.*

Above Paris *was known as the 'Aristocrat of the Atlantic' and this view of her being undocked at New York shows why.* **Below** *The* Paris *on fire in Le Harve.*

Franconia

Britain's famed Cunard Steamship Company lost over 200,000 tons of shipping during the First World War. Along with many smaller liners, the speedy 31,000-ton *Lusitania* was the victim of U-boat torpedoes. When the hostilities ceased at the end of 1918, Company directors at their Liverpool headquarters thought immediately of reviving their noted luxury passenger service and of replacement tonnage. There were different demands and projections, however, from those which the firm might have seen in 1914, when the conflict first started. In the decade ahead, during the 1920s, Cunard foresaw a lessening of traffic requirements. More moderate ships with more economical speeds would be the order of the day. While being given the giant 52,100-ton *Imperator* as part of a post-war reparations pact and which became the highly popular *Berengaria*, no new superliners were even considered until well into the later part of that decade. At that time, plans would begin for a pair of superships that would run the Atlantic's first twin-ship express service. The first of this pair, laid down in 1930, became the illustrious *Queen Mary* and was finally completed in 1936.

In 1919, Cunard planned for no less than 13 new passenger ships, all of them under 25,000

tons and none capable of much more than 17 knot service speeds. There would be five of the 20,000-ton *Scythia* class: the *Scythia* (1920), *Samaria* (1921) and *Laconia* (1922), and then the altered, improved *Franconia* (1923) and *Carinthia* (1925). Concurrently, six smaller sister-ship versions were ordered as the 14,000-ton *Alaunia* class. This group included the *Andania* (1922), *Antonia* (1922), *Ausonia* (1922), *Aurania* (1924), *Alaunia* (1925) and *Ascania* (1925). There were two final, but independent ships: the 12,700-ton *Albania* (1920) and the 16,200-ton *Lancastria* (1922).

Ordered from a good friend to Cunard, the John Brown Yards on the Clyde, the *Franconia* and her Vickers-built sister, the *Carinthia*, were—while part of an overall series of quite similar passenger ships—quite novel. From the very start, they had a dual purpose: half the year on the North Atlantic, carrying three classes of passengers including a high number in third class, and then long, luxurious winters on deluxe, all-first class cruises. This scheme represented one of the earliest designs for dual-purpose ships. With one of the largest fleets then on the Atlantic run, Cunard was well aware of the slumpish passenger loads on the North Atlantic in winter. Furthermore, they wanted to capture a profitable share of the increasing American cruise trade. Of special importance was the long-distance millionaire circuit. These twin ships could not have been more successful in their role as cruising liners. After the Second World War, when both were too old for such voyages as the Mediterranean, North Cape and Around-the-World, one of Cunard's first major decisions was to build a new liner purposely for luxury cruises. Completed as the *Caronia* at the end of 1948, she is rated as the first major liner to be designed and used for year-round cruise service. It was the infancy of the booming present day leisure industry, which has replaced the earlier port-to-port transport services.

The *Franconia* took her name from a previous Cunarder, an 18,100-tonner that was completed in 1910, but torpedoed and sunk in 1916. The new ship was launched at Clydebank on October 21 1922 and then delivered to the Cunard

Company in the following June. Her maiden voyage and regular service was between Liverpool, Cobh and New York. The *Carinthia*, having been built at Barrow-in-Furness, was commissioned in the summer of 1925.

The two ships used a rather simple design: a tallish single stack and twin masts. A set of kingposts were placed forward and aft, the promenade decks were left partially open (no doubt in consideration of their tropic cruise voyages) and there were 16 sets of double-nested lifeboats. Most noticeably, they could be seen as developments of the slightly earlier *Scythia* class. With the other post-war single-stack ships, all of them painted in Cunard's familiar orange-red and black funnel colours, they often made a most fascinating sight while berthed together at the Liverpool docks.

The *Franconia* and *Carinthia* were powered by two sets of Brown Curtis double reduction geared steam turbines, with a combined power of 12,500 shaft horsepower and driving twin screws at 90 revolutions per minute. Steam was supplied by six oil-burning boilers. Maximum speeds were given as 16½ knots. Their fuel capacities were listed as 3,204 tons of oil.

These ships were frequently refitted and improved, especially in consideration of the very demanding American cruise public. When the Depression began, in 1929, more and more ships turned to 'escapist' cruising, either on long-haul millionaire trips or on very short runs for as little as $10 a day. The *Franconia* was made more competitive. By the early 1930s most of her cruise cabins were given private bathroom facilities and there were strides made with her ventilation system.

Most of the *Franconia*'s public rooms were placed along her promenade deck. These included the two-deck high smoking room, done as a copy of the 15th century Toledo residence of El Greco; the American bar; the Early English style smoking room, another two-deck high space and with a central dome; and twin garden lounges, which made effective use of exotic flowers, palms and ferns. There was also a large library, a special chocolate shop, a writing room and a card room. An elevator connected most of her passenger decks. The dining room, done in Adam style, was located on D deck. There was a full health centre on F deck that included a pool, racquet court and modern gymnasium.

Following the Depression and after a major 1930–31 winter refit (when both ships were repainted with white hulls), the *Franconia* was sent almost entirely on cruises, mostly longer trips. She developed a very loyal following and numbered not only members of the world's millionaire set on her voyages, but such celebrated artists as Noel Coward, Cole Porter and Richard Rodgers and Oscar Hammerstein among her passengers. A number of famed songs and even musical productions were first created onboard the *Franconia*.

Best known and remembered are the *Franconia*'s early winter world cruises. She would leave New York, often at midnight, just after the Christmas–New Year holidays and then return as late as May or June. In a magazine advertisement from June 1931, the ship's next winter run was being publicised. 'Faraway, glamorous places have stirred your imagination! Bali, still in its primitive civilization; Macassar, flaming like a ruby on the jungle's edge; Bangkok's barbaric splendor; and Saigon, remote and so special! The *Franconia* includes them without extra cost ... and such unique highspots as Athens and the Holy Land ... and all the other highlights of a round-the-world voyage. 140 days, 33 ports and all at greatly reduced rates, beginning at $1,750. A perfect, proven ship, especially built for world cruising, ensuring direct docking arrangements at the majority of ports. Eastward from New York January 9th next.'

Some years later, for her January 1937 circumnavigation, the *Franconia* was listed as going the equivalent of 1½ times around the world. In 144 days, she would travel over 35,000 miles. Outbound from New York, her ports of call included Trinidad, Brazil, St Helena, South Africa, Madagascar, the Seychelles, India, Ceylon, the Straits Settlements, Malaya, Siam, Java, Bali, the Philippine Islands, China, Korea, Japan, the Hawaiian islands, California and Panama. Her fares had risen only slightly in six years, to $1,900 and up. Of course, for the *Franconia* (as well as the *Carinthia*), there were also numerous shorter, less expensive trips, such as seven days to Havana and return for $60 or two weeks to the Caribbean islands for $125.

Almost new—the Franconia *photographed on July 9 1923, leaving New York. Note 'Castle Stevens' in the background, the home of Colonel John Stevens who built a propeller driven steamboat before Robert Fulton's* Clermont.

The *Franconia* was called to war duty as the Nazis plunged into Poland, in September 1939. Painted over in grey and outfitted to carry over 3,000 troops, she was sent to the Mediterranean at first. Soon afterward, on October 5, she collided with the Royal Mail Lines' 22,000-ton *Alcantara*. Although neither ship was seriously damaged, both were sent to dockyards for inspection and repairs. A year or so later, on June 16, the *Franconia* was again damaged, this time during a German air raid off St Nazaire, France. Following further repairs, she resumed her war work. She took part in the landings on Norway, Madagascar and Sicily.

She was selected in the winter of 1945 for her most notable duty. At Yalta, she was to be the accommodation ship for Prime Minister Winston Churchill and his staff, during the strategic conference with President Roosevelt and Soviet Premier Stalin. Some of the British Prime Minister's favourite effects were brought down from London and placed in a completely refurbished suite of rooms aboard the *Franconia*. The ship also served as a communications centre and housed over 100 of the British government's attending staff. Included was a small army of secretaries, typists, telegraphers and security guards. Churchill, who had crossed previously during the war in the giant *Queen Mary*, seemed to enjoy the *Franconia*. Reportedly, he spent long hours soaking in his bath and worked from a specially created desk-shelf that was fitted across the ledges of the tub.

After the war, with an obvious change in conditions and passenger ship demands, the lease for the *Franconia* was extended and she was used in 'austerity' service with migrants, soldiers, war brides, children and refugees, sailing mostly to Canada. She was returned finally to Cunard in the summer of 1947, and then underwent her post-war refit. Two years later, in June 1949, she resumed commercial service although for year-round transatlantic sailings. For about nine months of the year, during the ice-free months on the St Lawrence River, she traded between Liverpool, Greenock and Quebec City. In deep winter, she went either to Halifax or to Halifax and New York. During one of these trips, in 1950, she went aground on Canada's Orleans Islands for four days. Finally towed free, she was temporarily repaired at Quebec and then sailed for home for more thorough patching. However, like her remaining fleetmates from the early 1920s, she was aging, slow and becoming mechanically troublesome.

When Cunard began to introduce a new quartet of liners for its Canadian service, namely the *Saxonia*, *Ivernia*, *Carinthia* and *Sylvania* of 1954–57, the older ships were gradually retired and sold for scrapping. The *Franconia* finished her schedules in December 1956. She then went directly to Inverkeithing in Scotland to be finished-off by T. W. Ward.

Gross tonnage: 20,158 (1923); 20,341 (1949)
Length overall: 623 feet
Width: 73 feet
Machinery: Steam turbines, twin screw
Speed: 16½ knots
Capacity: 221 first class, 356 second class and 1,266 third class (1923); approximately 400 all-first class for cruises (1931); 253 first class and 600 tourist class (1949)
Built: John Brown & Co Ltd, Clydebank, Scotland, 1923
Demise: Scrapped at Inverkeithing, Scotland, 1957

Above *The* Franconia's *main lounge photographed in 1937 when she was classed as a cabin class liner. Modest elegance but lots of solid comfort.* Below *A luxurious cabin on* Franconia *with real beds, wallpaper, full length mirror and more.*

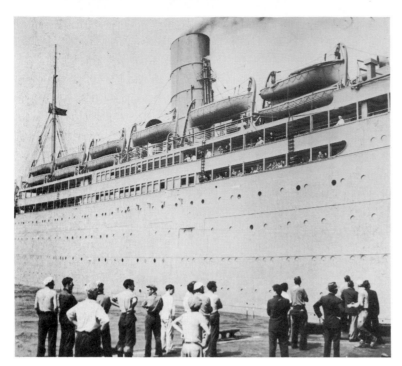

Left Franconia *leaves New York September 2 1939 for war service. A quick coat of grey paint was applied at her pier before she sailed.*

Below *A rare close-up photograph of the grounding off Quebec in 1950. Thousands were attracted to the scene to see the plight of the 20,000-ton vessel.*

High And Dry

Gripsholm

In the early 1920s, the Swedish American Line seemed to be content to use second-hand liners, such as the *Drottningholm*, acquired from the Allan Line, and the first *Stockholm*, originally built as Holland America's *Potsdam*. In 1923, they even obtained another former Holland America ship, the *Noordam*, which became the first *Kungsholm*. Company directors could foresee only the best of times ahead and therefore, with sufficient cash reserves in hand, ordered Sweden's first brand new liner. More importantly, however, while masked in a rather conventional design of twin funnels and masts, this new ship was to be a revolutionary: the North Atlantic's first motorliner.

Like several other maritime nations, including neighbouring Norway, the Swedish American Line had to seek an overseas shipbuilder for this project. The Armstrong Whitworth Yard at Newcastle in England was finally selected. Their passenger ship building experience had become better known, especially following orders from such notable firms as Cunard and P&O. The brand new Swedish flagship was completed in the autumn of 1925. Named *Gripsholm*, after Sweden's royal castle, she crossed to New York in November. Her diesel propulsion created particularly high press attention.

The *Gripsholm* was immediately successful and in rather quick time was joined by an even larger motorliner, the *Kungsholm* of 1928, which came from the illustrious Blohm & Voss Shipyards of Hamburg. Together, the two ships formed a comfortable, sturdy and dependable link on the transatlantic run, sailing between Gothenburg, Copenhagen, Halifax and New York. Furthermore, in the early 1930s, as the worldwide depression began to curtail normal passenger ship traffic, the Swedish American Line cast a serious eye to cruising as an alternative. It was, indeed, a very wise decision. To many ocean travellers, the company was actually better known and with an even higher repute for cruising.

The *Gripsholm* and *Kungsholm* not only sailed on short runs to Bermuda, the West Indies and Eastern Canada, but on special, long-distance cruises to the Mediterranean, the North Cape,

and even around continental Africa and South America. In addition, the *Gripsholm* was the first liner to sail from Gothenburg and have New York as one of her ports of call. She also made an annual cruise from Britain to South America. Quite appropriately, to increase their tropical flavour and decrease the temperatures onboard (air-conditioning was certainly non-existent on ships at the time), the Swedish-American liners were repainted with white hulls in 1932, replacing the earlier black.

The Second World War years were extremely favourable to the *Gripsholm*. Unlike most other liners, including the *Kungsholm*, she did not become a drastically altered, gun-equipped troopship, but the world's first 'Mercy Ship'. Her purpose: to carry exchange prisoners-of-war, children, diplomats, repatriated seamen and Allied nationals with neutral status. She retained her white colouring and wore huge identification markings along her sides. At night, her identity was a blaze of neon in the otherwise dark, sinister wartime seas. Officially operated by the International Red Cross, the *Gripsholm* travelled to ports throughout the world—including Rio de Janeiro, Montevideo, Lourenco Marques, Lisbon, Barcelona, Belfast, Liverpool, Marseilles, Alexandria, Port Said, Haifa, Piraeus, Naples, Palermo and even far-off Bombay. Most often, she was a

Gripsholm

welcome sight (and refuge) to exchange personnel. Between 1942 and 1945, the *Gripsholm* sailed over 120,000 miles and carried more than 27,600 passengers. Nine of these 'mercy voyages' were managed by the American Export Lines, a company with strong links to the Mediterranean and Middle East, but with limited passenger ship experience at the time.

Rather quickly returned to her Swedish-American owners and in need of comparatively minor repairs and refurbishing, the *Gripsholm* was among the first ships to resume commercial service on the Atlantic following the war. She first re-crossed to New York in fresh livery in March 1946. Among her first (and most famous) passengers was actress Greta Garbo, who returned to Sweden aboard the liner for her first visit since the late 1930s. In those 'boom years' of the late 1940s, a time complicated by a shortage of tonnage on almost all passenger routes, the *Gripsholm* was fully booked on almost every voyage regardless of direction. There was a new wave of westbound immigrants (to both Halifax and New York), business people and merchants, and a new era of tourism, begun mostly in America just after the war. The *Gripsholm* did not cruise during these years. Her Atlantic voyages were far more urgent (and profitable).

Time was taken, however, during the winter season of 1949–50 for the *Gripsholm* to be modernised. She was given a major face-lifting at Kiel in West Germany. Her original thin funnels were replaced by two of greater width and a more progressive dash of rake. The accommodation, while retaining the rich Old World, heavily dark-wood-panelled atmosphere, was reduced considerably. The original 1,557 berths in three classes was cut to 920, in a far more contemporary blend of 210 in first class and 910 in tourist. Furthermore, a new raked bow was fitted, extending the ship's overall length from 573 to 590 feet. Even her gross tonnage increased, from 17,993 to 19,105.

Within a few years, by the early 1950s, the *Gripsholm* had become the oldest member of the 'White Viking Fleet', the nickname for the Swedish American Liners. Although smaller and more of a combination ship, a new *Stockholm* was added in 1948, and then, largest of all, the

21,100-ton *Kungsholm* first appeared in late 1953. Consequently, the Swedes inventively found a new use for their ageing ship.

The West Germans, mostly in the form of the North German Lloyd, were very anxious to reopen a transatlantic passenger service to New York. Certainly, under strict Allied supervision, they were not permitted to build a new liner. In addition, suitable second-hand tonnage was not then readily available. The Swedes recognised the situation and approached the Lloyd about the *Gripsholm*. The result was a specially created, brief term partnership that produced the Bremen-America Line. Beginning in February 1954, the *Gripsholm* would begin sailing between Bremerhaven and New York, while retaining her Swedish name and white hull colouring, but with traditional North German Lloyd mustard-coloured stacks. It was all part of a sensible transition.

A year later, in January 1955, according to the agreement, the *Gripsholm* transferred to West German registry and was formally renamed *Berlin*. It was a significant occasion: the first German liner to sail commercially since that fateful autumn of 1939. The Bremen-America Line was promptly dissolved and forgotten, and hereafter trading came directly under the North German Lloyd banner. After all, it had been a full decade since the Nazi defeat and it was considered quite timely for a German ship, with rich ethnic overtones, to reappear on the bustling Atlantic. For the following four years, the *Berlin* sailed alone, mostly in direct service between Bremerhaven and New York, but with capacity loads of westbound immigrants and eastbound tourists.

In New York's Upper Bay, in July 1959, the *Berlin* met with her newly renovated successor, the 32,300-ton *Bremen*, the former French *Pasteur*. Considered the flagship of now growing West German merchant navy, the *Bremen* was a very luxurious, highly contemporary liner—close, in fact, to a new (and final) generation of transatlantic 'ships of state', such as Holland's 38,600-ton *Rotterdam* and Italy's 33,300-ton *Leonardo Da Vinci*. Certainly much smaller, and all while looking more and more dated, the *Berlin* became one of the Atlantic's 'grande dames'. Since her overall decor was almost original—complete with cage elevator, glossy dark woods and with a thick sense of Nordic heaviness about her, the *Berlin* seemed to be more and more of a ship from a very distant era. On one occasion, while berthed at New York, she sat between the likes of a new, flashier generation: the *Oceanic*, *France* and *Michelangelo*. However, the old ship was, to her very last days, impeccably maintained and quite popular.

In her final years, she took nine days to cross between Bremerhaven and New York. Occasionally, there was a call at Southampton. She also resumed cruising—from New York to Bermuda, the Caribbean and the St Lawrence River as well as from Bremerhaven to the Norwegian Fjords and to Madeira, the Canaries and West Africa. Her very last years included several Atlantic crossings to Montreal and Quebec City.

The *Berlin* departed from New York for the last time, on September 3 1966. She was then 41 years old. Following a short cruise from Germany, she was sold to Italian shipbreakers and dismantled at La Spezia.

Gross tonnage: 17,993 (1925); 18,134 (1927); 19,105 (1949); 18,600 (1955)
Length overall: 573 feet (1925); 590 feet (1949)
Width: 74 feet
Machinery: Burmeister & Wain diesels, twin screw
Speed: 17 knots
Capacity: 127 first, 482 second, 948 third (1925); 210 first, 710 tourist (1949); 98 first and 878 tourist (1955)
Built: Sir W. G. Armstrong, Whitworth & Co Ltd, Newcastle, England, 1925
Demise: Scrapped at La Spezia, Italy, 1966

The Gripsholm *arrives at New York on her maiden voyage.*

Gripsholm

Left Gripsholm *brings in 622 American men, women and children who had been prisoners in Japan. Her mercy trip ended on March 16 1944 at New York.*

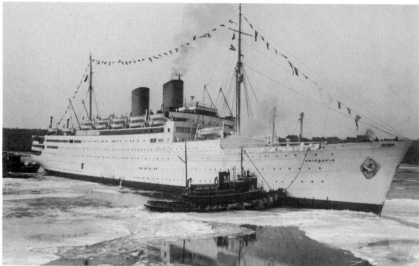

Left *Painted white and with new and wider stacks,* Gripsholm *returns to Swedish-American Line service after World War 2 (courtesy of Moran Towing).*

Left *Sold to North German Lloyd, she became the* Berlin *and returned to the black-hull styling (courtesy of Moran Towing).*

Right *Rare brochure detailing the wartime service of* Gripsholm *and* Drottningholm.

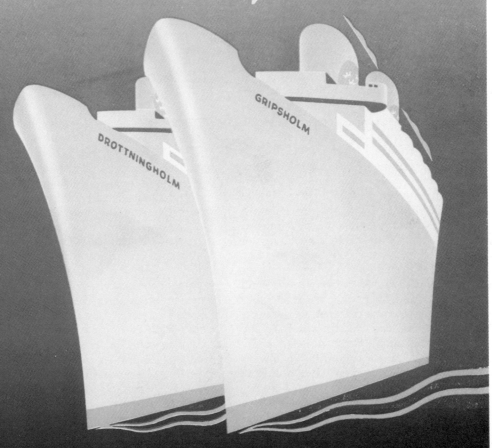

THE WHITE
VIKING FLEET

In war and peace

 SWEDISH AMERICAN LINE

Stella Polaris

If the first cruise-like voyage took place in 1846 and then Britain's P&O Lines offered the first commercial cruise eleven years later, such sailings were still much the domain of the rich and privileged by the 1920s. Millionaires, aristocrats and even exiled royalty appreciated long, leisurely and luxurious sailings, with all-first class amenities, fine cuisine and precision service. The more extensive and more diverse the trip, the better.

By the 1920s, there was much said and written about the world's great yachts, certainly about those owned by European royals, but also about those owned by the ever-rising number of American millionaires, moguls and tycoons. Although large ocean liners had their devoted following and popularity, the absolute ultimate in travel was a deluxe cruise in a smaller, more intimate ship, a commercial yacht if you will. Norway's Bergen Line was rather clever to recognise this and, apart from its normal steamer services across the North Sea from Bergen to Newcastle as well as along the fabled Norwegian coastline, they saw very bright days ahead in the future of luxurious cruising. They commissioned a new ship that was deliberately styled after a sumptuous yacht. She was aptly named *Stella Polaris*, 'the star of the north'.

Built in Sweden, at the Gotaverken Shipyards at Gothenburg, the new ship was scheduled only for cruise service. Fitted with very high standard accommodation, she could never be anything but first class. Some 160 crewmembers all but hand served the equal number of guests. There were four special deluxe suites, more than half of the other cabins had private bathroom facilities and as many as one-third of her staterooms were for single occupancy only. A small swimming pool was placed aft. Overall, the ship clearly resembled the yacht class. There was an ornate, scrolled clipper bow, twin masts, a single funnel and an all-white hull. From almost any angle, at almost any port, she looked handsome and serene.

The *Stella Polaris* worked a prescribed annual schedule. In winter, she most often cruised from New York on a trip around the world. As an example, in January 1937, she set out on a 110-day trip with passage rates beginning at $1,135.

She was routed through the Panama Canal and then set off to the South Pacific islands, the East Indies, around South Africa and then northward to Europe. Considered more complete than ever, she also featured special stopovers and overland excursions in southern India, the Seychelles, Madagascar, South Africa and West Africa. The voyage concluded at Southampton.

Each spring, from Britain, the 'little white yacht', as she was often called, spent the summer months in northern waters. From June until August, on mostly two-week sailings, she would sail to the majestic Fjordlands, to the North Cape for the Midnight Sun and even to more remote Spitzbergen and the Arctic pack-ice. Occasionally, she would go also into the Baltic for a visit to the northern cities, such as Helsinki and Stockholm. In summer during the late 1930s, her 12-day cruises were priced at $185, the 16-day runs from $229 and special 20-day voyages from $283.

During the Second World War, the beautiful *Stella* fell into Nazi hands. Mostly, she was very fortunate. After very limited and very brief trooping, she was moored permanently as an accommodation and recreation ship for German officers. When the hostilities ended in the summer of 1945, she was found to be in remarkably good and even seaworthy condition.

After a short stint of trooping between Norway and Scotland, she was returned to her builder's yard and thoroughly refitted and restored. She returned to cruise service in the summer of 1946. However, those prewar long-distance voyages were no longer quite as appropriate nor as financially successful for such a ship. Instead, while she resumed her summer schedules in Scandinavia, she spent her winters sailing to the Caribbean, first from New York and then from New Orleans. The only other change appears to have resulted from troubles prompted by the Norwegian Shipping Act of 1949. With more stringent regulations for Norwegian-flag passenger ships, the Bergen Line could no longer run the ship profitably and successfully. By 1951, arrangements were concluded to transfer her to the Swedish flag, to a newly created cruise-ship firm, the Clipper Line. The company's name was, in fact, inspired by the ship's superb clipper bow and her majestic appearance. These owners continued to be her operators until the end of her sailing career.

Writer C. M. Squarey appraised the *Stella Polaris* in the summer of 1953. He wrote, 'Considering that this ship is now 26 years old, I should like, at the onset, to pay her the tribute of saying that the passing of years does not fade her exterior beauty nor the passage of time dim the charms of her interior decor. Indeed, it seems that, like whisky, she grows better for maturing and verily is "still going strong". For sheer elegance of line, she stands supreme and I imagine that a duplicate will never be built again.'

Mr Squarey sailed in the ship on a short run from Tilbury to Bergen. 'We ran into a heavy head-on swell in the North Sea and her behaviour, considering she is a mere 5,200 tons, was incredibly good. She literally rode it like a duck, dipping and rising to it with a smoothness that had to be experienced to be believed; she certainly is a seakindly craft.'

Her facilities and accommodation especially delighted that author. 'Her layout has altered but little from the day she came out. The forward lounge with its vivid red carpet is a colourful and charming room. The Smoking Room with its bar is unmistakably Scandinavian in its atmosphere and has a fine selection of Scandinavian art. The Verandah Cafe aft, also with a bar and fine circular dance floor, is another well-thought-out room. Astern of that is what I best describe as a large quarter-deck covered with an awning around whose sides are wicker chairs with bright orange headrests and seats, creating a very pleasing effect. Just forward of the bridge, there is a large deck area which is an ideal spot for watching the ship making or leaving port.

'The dignified dining salon is a tremendous credit to those who originally designed it. It stands the test of time well; my only observation is that I think the curtains are not quite worthy of the room.

'The stewards, all of whom are at least bilingual, wear white monkey jackets, spotlessly clean (a new one issued every day) with a black tie and not only look smart but are really efficient in their duties. Those who like Swedish catering—

and who doesn't—will find the needs of their inner man particularly well satisfied in this ship.

'A notably happy atmosphere pervades the ship. What is an interesting fact about her is the extraordinary abundance of "repeaters" she carries. Having spent five days in her, I readily understand why so many of her passengers are loyalists; I hope one day I may join their ranks, for she is indeed a friendly ship—so friendly that I venture the guess that there are not many other ships that land their passengers more happy than the *Stella Polaris*.'

Indeed, as the *Stella Polaris* neared retirement, the Clipper Line was economically unable to replace her. Even converting a suitable secondhand ship seemed less than satisfactory. Fortunately, she was not scrapped. She was sold to the International House Company Limited of Tokyo for further use as a moored hotel, restaurant and yacht club. She was handed over in October 1969, and left Lisbon on the 28th of that month, bound for Osaka by way of the Panama Canal. Renamed *Scandinavia*, she survives to date, moored in mountain-surrounded splendour off Mitohama Beach, on Japan's western Izu Peninsular.

Gross tonnage: 5,209
Length overall: 416 feet
Width: 51 feet
Machinery: Burmeister & Wain diesels, twin screw
Speed: 15 knots
Capacity: 165, all first class
Built: Gotaverken Shipyards, Gothenburg, Sweden, 1927

Stella Polaris

Left *Postcard view of* Stella Polaris *when she was owned by the Clipper Line* (courtesy of Clipper Line).

Below *The classical lines of* Stella Polaris *are evident in this photo as she is anchored in one of the majestic Norwegian fjords* (courtesy of Clipper Line).

Right *Bought by the Japanese and made into a floating hotel-restaurant the lovely* Stella Polaris *became the* Scandinavia *and remained as beautiful as ever. She is moored at Mitohama Beach, on the Western Izu Peninsula.*

Below Stella Polaris *leaving on a cruise.*

Malolo

On June 26 1926, the hull of the new Matson liner *Malolo* slipped into the Delaware River out of the William Cramp Shipyards at Philadelphia. Great excitement prevailed. Not only was she the biggest liner yet to be completed by the Cramp Co, but to the officials and friends of the Matson Line, she was revolutionary. She was the first major liner to be built for the California/Hawaiian islands tourist service.

A year or so later, that excitement calmed somewhat. The fitting-out and completion coupled with the overall construction costs for the *Malolo* exceeded all estimates and resulted in the bankruptcy and closure of the Cramp yards. The new ship sailed out to sea for her trials on May 24. A day later, she was rammed by the Norwegian steamer *Jacob Christensen* in a dense Atlantic fog. The impact of the collision was estimated to be 14 times greater than that which sent the *Titanic* to the bottom 15 years earlier and greater than that which sank the *Empress of Ireland* in 1914. Miraculously, the *Malolo*—with her brilliant chief designer, William Francis Gibbs, on board— remained afloat, although loaded with 7,000 tons of sea water. She crept into New York and immediately began full repairs at a Brooklyn shipyard. The press coverage was intense, with the result that the ship became the 'unsinkable *Malolo*'. The great strides in compartmentisation in this ship allowed her to survive and led to even more significant advances in future ships, particularly with American liners.

By October of 1927, the *Malolo* was repaired and off on a trans-Panama Canal delivery cruise from New York to San Francisco. A month later, on November 16, she set sail on her first trip to Honolulu. It was an instant success story. While the Hawaiian islands were already growing in popularity, the addition of a luxury ship such as the *Malolo* was thought to be a tremendous stride. She showed rich profits. A second, even larger liner, the *Lurline*, joined the service in 1932 and therein created a famous Matson Line team.

Since the name *Malolo* was considered to be unlucky, at least by Hawaiian lore, the ship was renamed *Matsonia* in 1937, honouring the company founder. A year later, she was modernised and raised by a full deck. It was all part of the Matson policy of maintaining the highest possible standards. Then, a few years later, just after December 7 1941, it all suddenly changed. America went to war following the Japanese attack on Pearl Harbor. The *Matsonia* was called to duty by the US Navy and repainted in shades of sombre grey. Her voyages were confined to the Pacific theatres of war and, among others, she visited such remote spots as Tonga-tabu, Espiritu Santo, Tulagia, Finschafen, Oro Bay, Milne Bay, Morobe, Aitape and Eniwetok. By the time she was decommissioned, in April 1946, the USS *Matsonia* had steamed 385,549 miles, carried 176,319 passengers and served over 6.9 million meals.

The ship had a short stay at a crowded West Coast shipyard before reopening the Matson Honolulu service, but then only in a partially restored state. The true Matson luxury was temporarily set aside and replaced by the urgent need to transport post-war personnel: war brides, servicemen, children, reconstruction crews. Meanwhile, the *Lurline* was restored to her pre-war splendour and was ready for service in 1948.

Consequently, the *Matsonia* was withdrawn. The intention was to then fully refit her, but in the final appraisal, shipyard costs had risen to such an extent that such a refit had to be either deferred or cancelled. The 21-year-old ship went on the block and was sold, quite quickly to the Mediterranean Lines of Panama, a ship-holding subsidiary of the newly formed Home Lines, a firm with Greek, Swedish, Swiss, Italian and American links.

The *Matsonia* was renamed *Atlantic* and sent to the Ansaldo Shipyards at Genoa for rebuilding. The 700 or so first class berths of the Matson era were replaced with a more profitable, transatlantic complement of 349 in first class, 203 in cabin and 626 in tourist. The Home Lines' plan was to put the ship on the South Atlantic run, between Genoa, Rio and Buenos Aires, but then sudden currency problems in Latin America disrupted the idea. Instead, in May 1949, she sailed from Genoa and Naples to New York and, in doing so, made the first Home Lines' voyage to North America. The service prospered, especially during 1950, which was a Roman Catholic Holy Year in Rome.

The *Atlantic* was reassigned in February 1952, when she began service between Southampton, Le Havre and Quebec City. Her first voyages were, in fact, to Halifax, due to the heavy winter ice on the St Lawrence.

On December 23 1954, at the special request of the Greek government and in the presence of Her Majesty Queen Frederika, the *Atlantic* was renamed *Queen Frederica* at Piraeus for a newly created Home Lines subsidiary, the National Hellenic American Line. She hoisted the Greek colours and was refitted with yet another altered berthing pattern: 132 in first class, 116 in cabin and 931 tourist. On January 29 she departed from Piraeus via Naples, Palermo and Gibraltar for Halifax and New York, under the rather dubious title of the world's largest Greek-flag liner (the Goulandris-owned *Olympia* of 1953 at 23,000 tons was, in fact, under the Liberian flag at the time). Once at New York, the new *Queen* set sail on a 42-day Mediterranean cruise.

The ship seems to have done very well, especially popular with Greek travellers and west-bound immigrants, and was marketed by the Home Lines along with the *Homeric*, *Italia* and Hamburg Atlantic Line's *Hanseatic*. In 1960–61,

Above Malolo *at the fitting out berth of Cramp Shipyard, Philadelphia, USA, March 1 1927.*

Below *Departing from San Francisco in November 1929 for a round-Pacific cruise.*

the *Queen Frederica* was given a 2½-month refit at Genoa and once again her passenger capacity was restyled. This time, the figures read 174 in first class and 1,005 in tourist. At the same time, some 75 per cent of her cabins were given private toilets and showers.

The *Queen* was sold to the Themistocles Navigation SA, one of the Chandris Group subsidiaries, in November 1965. Her new part-time service was from Southampton to Australia and New Zealand via the South African Cape and then with only summer sailings on the Atlantic between the Mediterranean and New York. There were also some periodic cruises to Bermuda and the Caribbean. Her name remained the same and once again prosperity came her way. However, new, very strict safety standards came into effect in the United States in 1968. The 40-year-old *Frederica* would require several million dollars' worth of improvements, which to Chandris officials would be extreme. Consequently, on September 30 1967, she sailed from New York on her last transatlantic crossing. (She did, in fact, revisit New York one more time, but did not land or take on passengers.) The *Queen* was assigned to the Australian service full-time and occasionally undertook complete around-the-world voyages, sailing outbound via the Cape and then homewards via Panama.

In 1970, a charter from Sovereign Cruises Limited put the old *Queen* on seven-day summer cruises out of Palma de Majorca to Barcelona, Algiers, Palermo, Naples, Genoa and Cannes. The series was heavily marketed to British tourists on a fly'n'sail basis. Rather elaborate Sovereign logos were painted on the twin funnels.

As if exhaustion was finally setting-in, she was laid-up at Perama, near Piraeus, in the autumn of 1973. She had had 46 years of sailing. Three years later, in 1976, she featured in rumours that she was to be reactivated as a hotel-ship along the Suez Canal and then again (in 1977) that she was to be used as a floating prop in a new film on raising the *Titanic*. Neither proposal came to pass. The end was near. Scrap crews went aboard at her silent anchorage and small pieces were removed and lowered into barges. The entire process seemed painfully slow. Then, on February 1 1978, the beginning of her 51st year, she suddenly and dramatically burst into flames. Much of the remains of the *Queen Frederica* was a tangled mass of burned steel. The old ship was then finished-off forever.

Gross tonnage: 17,232 (1927); 17,226 (1937); 15,602 (1948); 20,553 (1952); 21,329 (1961); 16,435 (1966)
Length overall: 582 feet
Width: 83 feet
Machinery: Steam turbines, twin screw
Speed: 21 knots
Capacity: 693 first (1927); 349 first, 203 cabin, 626 tourist (1948); 132 first, 116 cabin, 931 tourist (1954); 174 first, 1,005 tourist (1961)
Built: William Cramp & Sons Ship & Engine Building Co, Philadelphia, Pennsylvania, 1927
Demise: Scrapping, then fire damage and then final demolition at Perama, Greece, 1977–78

Renamed Matsonia *she is rebuilt with new positioning of her lifeboats* (courtesy of Matson Lines).

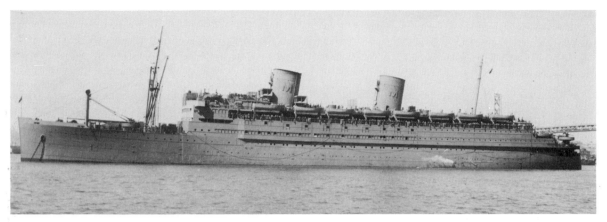

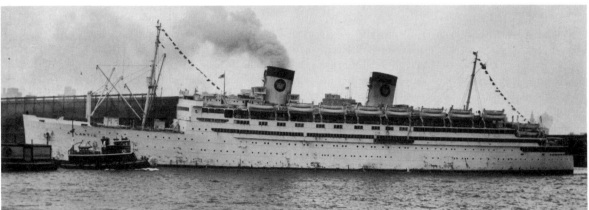

Top *She kept her name as a US Army troopship* (courtesy of US Army Signal Corps). **Above** *Bought by Home Lines she gets another name—Atlantic.* **Below** *Arriving at New York with still another name,* Queen Frederica, *she is now under the colours of the Chandris Lines.*

Vulcania

The *Vulcania* was the most successful Italian liner of all. She gave the most service, carried the greatest number of passengers and, when she was retired from nearly 40 years service as an Atlantic ship, she had a further six years in the Caribbean and then as a Mediterranean cruise-ship. Her story, which spanned some 46 years, ended with what was possibly the most prolonged near-scrapping of any major liner.

Designed as a part of a team of near-sisters, the *Saturnia* was launched first, in December 1925. The *Vulcania*, which was thought for a time to be called *Urania*, followed a year later, in December 1926. Built by the Cantieri Navali Triestino yards at Monfalcone, they were ordered by the Cosulich Line of Trieste for a dual-purpose: sailing from the Adriatic either to New York or to Rio de Janeiro, Santos, Montevideo and Buenos Aires. In fact, they were used mostly on the North American run. The *Saturnia* was commissioned in the autumn of 1927; the *Vulcania* just before the Christmas holidays in 1928.

Both ships worked one of the most extensive runs of all Atlantic liners. Carrying four classes of passengers (which was cut to three classes by the mid-1930s) as well as mail and general freight, they sailed on a monthly timetable between Trieste, Venice, Patras, Messina, Palermo, Naples, Gibraltar, Lisbon and then across to Halifax and New York. They were particularly

well known for their exceptional decor, which pointedly avoided the early era of Art Deco, but instead made stunning use of Rococo, Roman, Beaux Arts, even a Feudal style. In general, they were fashioned after what might have been a very good Italian hotel.

In 1932, both ships were part of the giant shipping merger organised by the Mussolini government. The passenger liners of the Navigazione Generale Italiana, Lloyd Sabaudo and the Cosluch Line were joined together, to become more competitive, to cut costs in the cruel depression and to form the consolidated Italian Line. Aside from their stacks being repainted in the new company colours, little else was changed for the *Saturnia* and *Vulcania*. They continued in Adriatic service, with the occasional detour for one-class cruising. Aside from the shorter trips to Bermuda and the Caribbean, there were also some extravagant winter jaunts through the Mediterranean. In February 1937, the *Vulcania* set off from New York for 60 days to the Azores, Madeira, Casablanca, Gibraltar, Lisbon, Tangier, Algiers, Cannes, Nice, Genoa, Ajaccio, Capri, Naples, Messina, Palermo, La Goulette, Malta, Tripoli, Port Said, Haifa, Beirut, Rhodes, Istanbul, Athens, Corfu, Cattaro Bay, Ragusa, Venice, Trieste, Patras, Naples, Palermo, Algiers, Gibraltar, Lisbon, the Azores and a return to New York. Minimum first class fares began at $685.

In 1935, the Italian Line made considerable changes and improvements in its overall passenger fleet. Among the major decisions was to re-engine both the *Saturnia* and *Vulcania*. Taken in hand at Monfalcone, their original Danish-built Burmeister & Wain diesels, which produced service speeds of 19 knots, were removed. They were replaced by brand new Italian-made Fiat diesels, capable of service speeds of 21 knots and a maximum of 23 knots. The new machinery in the *Vulcania* was said to include the most powerful heavy oil engines yet fitted to a ship. On her first trials afterward, she managed a most impressive 23.33 knots. The revised, accelerated service to the Adriatic could now be advertised as 'just 9 days to Venice and Trieste from New York'.

The competition was particularly intense in those otherwise sluggish mid-depression years. Otherwise, both ships continued in Mediterranean service until Italy entered the Second World War in the spring of 1940. However, they were used in early 1935 on special Italian government trooping voyages through Suez to East Africa. They played a major supportive role in the otherwise cruel Italian imperialist campaign. A year later, on October 19 1936, the *Vulcania* was nearly lost at sea. A serious fire erupted in her third class accommodation while the liner was en route from Naples to New York. Although several nearby passenger ships and freighters were asked to stand by, the Italian crew was eventually able to quell the blaze and the liner allowed to continue her westward voyage.

The *Vulcania* was one of just four major Italian liners to survive the Second War. The others included the *Saturnia*, *Conte Biancamano* and *Conte Grande*. Otherwise, the glorious Italian liner fleet was in ruins. Frequent wartime reports suggested, however, that the *Vulcania* was lost, either torpedoed, bombed or deliberately set afire. Laid-up in the summer of 1940, she seems to have made at least one troop voyage a year later, from Taranto to Tripoli, and still later was chartered to the International Red Cross to evacuate troops, refugees and prisoners out of East Africa. Just prior to the Italian surrender, she was laid-up, seemingly unharmed, at Trieste. On September 8 1943, manned by cadets from the Italian Merchant Marine Academy, she fled for safety. She sped from Venice for a neutral and then an Allied port. The *Saturnia* followed suit.

The *Vulcania* was finally taken over by the United States government and converted to an Army transport. Soon after the war ended, in 1945, the ship made several North Atlantic sailings, to Le Havre, Southampton and Liverpool, under the management of the United States Lines, and then returned to the Mediterranean, sailing both to war-torn Italy and more distant Egypt, for the American Export Lines. While both she and her sister-ship were laid-up for a time at New York, they were finally returned to the Italian government at the end of 1946. Immediate restoration began. The *Vulcania* resumed sailing in July 1947, some six months after the *Saturnia*. However, reflecting those enormous losses within the post-war Italian Line fleet, both ships could not return to the more lengthy Adriatic trade, but were needed instead on the express run between Naples, Genoa, Cannes, Algeciras and New York. In the 1930s, this same service was run by the giant *Rex* and *Conte Di Savoia*, but both of which were lost in action.

Not until the autumn of 1955, when the new sister-ships *Andrea Doria* (1953) and *Cristoforo Colombo* (1954) came into service, could the *Vulcania* (and *Saturnia*) be returned to their original terminal ports of Venice and Trieste. They resumed their most popular, well-booked pre-war service, touching on the same extensive list of ports and with roundtrip voyages often taking as much as 40 days. They were in use for nearly another decade.

As yet another pair of brand new express liners steamed into service, the super-ships *Michelangelo* and *Raffaello*, in the spring and summer of 1965, the two old motorliners were retired. They were replaced by a single ship, the *Cristoforo Colombo*, which was swung onto the Adriatic route from express service. Tugs, fireboats and newspaper commentaries sent off the *Vulcania* and *Saturnia* on their farewell Italian Line crossings. Having outlived all other national ships used on the New York run, they carried more Italian emigrants to America than any other ships. Their overall profits and revenues were said to be immense.

The two aged near-sisters sat for a time nested together, no doubt being inspected by some potential buyers. The *Saturnia* finished her days at the scrapyards of La Spezia, but the *Vulcania* found new life and further service (and profit) with the Grimaldi-Siosa Lines, another Italian passenger shipper. Refitted and then renamed *Caribia*, she was put on the 'double emigrant service', sailing from Southampton and then Vigo and Lisbon (where she loaded high numbers of Spanish and Portuguese migrants and workers) for such Caribbean ports as Antigua, St Kitts, Montserrat, Gaudeloupe, Martinique, Dominica, St Lucia, St Vincent, Barbados, Grenada, Trinidad, La Guaira, Curacao and Kingston (where she took on British-bound West Indian migrants). Her accommodation remained much the same time, although with slightly revised berthing figures in the three classes. Afterward, she was used

MOTOR VESSEL "VULCANIA"

(24.000 TONS, 21 KNOTS)

A grossly exaggerated representation of Vulcania, *issued by Cosulich Line in postcard form.*

permanently on seven-day cruises from Genoa to Cannes, Barcelona, Palma de Majorca, Bizerta (in Tunisia), Palermo and Capri. She began to sail only in summer and spent the off-season winters in lay-up.

Revised as a one-class ship, her accommodation was, in fact, sold in four categories: 'Deluxe, Increased Comfort, Tourist and Youth Special'. For these weekly cruises, fares began at $300 in deluxe, $157 in increased comfort, $93 in tourist and $84 in youth special for the 1968 season. She again became a very popular ship and was used by even more American passengers as part of air–sea Mediterranean tours. It is, of course, most difficult to predict how much longer the *Caribia* would

have survived. Her demise began when she struck some submerged rocks off Nice, on September 24 1972. Badly holed, her engine room was flooded. She was patched temporarily, placed under tow and then brought into La Spezia, to an anchorage that was quite close to Italy's biggest scrappers. In evaluating the 44-year-old liner, it was obviously the end of her long commercial career. Simply, she was far too old to repair and restore.

In January 1973, the former *Vulcania* began a most extensive series of delays, all while bound for the junkheap. She was sold to those La Spezia scrappers, but then resold to Spanish breakers. Nine months later, in September, she was moved to Barcelona. Left untouched, she was then resold to a Taiwanese firm, who had her towed out to Kaohsiung. She completed the long, slow journey to the East, only to develop a serious leak and sink in the outer reaches of Kaohsiung harbour. It was an extraordinary ending for such a successful ship.

Gross tonnage: 23,970 (1928); 24,469 (1935); 24,496 (1947)
Length overall: 631 feet
Width: 80 feet
Machinery: Burmeister & Wain diesels (1928–35); Fiat diesels (from 1935). Twin screw
Speed: 19 knots (1928–35); 21 knots (from 1935)
Capacity: 279 first class, 257 second class, 310 third class and 1,350 fourth class (1928); 319 first class, 460 second class, 310 intermediate class and 700 third class (1932); altered to first, tourist and third class (1934); 232 first class, 262 cabin class and 958 tourist class (1947); 337 first class, 368 cabin class and 732 tourist class (1966)
Built: Cantieri Navale Triestino, Monfalcone, Italy, 1928
Demise: Sunk at Kaohsiung, Taiwan, July 20 1974, while inbound for a local scrapyard

Above right *Launching the* Vulcania *at Monfalcone, Italy. Her displacement tonnage of 36,500 tons was given out to prove that she was the world's largest motorship at the time.*
Right *From left to right,* Olympia, United States, America, Independence *and* Vulcania *(courtesy of New York Port Authority).*

Above Vulcania *undocking in winter* (courtesy of Moran Towing).

Left *The* Vulcania *at Naples in 1964 during a strike.*

Left *As* Caribia *the famous old motorship sailed first as an Atlantic liner to the Caribbean then later as a Mediterranean cruise ship* (courtesy of Luis Miguel Correia).

Empress of Japan

Few liners have had three quite separate, but most distinguished and popular careers. One such ship was the *Empress of Japan*, which spent the 1930s as the fastest passenger ship on the Pacific. Then, in wartime, having been renamed *Empress of Scotland*, she was a valiant trooper. Afterwards, her owners placed her on the North Atlantic, their royal three-funnel flagship. Her third and final career was as the totally rebuilt *Hanseatic*, a glorious bid by West Germany to re-enter the luxury liner business following the devastation of the Second World War.

The *Empress of Japan* was built for the great Canadian Pacific Company, by the Fairfield Shipyards of Glasgow, and completed in the spring of 1930. Designed to be the fastest and most luxurious liner yet for the Vancouver–Far East service, the ship was given a regal sounding name, honouring Imperial Japan. Emerging as a handsome ship, the new *Empress* was, in fact, a refined, smaller version of the giant *Empress of Britain*, which was then still building at the John Brown Yards at Clydebank. The Pacific ship had a more 'relaxed' profile, however, with three evenly slanted funnels (the third was a dummy). The big *Empress of Britain*, while an imposing, majestic ship, seemed more rigid and unctuous in style.

The *Empress of Japan* was richly appointed. Her decor strongly reflected the new age of what has been more recently termed Art Deco, but without a severity that excluded warmth and comfort. Certainly, the accommodation was made more endearing by the added touches: scattered soft-chairs, area carpets, potted palms, silk pillows. The berthing was arranged in prescribed Pacific fashion: 399 in first class, 164 in second class, 100 in third class and 510 in 'Asiatic' steerage.

After completing her sea trials, the new *Empress* was delivered to Canadian Pacific and sent on an introductory sailing to the St Lawrence. After all, she was to be one of the main ingredients of a near-worldwide service: across from Britain by trans-atlantic *Empress* to Montreal, then by rail to Vancouver by Canadian Pacific train and finally out to the Orient by one of the Pacific *Empresses*. It was then one of the finest, most comprehensive transportation networks available. It was certainly a serious rival to the ships of P&O and Blue Funnel, which used the Suez route out to the Far East. The *Empress of Japan*'s Atlantic crossing hinted at her future. She set a record, between Liverpool and Rimouski, of five days, five hours. Applauded, praised and deemed most appropriate, she then returned to Southampton and set sail for Hong Kong via the Suez Canal. Arriving at Vancouver for the first time in August 1930, she averaged a very commendable 21.04 knots on her first eastward crossing of the Pacific. In the following spring, in April, she established a record of 7 days, 20 hours and 16 minutes between Yokohama and Victoria. This represented an average speed of 22.27 knots. In May 1935, during a sailing via Honolulu, she averaged 22.16 knots. On yet another occasion, while travelling between Victoria and Honolulu, she achieved 22.37 knots.

Remarkably, the *Empress of Japan*'s record runs were not broken until some 30 years later by the American freighter *Washington Mail*.

Following the outbreak of war in that fateful summer of 1939, the speedy *Empress* was among the first ships to be requisitioned for military duty. Her identity soon became less apparent, being covered in layers of grey paint and with her name obscured. In service by November, she was to serve her government for some eight years. Later moved to the South Pacific, she took part in at least two very notable convoys. The first departed from Australia and New Zealand in January 1940, and included three columns of converted troopers: the cruiser HMS *Kent* led the *Empress of Japan*, *Empress of Canada*, *Orcades* and *Rangitata*; the battleship HMS *Ramillies* led the *Orion*, *Orford* and *Dunera*; and the French warship *Suffren* led the *Strathaird*, *Strathnaver*, *Otranto* and *Sobieski*. The convoy stopped briefly at Fremantle for fuel and water, and then at Colombo, before proceeding to Aden and Port Said. At Colombo, the group had been joined by the converted French liner *Athos II*, HMS *Sussex*, HMAS *Hobart* and the aged aircraft carrier HMS *Eagle*.

In the following May, the *Empress of Japan* was part of one of the biggest troopship convoys of the War. Named Convoy *US 3*, it included the *Queen Mary*, *Aquitania*, *Empress of Britain*, *Mauretania*, *Andes*, *Empress of Canada* and, of course, the *Japan*. The combined tonnages of these seven liners was 277,345. In Robert Turner's excellent *The Pacific Empresses*, he included a recollection from May 10 1940: 'After an uneventful voyage, the convoy arrived Fremantle, Friday 10th May. *Mauretania*, *Andes* and the three cruisers going alongside first. *Queen Mary*, *Aquitania* and *Empresses of Britain*, *Canada* and *Japan* anchoring in Gage Roads, where we remained all night. Next morning, the three *Empresses* proceeded into the harbour and Fremantle was the scene of a unique spectacle: three CP *Empress* ships laying end on end at one time. Special trains came right down to the wharf and transported the troops to Perth, which was enfete to greet them. . . .'

The *Empress of Japan* was ordered to home waters in the autumn of 1940. She was actually part of the same extended convoy, which included the flagship *Empress of Britain*. She was hit by a Nazi patrol bomber off northwest Ireland on October 26, burned badly, and then torpedoed two days later by an enemy U-boat. The *Empress of Japan*—suddenly elevated to company flagship and largest vessel—was just days behind. On November 9 1940, also off the north coast of Ireland, she was sighted by a Nazi bomber. Fortunately, all intended bombs missed the speeding liner. One bomb, however, exploded very near to the stern and knocked-out power onboard the ship. Working mostly in darkness, the engineers later assessed that the rudder was off balance and that the shaft bearings and main condenser were also damaged. The *Empress of Japan*, although wounded, limped to her River Clyde destination.

In October 1942, prompted by Japan's entry into the war, the *Empress of Japan* aptly became the *Empress of Scotland*. Her name seemed far removed from her original trade. Not decommissioned until as late as 1948, she steamed over 500,000 miles during the war, made three around-the-world trips and carried over 200,000 personnel. Returned to the Fairfield Yards at Glasgow, she was elegantly refitted, but not with the same original intention. Canadian Pacific decided to abandon its transpacific liner operation. Consequently, the *Empress of Scotland* was restored as flagship of the North Atlantic run.

With the most obvious difference being the addition of Canadian Pacific red-and-white chequers on her three funnels, the reconditioning was completed in May 1950 and the liner sent on her inaugural trip from Liverpool and Greenock to Quebec City. Her berthing figures had been greatly altered to suit the Atlantic trade, being 458 in first class and a rather scant 205 in tourist class. Indeed, her most distinguished passengers came aboard in November 1951. She carried Her Royal Highness Princess Elizabeth and the Duke of Edinburgh, and their party homeward from a highly successful North American tour. They boarded from a specially arranged stop at Portugal Cove in Newfoundland and then disembarked six days later at Liverpool. One of the Royal Trains was waiting and later delivered the King's daughter and her husband to London. (Sadly, within three months, King George VI would be dead and the young Princess Elizabeth would become Queen.)

In May 1952, the towering twin masts on the *Empress of Scotland* were cut down by 40 feet each. She could now make the bridge clearance needed to proceed directly to Montreal. Also, she gradually resumed Canadian Pacific's famed cruise service. Mostly, these were on two and three-week winter trips from New York to the West Indies and South America.

By the end of the 1957 summer season, the *Empress of Scotland*—the last surviving three-stacker apart from the *Queen Mary*—was made redundant. Canadian Pacific had just added two new sister-ships, the 25,500-ton *Empress of Britain* and *Empress of England*. The pre-war *Scotland* no longer fitted in the sailing patterns. Running her last crossing in November, she was laid-up, first at Liverpool and then at Belfast. Then, in rather quick time, she was sold for £1 million to a newly formed West German firm, the Hamburg Atlantic Line. Provisionally renamed *Scotland*, she was sent directly to the Howaldtswerke Shipyard at Hamburg.

Gutted and then largely rebuilt and modernised, the former *Empress* reappeared on the transatlantic shipping scene as the streamlined, twin-funnel *Hanseatic* in the following July. The accommodation had been greatly enlarged, to 85 in first class and 1,167 in tourist. Engaged in single-ship service between Cuxhaven (Hamburg), Southampton, Cherbourg and New York, this virtual new ship attracted considerable attention and was briefly noted as the largest German liner in nearly two decades. (The 32,300-ton *Bremen* outstepped her a year later.) The ship's actual gross tonnage had increased from 26,313 to 30,029.

During the winter months, the *Hanseatic* went cruising. She was among the first large passenger ships to be based at Port Everglades, Florida for Caribbean trips. In November 1961, she made the first 'nowhere cruise' out of New York since 1939. A sell-out voyage, it was scheduled over the American Thanksgiving holiday, sailing on Wednesday at 6.00 pm and then returning at 4 o'clock on Friday afternoon. Co-author Miller was aboard as one of the teenage passengers. There were only three fares: $75, $85 and $95. In addition, the *Hanseatic* also cruised from Cuxhaven to the Fjords and the Baltic, and from Genoa within the Mediterranean and to West Africa.

Having become a very popular and successful ship, she met with a most untimely end. On September 7 1966, just hours prior to her departure from New York's Pier 84, at the foot of West 44th Street, she caught fire and was seriously damaged. Smoke poured from her upper-deck windows, portholes and ventilators. Firefighters were especially cautious, however, not wanting to repeat the *Normandie* tragedy, which was so overloaded with water that she capsized at her berth. Without injury to either passengers or staff, the *Hanseatic* was moved within two days to the Todd Shipyards at Brooklyn's Eire Basin. Her owners, fire inspectors, engineers and insurance agents examined the 36-year-old liner. The findings were disappointing. While the actual fire damage could be repaired, the smell of smoke had permeated throughout the ship. It lingered everywhere. She would have to be stripped, cleaned and refitted thoroughly. To the German accountants, this would be uneconomic against her age.

With her engines still immobilised, she was towed several weeks later to Hamburg, arriving there on October 10. She was then sold to local scrappers, Eisen & Metall A/G. Months later, in June 1967, co-author Miller was travelling aboard the *Homeric* of the Home Lines, a company related to the Hamburg Atlantic Line. Numerous deckchairs were marked for the *Hanseatic*. They had obviously been removed from the ship just prior to her final departure from New York. Ironically, six years later, in July 1973, the *Homeric* was also damaged by fire. Again, the thick smell of smoke had spread throughout the ship and, once again, because of her age, she had to be scrapped.

Gross tonnage: 26,032 (1930); 26,313 (1948); 30,030 (1958)
Length overall: 666 feet (1930); 672 feet (1958)
Width: 83 feet
Machinery: Steam turbines, twin screw
Speed: 21 knots
Capacity: 399 first, 164 second, 100 third, 510 steerage (1930); 458 first, 250 tourist (1948); 85 first, 1,167 tourist (1958)
Built: Fairfield Shipbuilding & Engineering Co, Glasgow, Scotland, 1930
Demise: Fire damage at New York in September 1966; then towed to Hamburg and scrapped

Left *The US Coast Guard took over* Empress of Scotland, *the name given to* the Empress of Japan *after the attack on Pearl Harbor (courtesy of US Coast Guard).*

Right *A superb bow view of* Empress of Japan, *one of the most handsome of great liners.*

Left *The* Hanseatic *was a very popular cruise ship. She is seen here berthed at La Guaira, Venezuela, during a winter cruise from Florida (courtesy of Everett Viez collection).*

Johan Van Oldenbarnevelt

The *Johan Van Oldenbarnevelt* was among the most popular and beloved of all Dutch passenger liners. She and her sister-ship, the *Marnix Van St Aldegonde*, were not only the largest passenger ships yet to be built in the Netherlands and the flagships of the colonial East Indies trade, but they also had two of the longest names ever to be put to sea. The *Van Oldenbarnevelt* was named after the founder of the East India Company and the architect of Dutch independence from Spanish rule. The *St Aldegonde* took her name from the chief adviser to William of Orange and the supposed composer of the Dutch National Anthem.

Both were designed as progressively larger and improved continuations of earlier Nederland Line colonial motorships, this new team was ordered from the Netherlands Shipbuilding Company yards at Amsterdam. The *Johan Van Oldenbarnevelt*—or the '*JVO*' as she was more commonly known—was laid down in June 1928, launched a year later, on August 3, and then was ready for trials in March 1930. Fitted with twin Sulzer diesels, she was designed to make 17 knots maximum while in service. Delighting both her builders and owners, she reached 19 knots during her trial runs. Then, soon after being signed over, she was selected for special duty: a short cruise with distinguished guests from Amsterdam to Ijmuiden and return. The occasion was the dedication and opening of the new North Sea

Lock, then the largest sea lock in the world, in the North Sea Canal. The guest list was headed by Her Majesty Queen Wilhelmina, Prince Hendrik and their daughter, Crown Princess Juliana. Few liners have started their careers as something of a royal yacht.

Unfortunately, the maiden trip outbound was slightly interrupted. After leaving Amsterdam on May 6, she collided in the North Sea Canal with the 3,854-ton Dutch freighter *Reggestroom*. Although the impact was slight, both ships had to be taken in hand by tugs and brought into Amsterdam harbour. Shipyard crews worked around-the-clock on the new liner and had her repaired within three days. Using her reserve speed, she cut short her maiden call at Southampton, reached Genoa a day late and yet was almost exactly on time for Port Said. When she finally reached Batavia (present-day Jakarta), she was firmly established as the new queen of the East Indies trade.

The *JVO* had six main passenger decks, which included such facilities as a hospital, swimming pool and gymnasium (located just forward of the first squat funnel), a nursery, music room, three dining rooms and considerable open-air promenade deck space, especially useful for the steamy passages through the Mediterranean, Red Sea and Indian Ocean. The berthing was flexible, adjusted according to demand: 245 to 300 in first class, 246 to 367 in second class, 64 to 99 in third class and a firm 48 in fourth class. This accommodation ranged from two deluxe suites on B deck to the fourth class space, which surrounded the crew accommodation on F deck. In addition, the *JVO* could take 1,000 tons of cargo in five holds, which were serviced by a dozen three-ton deck cranes that sat on the open decks like mounted guns.

These new ships were improved, more luxurious versions of two earlier Nederland liners, the 14,600-ton *Pieter Corneliszoon Hooft* of 1925 and the 15,600-ton *Christiaan Huygens* of 1928. The decoration in the new sisters represented the colonial wealth and brilliance of the East Indies. In the Smoking Room aboard the *JVO*, the brown panelling was covered in antique gold leather and

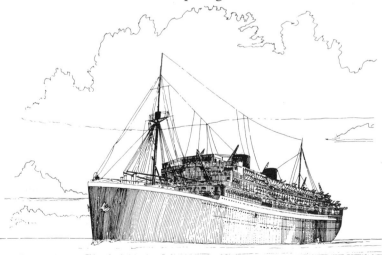

included a prominent portrait of Johan Van Oldenbarnevelt. All of the furniture was done in ebony, with inlays of tin in most of the chairs. The ceiling was done in a red coppered tone and rose above beams of beaten copper. Large arched windows flooded the room with natural light. The two-deck high social hall was lined in padouk, again inlaid with tin and with carved teak doors and panels completing the decor. The dining room was done in white-painted mahogany with ebony Venetian blinds that included stainless steel decorations. A tapestry was placed at the far end of the restaurant and depicted old Amsterdam. Every cabin was outside, either directly or through a long corridor that connected to a porthole.

The two ships sailed in continuous colonial service throughout the 1930s trading from Amsterdam to Batavia in 29 days and then reversing course. The *Marnix Van St Aldegonde* was damaged by fire while in the western Mediterranean, on October 8 1936 and was forced into Ajaccio on the island of Corsica for temporary repairs. Although one of her cargo holds was flooded, she was able to continue her outward voyage to Java. Less than a year later, on July 31 1937, the *JVO* was hit by some shells while sailing close to the Spanish coast. Fortunately, there was only slight damage.

In that tense summer of 1939, the *JVO* was chartered for one roundtrip voyage to New York for the Holland–America Line. Detoured to Rotterdam, she was booked to capacity with anxious passengers, tourists and refugees, all fortunate to escape the threatening Nazi war machine. Thereafter, she was rerouted via South Africa on her voyages out to the East. By early 1940, her operations were modified still further. Together with the *Marnix Van St Aldegonde* and two Rotterdam Lloyd liners, the *Dempo* and *Sibajak*, the Batavia service was run from still-neutral Genoa. Dutch passengers were delivered to that northern Italian port by rail. However, there were far more drastic changes ahead.

When Rotterdam was bombed on May 14 1940, the *JVO* was in the Red Sea and bound for the Mediterranean. Abruptly, she was ordered to reverse course, return to the East Indies and adopt Batavia as her homeport. Once there, she became the first Dutch merchant ship to sail with a military escort while in Eastern waters. The *JVO* and those three other Dutch liners from the Genoa service were promptly transferred to the Java–New York Line, which ran emergency services between the United States and the Dutch East Indies via the Cape. Although these ships still carried passengers, including many worried evacuees, cargo was the immediate and most pressing purpose. Aboard the *JVO*, cargo was even stacked in the public rooms. She was officially transferred to the Allies on January 20 1941 and converted at New York to a wartime trooper with space for 4,000 personnel. She was given over to the British government, who placed her under the management of the Orient Line, but was again given different registry, this time at Willemstad on Curacao in the Dutch West Indies.

The *Johan Van Oldenbarnevelt*'s war record is quite impressive: 33 voyages, 281,000 miles and a list of over 72,000 passengers. Her sister-ship was less fortunate, however. The *Marnix Van St Aldegonde* was hit by an aerial torpedo off Algeria, on November 6 1943. While there was no loss of life among the 3,000 troops and crew aboard, the abandoned and badly damaged Dutch liner sank the following day, not far from the shores of Phillippeville.

The *JVO* travelled extensively throughout the war years, to Iceland, the Mediterranean, West Africa, the Suez and India. However, there was one annoying problem: her engines were troublesome. In June 1943, she was laid-up at Liverpool's Langton Dock for 11 months for necessary repairs. She finally returned to a liberated Holland in August 1945, when inbound with returning troops from Bombay, she proceeded from Southampton to Rotterdam. A call at her former homeport of Amsterdam would have to wait as the North Lock of the North Sea Canal was damaged badly by the retreating Nazis. Months later, in March 1946, she was handed back to the Dutch government and finally berthed at the Nederland Line's Javakade at Amsterdam.

While her colonial work was interrupted by the Indonesian struggle for independence, the *JVO* was called-up by her government, to carry troops out to the troubled Eastern islands and then return with the evacuating Dutch. This work continued until mid-1950. Immediately thereafter, she was

A busy scene at the Netherlands Shipbuilding Yards on July 28 1929. The Johan Van Oldenbarnevelt *is to the left and well under way while her twin sister,* Marnix Van Aldegonde *is under construction on the right* (courtesy of Nedlloyd).

given another task: to carry fare-assisted Dutch emigrants out to either South Africa or Australia. It proved a successful and useful new career for the former queen of the Eastern colonial run.

Refitted by the Amsterdam Drydock Co during the winter of 1951–52, her original berthing of about 770 passengers in four classes was changed to 1,414, all in a single austerity class. The cabin accommodation was rearranged completely with very few double and triple rooms, 200 four-berth cabins, 50 with five or six berths and 13 large dormitories. All of the staterooms were fitted with washstands and cold running water only. While many of the original public rooms were restored, new amenities included a cinema, hairdressing salons and two passenger laundries. Her diesels were, however, still worrisome. On her trial runs in January 1952, she barely managed 15½ knots. But there were further troubles for the *JVO*. On her first Australian trip, sailing out to Fremantle, Melbourne and Sydney via the Suez, she had no less than four fires. One was discovered during a special call at Antwerp and another off the Isle of Wight. The latter blaze caused her Master to reverse course and return to Amsterdam for inspection and temporary repairs.

During the 1950s the *JVO* occasionally strayed from the busy Australian migrant trade. She made a number of student sailings across the North Atlantic, to both Quebec City and to New York. The arrangements for these trips were handled by another very prominent Dutch shipper, the Holland America Line. I [WHM] recall seeing her at New York in 1958. She was a most unexpected sight, almost unrecognisable. At first, I thought that she was Cunard–White Star's *Britannic*, which also had twin squat stacks. At the time, she was berthed in the partially obscured north berth of Holland America's 5th Street pier in Hoboken. In complete irony, another Dutch East Indian liner, the *Willem Ruys*, was in the south slip. While it was very rare to see the *JVO* it was indeed a very special occasion to see two of these very distant liners at the same time. Both were running student and low-fare tourist crossings from Europe.

By the late 1950s however, Dutch passenger ship operators were preparing for some changes. It had been decided that the once-rival Nederland Line and Royal Rotterdam Lloyd would merge the services of their three surviving liners, the *JVO*, Nederland's 20,500-ton *Oranje* from 1939 and Rotterdam Lloyd's 23,100-ton *Willem Ruys* of 1947. Each of the ships would be modernised and upgraded, and a special around-the-world service started. In the winter of 1959, the 29-year-old *JVO* was again sent to the Amsterdam Drydock Co, this time for a £400,000 refit. Her berthing plans were rearranged for 1,210 all-tourist class passengers, carried in 247 doubles, 90 triples, 81 four-berth and a few dormitories. More cabins were given private shower and toilet. While some new public rooms were added, the original lounges and salons again kept their distinctive earlier decor, which was especially popular with Dutch travellers. Air-conditioning was added as was a second deck pool, which replaced an aft cargo hatch.

The biggest changes were made to the exterior of the ship, however. A new dove-grey colouring was used on the hull, replacing the original black. Her funnels were heightened and given more contemporary domed tops. The foremast was halved, the mainmast removed completely and a new signal mast placed above the bridge. Her new routing was on three-month eastabout world voyages, sailing from Amsterdam and Southampton to Palma de Majorca, Genoa, Port Said, Suez, Colombo, Fremantle, Melbourne, Sydney, Wellington, Auckland, Suva, Papeete, Callao, Cristobal, Port Everglades and occasionally New York and then homewards to Amsterdam. Unfortunately, this new service was less than a success.

The *JVO* was withdrawn from her world voyages in the autumn of 1962. One of her last assignments was to serve as a hotel-ship at Fremantle for the Seventh Commonwealth Games at Perth. Another Dutch passenger vessel was used as well, the converted Victory freighter *Groote Beer*. In February 1963, the *JVO* left Sydney, empty and in the hands of a delivery crew, for Genoa. The Dutch flag was lowered for the last time and, with the official transfer enacted, she raised the colours of Greece for the big Goulandris Group, who owned the Greek Line passenger fleet. Registered to a subsidiary, the Ormos Shipping Company, she was renamed *Lakonia* and refitted at the Mariotti Shipyards in Genoa. With Greek themes now applied throughout her decoration, with her pool extended in size and with all cabins being given beds instead of bunks, she was prepared for a year-round cruise service (12–16 days) from Southampton to ports in the eastern Atlantic—Vigo, Lisbon, Gibraltar, Madeira, Teneriffe, Las Palmas and Casablanca. She was scheduled for 17 cruises between April and November 1963, and 27 trips between Christmas 1963 and November 1964. Her winter-time partner would be another Greek Line ship, the *Arkadia*, the former *Monarch of Bermuda* of 1931.

The *Lakonia* developed a certain popularity, but was, once again, not without her problems. Her engines again proved faulty and, by September, she was running 1–2 days off schedule because of delays. Taken in hand by the Thornycroft Shipyards at Southampton, she was said to be improved considerably. Her next trip was a fully-booked Christmas sailing, leaving Southampton on December 19 with 1,036 passengers and crew aboard. Sadly, this was to be the final voyage of the 33-year-old ship.

The day before reaching Madeira, on December 22 1963, fire broke out in the hairdressing salon and spread rapidly. Quickly, the ship was filled with smoke. The initial error was the complete lack of fire detection until the eruption had reached hazardous proportions. An SOS was flashed to all nearby ships, with responses coming from the carrier HMS *Centaur*, American Export's *Independence* and three freighters, the *Montcalm*, *Mehdi* and *Rio Grande*. Evacuating the flaming *Lakonia* was chaotic: some boats were lowered with great difficulty, others leaked once they reached the chilly waters of the Atlantic and then a davit collapsed and dropped a fully-loaded boat into the sea. After midnight on the 23rd, the completely abandoned *Lakonia* was burning from end to end.

Survivors were picked-up from lifeboats, rafts and lifelings by the rescue ships, which later included two other liners, Belgium's *Charlesville* and P&O's *Stratheden*. The *Lakonia* was left to drift and to burn herself out. On the 24th, two muscular ocean-going tugs, Holland's *Poolzee* and Norway's *Hercules*, attempted to put the scorched hull under tow. It was a difficult and tender process. The *Lakonia* began to list and while cautiously destined for Gibraltar, she heeled over and sank on the 29th. Her long career was over. The Christmas cruise tragedy claimed 130 lives and began an international study (later extended to two further disasters in North American waters, the cruise-ships *Yarmouth Castle* and *Viking Princess* in 1965 and 1966 respectively) for stricter safety standards for elderly passenger ships. By 1968, with these regulations in effect, many older liners were sent rightfully to the scrapheap.

Gross tonnage: 19,040 (1930); 19,429 (1937); 19,787 (1951); 20,314 (1959)
Length overall: 608 feet
Width: 74 feet
Machinery: Sulzer diesels, twin screw
Speed: 17 knots
Capacity: Approximately 366 first class, 280 second class, 64 third class, 60 fourth class (1930); 1,414 all tourist class (1951); 1,210 all tourist class (1959)
Built: Netherlands Shipbuilding Co, Amsterdam, Holland, 1930
Demise: Caught fire on December 22 1963, while some 200 miles off Madeira; later abandoned and then placed under tow. Sank on December 29 while 250 miles west of Gibraltar

Her Majesty Queen Wilhelmina and Crown Princess Juliana aboard the 'JVO'. She was used as the 'host ship' for the opening of the North Lock at Ijmuiden (courtesy of Nedlloyd).

Serving as Lakonia *for the Greek Line, the ship was destroyed by fire during a Christmas cruise in 1963* (courtesy of Roger Sherlock).

The Johan Van Oldenbarnevelt *was fitted out with a great amount of highly stylised dark wood panelling. The main lounge is a fine example of her unique decoration* (courtesy of Nedlloyd).

Morro Castle

Many memories rush to the surface when I (FOB) think of the *Morro Castle*. In 1930, when I was 14 my parents took me from our home in Long Island to Washington. This trip involved two boat trips. The first was a two-night coastal voyage on the Old Dominion Line's little one-stacked coastal steamer *Hamilton*, my first sea trip. A most embarrassing experience occurred on this voyage. My hat blew overboard, and, being a sickly child, I was told by my mother that I could not go out on deck again unless we found a new hat. Loving ships I could not bear to miss the opportunity to see others from the vantage point of the deck, so I agreed to wear one of her hats made to look something like a beret.

During our one day's stay at Newport News, my father arranged for us all to visit the Newport News Shipbuilding & Dry Dock Co yard. We saw two huge unpainted hulls being worked on at the fitting out dock. They were the *Morro Castle* and her sister, the *Oriente*. Although cameras were not permitted, I managed to secrete my old box camera on my person and took a few snapshots, very fearfully. For years I would think that because of this I had somehow jinxed the poor *Morro Castle*. We went from there on to Washington on the overnight Potomac River steamer *District of Columbia*.

Before recounting my other personal links with the *Morro Castle*, a few words about her as a ship, gleaned from old newspaper clippings and company brochures. The *Morro Castle* was finished in the summer of 1930 and on August 19 of that year an inspection and luncheon for local VIPs in the New York area was held. An impressive-looking engraved invitation invited these people to board the liner at Pier 13, East River, at 1 o'clock. One such invitation went to Russel J. Baker, of the American Steamship Owners Association, 11 Broadway, and was promptly filed for posterity. I worked for this outfit and when it folded up I acquired their *Morro Castle* file.

As a boy I wrote to many ship lines for their literature and saved everything I received, starting with the *Belgenland* world cruise brochure in 1924. One of the most interesting folders I got in this way 55 years ago was the first big brochure issued for the new *Morro Castle* and her sister. Although I did not think so then, it seems a bit sombre looking today, being done in grey and black. The first eight pages showed artist's conceptions of the new liner's public rooms and deck spaces. Then a 24-inch long page opened up featuring an 8 × 16 inch artist's conception of the new liners and a block of copy giving their size and luxury and stressing their safety features:

'The ships are protected throughout with proven safety devices of the latest type, including radio sending and receiving sets, radio direction finders, automatic electric fire alarms, automatically operated fire-doors, electrically controlled bulkhead doors, automatic detecting and chemical fire extinguishing systems, fathometers, Watchmens' Clock System, complete Sperry Gyroscope System, including automatic steering, powerful fog siren, searchlight, helm indicators, tachometers, and embody structural safeguards of an advanced nature, which contribute toward making these vessels the safest afloat.'

Perhaps the shipyard's pride in the safety side of their new products influenced the line in including

these facts in its first big folder. Certainly it became company policy thereafter to say little or nothing about safety and the ship's safety features in its brochures for fear of worrying the passengers. For the same reason fire drills were not well attended by the crew and very little effort was made to encourage passenger participation.

The new ships were proudly described as *T.E.L. Morro Castle* and *T.E.L. Oriente*, meaning turbo-electric liners. The turbo-electric propulsion system had been publicised widely by the US Navy in their huge aircraft carriers *Lexington* and *Saratoga*. The first major American liners to have this system were the three Panama Pacific Line steamers *California*, *Virginia* and *Pennsylvania*. In due course the *Normandie* would be built with turbo-electric drive. The brochure listed the many 'exceptionally comfortable and luxurious' features of the new ships, including 'modern beds, running hot and cold water, mechanical ventilation and heating by the Thermo System, electric bed and reading lamps, telephone and annunciator systems'. The term 'annunciator' went back as far as the Collins liner *Baltic* of 1850. It referred to buzzers to summon room service. The *Morro Castle* was ahead of her time on the score of private facilities: 'Many rooms have both toilet and shower, others have toilet only, a considerable number have private bathrooms, while public baths and toilets are conveniently located on all decks. . . .'

The ships certainly had many luxuries, but wall fans in all public rooms showed that the era of air-conditioning on ships was still not at hand. The main lounge and the dining salon were both two-deck high rooms with plenty of airy space and tall columns. Watteau and Fragonard style murals in the lounge suggested a French atmosphere. The smoking room was meant to suggest the Italian Renaissance period, and featured a large electric fireplace, heavy armchairs and wood panelling. A light and airy deck ballroom aft on the promenade deck was glass enclosed and spread the entire width of the ship. A band stand aft was flanked by window box ferns. The dining salon had murals based on Greek mythology, and was decorated with two-deck high fluted pilasters. A small children's playroom was designed like a courtyard with bright awnings and rustic furniture and

described as having 'a decided appeal for the youthful traveler'.

The writing room, which would live to have frightful connotations, 'is of the Classical French style, with furniture following the Empire design'. It was a smallish room forward on the port side with large hanging paintings of pine trees and outdoor scenes. Small double-seat writing desks lined the walls. The room was done in white with a many-squared carpet. It looked out on the glass-enclosed promenade. This is where testimony had it that the tragic fire that destroyed the liner began. News stories hinted that one disgruntled crew member had planted an explosive pen in one of the desks. Other stories would tell of drunken passengers flipping lighted cigarettes into waste baskets the evening of the disaster.

In 1931 a variety of 9, 10, 13, 16 and 17-day cruises were offered in addition to the *Morro Castle*'s regular service to Havana. Prices ranged from $145 to $477 and cuisine and luxury were emphasised in the cruise literature. An Easter cruise offered the next year was publicised in a couple of double-page spreads 21 × 14 inches in size with ten photographs each showing life aboard. Italicised captions were done in the best Madison Avenue style: 'The pastry chefs have the subtle touch that makes them artists', and 'Mask parties will be another gay feature. Here you may show your genius in costume designing', and 'These boys furnish concert and dance music of the best'. The ship line hired the Barbary Coast Orchestra of Dartmouth College for the cruise. No reference in the folder was made to safety. The cruise was of nine days duration and prices began at $95. The brochure began: 'Havana, Miami, Nassau! Three prime favorites! And the fourth is the *Morro Castle*—one of the most popular cruise-ships of recent seasons!'

A 'Winter Cruise to Havana' cruise folder was done with a cover of orange and tan showing a scantily dressed Spanish dancer with blue shawl and wide billowing skirt, high enough to reveal a fancy garter. The back of the folder's cover showed the twin liners in stylised drawings with sharp stems, twin stacks and splashing bow waves, again done in orange, tan and brown, with a touch of light blue and white, a most unusual colour scheme hinting at the joys of warm, Spanish

Havana. Apparently the idea was to show that you would be entertained every minute of the trip: 'You'll have to step lively to keep up with all that's doing on these Havana Winter Cruises. The Cruise Directors know how to entertain and will keep you tuned to concert pitch. Days are filled to overflowing with every kind of shipboard sport and activity imaginable. . . . It's a fiesta and carnival of fun every day and every night on shipboard on these Havana Winter Cruises.'

The ships did not have a regular swimming pool, but someone thought up the idea of piping in salt water and having what amounted to an outside shower for one and all on deck. . . . A photo shows five models standing and sitting under three large sprays of water supported on a pipe on a sports deck. Some years later the *Oriente* would have a tiny outdoor pool installed.

A wine list saved by some 1934 passengers showed that a bottle of 1923 Ch Heidsick Champagne could be had for $6. Cocktails cost 25 cents and a Tom Collins or a Whiskey Sour each cost 30 cents.

I was returning from my first voyage to Europe in the late summer of 1934, a tourist third class passenger aboard the US Lines' *President Roosevelt*. One day there was a Fire Drill and I sensed that it was an unscheduled one for which the crew were unprepared. There had been an earlier one a few hours out of Le Havre. The drill gave me great pleasure on two counts. My lifeboat station was on the cabin class promenade so I had a legitimate reason to go into this upper class area. As I stood under my boat with my life jacket on I saw several cabin class passengers ignoring the drill in a sophisticated way and looking at me as if to say look what has come up from the depths. Then, to my delight, along came crusty old Captain John F. Jensen with his coterie of officers to inspect things. He gave the lolling cabin class passengers a good tongue-lashing and ordered them down to their cabins at once to get their life jackets. They obeyed. It felt great to see it all happen. There was, however, no explanation of 'why' the sudden fire alarm and drill. Several days later when we docked at New York the first words my waiting parents said to me were: 'Wasn't it horrible about the *Morro Castle* fire!'

The destruction of this fine vessel will remain

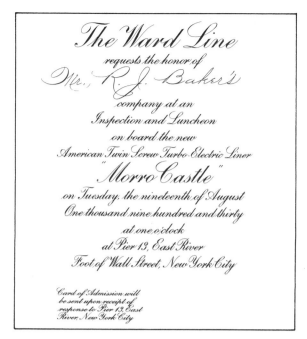

An invitation to 'Inspection and Luncheon' aboard the Morro Castle.

one of the great tragedies of the history of the American Merchant Marine. How so fine a ship, so new and so well equipped could burn with such a high loss of life has never been properly explained. Many TV shows and at least three books on the subject have far from solved the riddle of this disaster.

Years later the president of the Cuba Mail Line, the new name Ward Line chose after the fire, told me that despite the lengthy Congressional hearings, the long trial of the ship's officers and the many 'great changes' in safety regulations, the line was not required to alter or improve the sister-ship *Oriente* in any way, shape or form.

Gross tonnage: 11,520
Length overall: 508 feet
Width: 70 feet 9 inches
Machinery: Turbo-electric, twin screw
Speed: 21 knots
Capacity: 500 first, 50 third
Built: Newport News Shipbuilding and Drydock Co, 1930
Demise: Burned and scrapped in Baltimore 1935

Left *The* Morro Castle's *two deck high dining saloon.*

Left *Saluting her namesake, Morro Castle, Havana, the new* Morro Castle *makes a record first trip in 1930.*

Left *Dancing aboard the* Morro Castle *in the deck ballroom aft.*

Above *Lifeboats that could not be used.*

Right *The fire! Note the seamen on the foredeck trying to saw through the anchor chain so that the ship could be towed. A lifeboat can also be seen under the bow.*

Borinquen

In the years up to the Second World War, the American merchant marine included a large fleet of both coastal and Latin American passenger ships. There were such shippers as the Clyde Line, Morgan Line, Red 'D' Line, Ward Line and Colombian Mail Line. Another was the New York & Puerto Rico Steamship Company. Their ships provided three lucrative services: roundtrip cruises for American tourists, normal port-to-port service for one-way traffic and, equally importantly, for cargo with both general freight and the mails.

These ships with their diverse house-flags have been rather poorly recorded. Primarily because they were under 10,000 tons and did not make long-distance trips, they were well overshadowed by the big transatlantic queens and others on the long-haul overseas routes to South America, Africa and Australia. Most unfortunately, however, this part of the American fleet was mostly gone by the late 1940s, either because of war losses or, more importantly, the intrusion and protected interests of the airline, railroad and trucking industries. One of the larger ships of this group, the *Borinquen* of 1931, returned to something of her original service and then went on to a more diverse career,

as both an Atlantic liner and Florida cruise-ship.

The *Borinquen* was the finest passenger ship to be built for the New York & Puerto Rico Steamship Company. Built by the Bethlehem Steel Shipyards at Quincy, Massachusetts, she was fitted out alongside three much larger American beauties, Matson's famed trio of the *Lurline*, *Mariposa* and *Monterey*. Despite the bitterness (and loss of business) from the Depression, these building orders had actually been placed in the late 1920s and then continued forward. Certainly, all of these ships—as well as almost all those in service— would be receiving fewer passengers than expected. The *Borinquen* was placed on a two-week service between New York, San Juan in Puerto Rico and Ciudad Trujillo in the Dominican Republic.

Her pleasant accommodation was balanced between 261 in high-standard first class quarters and 96 in second class. Throughout the 1930s, she was a familiar fixture at New York Harbor, sailing from an unusual berth at the foot of Wall Street in Lower Manhattan, along the East River. Aside from other passenger ships and freighters, she was often docked just across from the Ward Line's two-funnel *Oriente*, which was on the Havana service, and opposite the Brooklyn slips of such Grace liners as the *Santa Barbara* and *Santa Maria*.

Like most American-flag ships, which were still neutral, the *Borinquen* continued sailing well after the Nazi attack on Poland in September 1939. In fact, she was not called to emergency government duty until December 31 1941. Although it was over three weeks since the Japanese attack on Pearl Harbor and since the United States was declared to be officially at war, she was preparing to sail, on that New Year's Eve, on yet another luxury cruise to the Caribbean. In January, she was allocated to the American War Department and given the duty of taking members of the Corps of Engineers to various overseas destinations. In February, on her first military voyage, she sailed to Iceland. In April, for the longest voyage of her career, she went not only to Iceland, but to England and then on a distant journey southward to Freetown, Capetown and Durban.

136

In 1943, the *Borinquen* made a continuous series of crossings to Oran, often heavily loaded with troops. With various modifications, her capacity had been increased from 357 in peacetime to 1,289 during the war years. Afterward, there were some Northern passages, to Belfast, Southampton and Le Havre. In the latter part of 1945, she returned to the Mediterranean, travelling to Marseilles and the Italian port of Leghorn. Her last government trip came in January 1946, a westbound sailing from Le Havre to New York with returning troops. The US Army returned her to the War Shipping Administration, a New York City-based intermediary, who then returned her to new owners, the Agwilines Incorporated. The original New York & Puerto Rico Steamship Co had been bought out and consequently lost its identity.

There seems to have been some indecision as to the exact use for the *Borinquen*, the sole survivor among her pre-war fleetmates. She was sent to lay-up, anchored in an unusual location off City Island, in the northeast reaches of New York Harbor. After considerable study, her owners decided to reactivate her for something of her earlier service, 12-day cruises to Puerto Rico from New York. In December 1946, she was sent to the Bethlehem Steel Shipyards at Hoboken and given a $1.5 million restoration, an amount that was greater than her total construction cost some 15 years earlier. She resumed commercial sailings in the following June, with roundtrips costing $150.

The little *Borinquen* was not a huge success and, within two years, was transferred to another American steamship firm, the Bull Line. They too were active in Caribbean service and saw bright days ahead for a year-round Puerto Rican cruise service. The ship was renamed as the *Puerto Rico*. However, the results were again less than favourable. In early 1953, she was laid-up at New York, along the Brooklyn waterfront, with little hope for continued service under the Stars and Stripes. American labour was becoming increasingly expensive, she offered only single-ship service and then, as if to add further complication, airline services to the Caribbean had developed. The Bull Line continued thereafter only with 12-passenger freighters.

In January 1954, in a rather unlikely move, a new transatlantic firm, the Arosa Line of Switzer-land, bought the ship for extensive conversion. Renamed *Arosa Star*, she was taken to Bremer-haven to be fitted with enlarged accommodation for 38 in first class and 768 in tourist. The Arosa Co then just two years old, had one other ship, the 8,900-ton *Arosa Kulm*, the former *American Banker* of the United States Lines. She too had been converted to a high-density tourist class ship. At the time, in the mid-1950s, the Arosa Line offered some of the lowest priced passages on the North Atlantic, beginning at $150 in a dormitory for nine days between Bremerhaven and Quebec City.

The *Arosa Star* first appeared in May 1954, having completed her $1 million renovations, which included a new raked bow. Her operations thereafter became quite diverse. In the summer, she sailed on the Atlantic, trading mostly between Bremerhaven, Le Havre, Southampton, Quebec and Montreal. Occasionally, there were special sailings to either Halifax and/or New York. There were also winter cruises: from New York to Bermuda and the Caribbean, from Miami to Nassau and Havana and some special charter trips from North European ports to the Mediterranean. Her owners progressed as well. In the summer of 1955, they added the 20,100-ton *Arosa Sun*, formerly the *Felix Roussel* of France's Messageries Maritimes, and then their fourth and last liner, the 17,400-ton *Arosa Sky* (which joined in spring 1957), another one-time Messageries Maritimes liner, *La Marseillaise*. Soon afterward, however, the entire Arosa company fell on hard times.

A coupling of problems included financial over-extension, mounting fleet expenses and a declining low fare market on the Atlantic. Furthermore, while seeking an alternative in the Caribbean cruise trades, the Arosa reputation was scarred by several small, but newsworthy shipboard fires, passenger reports of unsafe conditions onboard and unhappy crew members who were demanding back wages. It became more and more unpleasant, and more and more obvious. In a bid for emergency 'working capital', the *Arosa Sky* was sold off in October 1958, after little more than 15 months service, to Italy's Costa Line and renamed *Bianca C*. But, within two months, in December, the cruel axe fell. Each of the three remaining Arosa ships were seized and impounded for debts: the *Arosa Kulm* at Plymouth, the *Arosa Sun* at

Bremerhaven and the *Arosa Star*, the former *Borinquen*, at Bermuda. Each of the ships would be auctioned-off and the Arosa Co disbanded.

In June 1959, while still idle at St Georges, Bermuda, the *Arosa Star* found yet another buyer. Changing hands for a scant $510,000, she went to Mr William Lovett, the owner of the Piggly Wiggly supermarket chain and creator of a Panamanian holding firm, McCormick Shipping Company. The ship was towed to Jacksonville, Florida and thoroughly refitted. Mr Lovett sailed her under the banner of the Eastern Steamship Lines of Miami as the *Bahama Star* on three and four-day cruises to Nassau. She would depart from Miami twice weekly, on Mondays and Fridays. Fares for the three-day trips began at $59 and for four-days at $69.

While lacking such obvious cruise-ship amenities as lido decks and circular outdoor pools, private cabin plumbing throughout and even complete air-conditioning, the *Bahama Star* was nevertheless a great success. Miami had not yet grown into the major cruise-port that it is today and this older ship then rated as the largest and grandest on the Bahamas trade out of Florida. Her Eastern fleetmates were, in fact, two other former American passenger ships from the pre-war coastal trades, the 5,000-ton sisters *Evangeline* and *Yarmouth*.

Years later, on November 13 1965, it was the *Bahama Star* that heroically rescued 378 survivors from the burning *Yarmouth Castle*, the former *Evangeline*. It was this disaster among several others at the time that would, in fact, prompt legislation and strict safety regulations that would spell the end for the veteran *Bahama Star*. Captain Carl Netherland-Brown, master of the affectionately-dubbed *Star*, recalled, 'She was a wonderful old ship, which we all loved. She was easy to handle, ideal for the overnight trade between Miami and Nassau and was assuredly the catalyst for the enormous success of Florida cruising today. In 1968, when the new International Safety Standards came into effect, we so regretted that it would be totaly uneconomic to upgrade the 37-year-old *Star*. She simply had to go.'

The *Bahama Star* was retired in November 1968, almost to the very last moment before the new passenger ship regulations took effect. Her original steam chime whistle was nostalgically removed and placed aboard her successor, the *New Bahama Star*, just purchased from the Zim Lines after having been their *Jerusalem* of 1957. The older ship was put up for sale. At first, there were rumours that the Indonesians would buy her for inter-island services out of Jakarta, then that some other interest wanted to dismantle the ship and then reassemble her for use on some Central American lake, and finally that the otherwise unknown Western Steamship Company, another Panamanian line, would use her in some overseas cruise service. That latter idea was shelved when she was leased instead to a California firm, who wanted her as a floating hotel and restaurant in Channel Islands Harbor at Oxnard.

Brought out to California via Panama, refitting hardly began when, on April 13 1970, the ship was lashed by a ferocious hurricane, capsized and then wrecked. Canted over and partially flooded, she was beyond repair and had to be broken-up on the spot. That summer, just short of her 40th year, there was yet one further historic notation: a fire aboard while being scrapped.

Gross tonnage: 7,114 (1931); 9,070 (1954)
Length overall: 429 feet (1931); 466 feet (1954)
Width: 60 feet
Machinery: Steam turbines, twin screw
Speed: 15 knots
Capacity: 261 first class and 96 second class (1931); 1,298 wartime troops (1942); 38 first class and 768 tourist class (1954); 806 all-first class (1959)
Built: Bethlehem Steel Co, Quincy, Massachusetts, 1931
Demise: Wrecked off Port Hueneme, California, on April 13 1970; later scrapped on the spot

Top right *Taken over for war service she became USAT* Borinquen (courtesy of US Army Signal Corps).
Centre right *Sold to Bull Line she got a new smoke stack boasting the letter 'B' and a new name—*Puerto Rico.
Right *Sold again she became the* Arosa Star *of the Arosa Line. Here she is seen, freshly refitted for transatlantic service, in the icy winter waters at Bremerhaven (courtesy of Arnold Kludas).*

Above *The sad end of a lovely lady*—La Janelle, *as she was named at the time, aground off California* (courtesy of J. Fred Rodriguez).

Left *A dramatic photograph of the half-sunk* La Janelle *taken by the adventurous and skilful photographer J. Fred Rodriguez in August 1970.*

Colombie

The famed French Line, the Compagnie Generale Transatlantique, is certainly best known and remembered for its luxurious transatlantic liner service to New York. Readily, ships like the giant *Normandie*, the celebrated *Ile De France* and, more recently, the longest liner of all, the *France*, come to mind. However, these French owners also ran two other passenger services: across the mid-Atlantic to the Caribbean islands and on the Mediterranean Sea from Marseilles to North and West Africa. In the late 1920s, soon after commissioning the brilliant *Ile De France* and while planning for the succession of the *Lafayette* (1930), *Champlain* (1932) and then the immortal *Normandie* (1935), the company also ordered its newest passenger ship for the Caribbean trade. She was the *Colombie*, which was commissioned in the late summer of 1931.

Based at Le Havre and with service calls at Southampton, the West Indian liner route travelled to Guadeloupe and Martinique, with occasional stops at such other ports as Trinidad, Barbados, San Juan and even periodically to French Guiana. Additionally, the yacht-like *Colombie* was sent cruising, from Le Havre to the Norwegian fjords and northern cities or to West Africa and the Mediterranean. Her most unusual cruise was undoubtedly a transatlantic crossing to New York, in August 1939, especially for the World's Fair.

While most of the other larger French liners were promptly laid-up, the *Colombie* continued in erratic service through that perilous autumn of 1939. However, early the next year, when the Atlantic was considered quite unsafe, the ship was kept for safety at Martinique. Later moved to Casablanca, she was seized by the US government in December 1941, just after the attack on Pearl Harbor. At the same time, the idle *Normandie*—laid-up at her New York pier since August 1939—was taken as well, to become the USS *Lafeyette*. The *Colombie*, repainted in deep shades of grey, was brought across to New York in April 1943. Placed under partnered operation of the American War Shipping Administration and the exiled French Line headquarters at New York, she was given over to the Arthur Tickle Engineering Company in Brooklyn and converted to a wartime trooper with a capacity of 2,683 (a dramatic increase over her 491 peacetime berths).

The *Colombie* left New York on her first trooping voyage on October 21 1943, bound for Glasgow with invasion forces. This was followed by a trip to Belfast and Gourock. During the ensuing nine months of 1944, the ship made six voyages between New York and the Clyde, sailing once via Boston. Returning to Norfolk in September 1944, she then proceeded to the Mediterranean, to Naples, Leghorn and Gibraltar. She returned to New York in October and departed again, in early November, to Gibraltar and Naples via Norfolk. She returned to New York in December and was taken in hand for conversion to a hospital ship.

The demand for specialty hospital-ships in 1945 was staggering. Among many others, the compact *Colombie* was a perfect selection. She returned to the Arthur Tickle yards in Brooklyn and was refitted to handle 828 patients. The transforma-

tion took four months, with the vessel ready in time for VE Day. Renamed *Aleda E. Lutz*, in honour of Lieutenant Aleda E. Lutz, a US Army nurse killed in a plane crash in southern France in November 1944 after having participated in 190 missions to evacuate wounded personnel. This role for the former French liner was not a success. After leaving New York in April, she made a roundtrip to Europe and was then assigned to the port of Charleston, South Carolina. Another trip to Europe followed, but then, in a flash decision, she was ordered out to the Pacific. In preparation, she returned to New York for special outfitting at the Todd Shipyards in Brooklyn's Eire Basin. In December 1945, she set sail for Manila. Unfortunately, while at Honolulu, considerable mechanical problems were discovered. Her Pacific duty had to be cancelled. She was ordered to return to the United States at a reduced speed, without passengers and for official disposal.

The *Aleda E. Lutz* sailed sluggishly from Honolulu to New York via Panama in the late winter of 1946. The voyage took nearly 60 days. She was returned to the French Line on April 11, while berthed at Pier 88; immediately, she hoisted the tricolour and reverted to her original name. The *Colombie* was leased to the French government, kept her hospital-ship colours and fittings, and was sent out to troubled Indo-China for special duty.

The *Colombie* had nearly two years of further military service before being released for commercial service. Overworked and in need of a complete modernisation and redecorating, the ship was then sent to the De Schelde Shipyards at Flushing in the Netherlands. Within an extended two-year refit, her original twin funnels were removed and replaced by a single tapered stack. Her passenger quarters were upgraded and the configuration modified to 192 in first class, 140 in cabin class and 246 in tourist class. She resumed her West Indies sailings in November 1950. Previously, her place had been taken by the chartered Greek Line passenger ship *Katoomba*, a coal burner that dated from 1913 and which was formerly an Australian coastal liner.

Writer C. M. Squarey appraised the *Colombie* soon after her post-war maiden sailing: 'Here is a ship running in a trade that requires her to be snug and cozy for about one-third of the voyage, and then cool and airy for the other two-thirds. One answer to that problem may lie in air-conditioning —with which equipment this ship is fitted in part—but the layout and design of her first class accommodations gives me the impression that even without air-conditioning she would be a good ship on which to spend sun-drenched, tropical days and moonlit, tropical nights.

'A charming feature of the *Colombie* is her Winter Garden, where the windows are well down to deck level and so permit a good visibility when reclining in the exceptionally comfortable, green-colored garden chairs. The salon adjoining the "Jardin d'Hiver" makes a pleasing impression on one because of the simplicity of its style of furnishing. The Smoking Room, a deck higher, with its off-white leather chairs and its attractive bar, has a pleasant, masculine atmosphere about it. The dining saloon runs true to French Line form by having an imposing stairway descend into it.

'The cabins are pleasantly furnished, and a unique feature is the fact that all beds are at least three feet wide, which is about six inches more than you find on most ships.'

Mr Squarey elaborated on the Caribbean passenger trade as well. 'Recently, there has been renewed agitation about the lack of tonnage in the West Indies trade. Pre-war, the French, the Dutch, the Germans and the British were on that berth. The British have built since the war but one new ship for that run; the French Line have two ships under construction [the *Antilles* and *Flandre* of 1952–53], each of 20,000 tons gross and a designed service speed of eighteen knots. It is, perhaps, natural to say that one would like to see the British flag flying more strongly. How long it may is unpredictable, but there has been, and still is, a strong demand for space to the West Indies, and there are certainly many people who would like to go there for a visit, but finding its accessibility so bad, head off elsewhere. From what I am told, the West Indies trade is not a profitable one for shipping. It may not have been, but I still cannot help feeling that two good modern ships, really attractively appointed, backed up by a good advertising campaign, backed up by agents and backed up by the Caribbean Tourist Committee, should be pretty sure of carrying high load factors the year round and could command good fares. Good luck to the French Line.'

The *Colombie* sailed alongside the larger 19,800-ton *Antilles* in year-round service to the Caribbean and the pair was joined during the winter months by the latter ship's sister, the *Flandre*. As suggested by Mr Squarey, many passengers, both French and British alike, made roundtrip sailings as a form of full cruise. Occasionally, the *Colombie* was also sent on one-class summer cruises, to the Fjordlands and to the Mediterranean. However, soon after the *Flandre* was placed on the West Indies trade full-time, at the end of 1962, the older ship became less important and less profitable. She ran more cruises.

Finishing her last winter season in 1963–64, she went to the block. Her new owners were the rapidly expanding Typaldos Brothers of Greece. In short time, they were creating one of the biggest passenger and cruise fleets in the Mediterranean. Along with such veteran ships as Australia's *Taroona* and the former Grace liners *Santa Rosa* and *Santa Paula*, the *Colombie* was acquired for European tourist services. In particular, the Aegean and eastern Mediterranean were rapidly gaining in popularity.

Little was done to the former French liner, with the obvious exception of repainting her funnel, altering her capacity into approximately 600 one-class berths and redubbing her with a new name. *Atlantic* was first suggested, but this conflicted with the American Export liner of the same name and which operated in the same waters. Furthermore, there were some reports that the ship would spend the summer of 1964 at New York, while under charter to the Caribbean Cruise Lines for seven-day cruises to Bermuda. While these never materialised, she re-entered service as the *Atlantica*. Her general routing was from Venice to Piraeus, the Greek isles, Istanbul and Haifa. It was a popular two-week cruise run.

On December 8 1966, the Typaldos ferry *Heraklion*, the former Bibby combination liner *Leicestershire*, sank during an Aegean storm. With little more than 15 minutes for evacuation, there were 241 casualties. In the official inquiries that followed, the ship was found to be loaded unsafely. In retribution, the Typaldos Brothers were sent to prison and their fleet disbanded, being seized mostly by the National Bank of Greece. The *Atlantica* was among the group and was sent to an anchorage in Perama Bay, near Piraeus. She would never sail again. While there were reports that she was scrapped in 1970, she was, in fact, only partially dismantled. Four years later, in May 1974, her remains were towed to Barcelona and finished-off.

Gross tonnage: 13,391 (1931); 13,803 (1950)
Length overall: 509 feet
Width: 66 feet
Machinery: Steam turbines, twin screw
Speed: 16 knots
Capacity: 201 first class, 146 second class and 144 third class (1931); 192 first class, 140 cabin class and 246 tourist class (1950); approximately 600 one-class (1964)
Built: Ateliers et Chantiers de France, Dunkirk, France, 1931
Demise: Partially scrapped in 1970 at Perama, Greece; remains scrapped in 1974 at Barcelona

A postcard of the French Line's Colombie *at Le Havre in her original paint scheme with black hull. Her highly distinctive appearance marked her as a French ship—no two French liners were ever alike and all of them were different from other ships.*

Above Colombie *became an American troopship after the United States entered World War 2 (courtesy of US Coastguard).*

Left *An aerial view of New York August 27 1939. The German liners* St Louis *and* New York *are near the bottom at Pier 86. The French ships* De Grasse *and* Colombie *are together at Pier 88. Italy's all white* Roma *is at Pier 92 and at the very top is Sweden's* Drottningholm, *berthed at Pier 97 (courtesy of French Line).*

Right *Later in the war she was converted for use as a hospital ship and became the* Aleda E. Lutz *(courtesy of Alfred Palmer).*

Below *Modernised after the war, and now boasting one huge French Line stack, she is again named* Colombie.

Lurline

In the early 1920s, the Matson Line of San Francisco ran a passenger service to Honolulu with such combination ships as the 6,700-ton *Wilhelmina*, the 9,400-ton *Matsonia* and the 9,800-ton *Maui*. Several years later, in 1927, the company commissioned its first luxury passenger liner, the 17,200-ton *Malolo*. She was the pioneer ship of the Hawaiian cruise trade. She was also an instant and spectacular success. Only better times could be ahead.

Within two years, by 1929, Matson was projecting not only for an additional larger liner for the Honolulu run, but to extend such luxurious ships to the South Pacific and Australia. Consequently, a trio was designed, which would become three of the finest, best looking and most enduring passenger ships ever built. In some ways, they were as successful to the Pacific as some of the famed Cunarders and French liners were to the Atlantic. To the Hawaiian islands and the South Seas, they were without serious rivals. At some 18,000 tons each and measuring some 631 feet long, they were named as the *Mariposa*, *Monterey* and finally the *Lurline*.

All were ordered from the Bethlehem Steel Company, from their yard at Quincy, near Boston in Massachusetts. The *Mariposa* came first, being launched in July 1931 and placed in service in the following January. The *Monterey* went down the ways in October 1931 and was commissioned in May of the next year. Both of these ships, while operated under the Matson Line banner, were formally owned by the Oceanic Steamship Co, which had interests in the southern Pacific. Their routing was from San Francisco and Los Angeles to Honolulu, Pago Pago, Suva, Auckland, Sydney, Melbourne and then return via the same ports. The last of this trio, the *Lurline*, was launched in July 1932 and then entered service (on a special South Pacific–Far East cruise) in the following January. She was later paired with the popular *Malolo* on the Honolulu run from San Francisco and Los Angeles.

The *Lurline* became the most popular and beloved liner ever to sail on the Honolulu service. She received rave notices from all quarters, even from the marine design and engineering quarter.

In one publication, she was called 'a beautiful example of modern craftsmanship in build and design, especially built for tropical travel'. Together with her sisters, the *Lurline* was the first large liner to have her entire sides heavily insulated with a cork lining to exclude the heat from the sun in tropical climates. Every six minutes, the air in every stateroom, in both first and cabin class, was changed. The passengers could control this 'noiseless' system at will.

The restaurants had air-conditioning, then a new shipboard system that not only regulated the temperature but the humidity as well. In exploring the ship's innards, one critic wrote, 'The first class dining saloon is a gorgeous room with brilliant murals by artist Paul Arnat, capturing the spirit of the sea in original vistas of old time clippers and palm fringed isles. Every first class stateroom has full-length mirrors, wardrobes, dressing tables, ice water thermos bottles, electric fans, ample baggage space, private telephone and private bathroom facilities. The lounge is unusually large and decorated with restraining smartness and unusual artistry. The smoke room is a fascinating space equipped with a bar close at hand. There is also a gentlemen's club room, from which the ladies are excluded; a quiet library; a gay verandah cafe-Bohemia; a capital gymnasium; deck tennis courts; clay pigeon shooting; two large swimming pools and children's playrooms.'

The *Lurline* and her running-mate *Malolo*, which was renamed *Matsonia* in 1937, continued in uninterrupted service until early December 1941. In Fred Stindt's excellent *Matson's Century of Ships*, first published in April 1982, he recorded, 'On the morning of December 7 1941 [the day of the Japanese attack on Pearl Harbor], the *Lurline* was homeward-bound from Honolulu on her regular run. News of the Japanese attack was handed to Commodore Berndtson by the wireless operator at 10:15 am, the ship's time.

'The *Lurline* was immediately diverted from her course, her speed increased to full ahead, and her crew instructed to secure her watertightness below and for the necessary blackout. Naval and military officers aboard were gathered together and a staff formed to enforce military security. At 5:00 pm the passengers were gathered together in the ship's lounge, and Commodore Berndtson briefly explained the nature of the emergency, requesting the co-operation of all in maintaining the blackout.

'The tense race for safety will be remembered a lifetime by those aboard—the great white ship shining in the bright moonlight, racing for home at her full 22 knots while her passengers in life jackets scanned the horizon, hoping for a protective blanket of fog or a heavy rainstorm.

At 2:00 am the morning of December 10th, the *Lurline* slipped under the Golden Gate Bridge, just as the air raid sirens plunged the City into darkness for the second time that night. She docked at 3:27 am and by day-light the passengers were cleared completely through necessary inspections.'

Repainted in military greys and outfitted to handle some 4,037 wartime troops, the *Lurline* was assigned to the US Navy for the duration of the hostilities. In early 1942, she made three further trips to Honolulu and then, in April, sailed outwards to Adelaide. A year later, in early 1943, she steamed out to Noumea and Suva, then on a roundtrip to Auckland and finally on a more diverse round voyage to Honolulu, Samoa, Noumea, Melbourne and Wellington. In September 1944, she continued onwards to distant Bombay, travelling via Noumea, Brisbane and Fremantle and then returned via Melbourne. At the end of the year, she went to Honolulu, Pago Pago and Guadalcanal. During 1944, the *Lurline* sailed mostly to more remote Pacific ports: in January, to Espiritu Santo and Guadalcanal; in March, to Milne Bay and Sydney; in April, to

Honolulu, Espiritu Santo, Finschhafen and Milne Bay; in June, to Brisbane, Milne Bay and Oro Bay; in August, to Lae, Oro Bay and Brisbane; and in October, to Noumea, Oro Bay, Milne Bay and Hollandia.

In June 1945, the *Lurline* made her only wartime diversion. She passed through the Panama Canal and went to Gibraltar and Marseilles, to load troops for the Far East. Returning, she again passed through the Canal and steamed directly for Honolulu and then onwards to Ulithi, Manila, Leyte, Hollandia and Brisbane. In November of that same year, she crossed to Tokyo and Nagoya. Her final military voyages, made in the spring of 1946, were two roundtrips to Honolulu. Immediately thereafter, the *Lurline* was sent to the United Engineering Shipyards at Alameda, just across the bay from San Francisco and a facility owned by the Matson Company.

Moored just aft of her pre-war sister-ship *Monterey*, the twin liners became a mass of scaffolding and were alive with work crews. Unfortunately, efforts for the *Monterey* were soon abandoned. In re-appraising the costs of these twin restorations, the estimates for each ship were nearly three times what they cost to build originally. Two ships were quite unaffordable at the time. When the *Lurline* was commissioned, in 1933, she had cost $7.9 million; her two-year refit in 1946–48 cost $19 million.

The beautiful *Lurline* resumed Honolulu service in April 1948, but on a singlehanded schedule. Although briefly returned to post-war service, the earlier *Matsonia* (ex-*Malolo*) was sold off, again to avoid the staggering American refit costs, to the Home Lines becoming their *Atlantic*. The other Matson sister-ships, the *Mariposa* and *Monterey*, were both laid-up at the otherwise quiet Bethlehem

Lurline

Shipyards at Alameda. Some years later, in late 1953, when it was felt that the *Mariposa* would not be restored, she was also sold to the Home Lines and became their *Homeric*. The *Monterey* remained in lay-up for nearly a decade, until 1956, when she was thoroughly refitted and then reactivated for Matson's Hawaii service as the *Matsonia*.

While the *Lurline* remained as popular as ever, it became increasingly clear that two large liners on the Honolulu service in face of aircraft competiton (and increasing American labour costs) were fast becoming unprofitable. Since the former *Monterey*, as the *Matsonia*, had the most recent renovations and improvements, she was selected to remain in service. (In fact, soon afterward, she was renamed *Lurline*, a name thought to be far more favoured.) The original *Lurline* was offered for sale in the summer of 1963.

American passenger ships have been exceedingly popular with Greek shipowners, particularly the Chandris Group, in recent decades. High maintenance and their spacious design (which is easily adaptable to greatly increased capacities) are their most obvious selling points. Chandris saw great promise in the *Lurline* and bought her on September 3 1963. Registered to a Chandris subsidiary, Marfuerza Compania Maritima S/A, she was sent to Britain's Smith's Dock Company at North Shields and extensively refitted for the booming Australian immigrant trade. Rechristened *Ellinis* (for 'Greek Lady'), her cabin accommodation was more than doubled, from Matson's 761 first class berths to 1,642 all-tourist class for Chandris. Her bow was raked in more modern fashion and extended by 11 feet, from 631 to 642 feet overall. Completed in just under three months, she left Piraeus on December 30 on her first migrant sailing to Australian ports.

The demands on Chandris liners such as the *Ellinis* were such that in short time the 33,500-ton *America* of the United States Lines was purchased as well. Following more special alterations, her capacity increased from 1,046 to 2,258 berths. Leonard Weir served aboard the *Ellinis* and *Australis* (ex-*America*) during these peak years and recalled, 'Outbound, we were usually full-up to every last berth. Most of the migrants were going out on a £10 fare-assisted plan, for resettlement in Australia. To Chandris accountants, if the ship sailed full on the outward trip, the homeward voyage was already paid for. Homebound, while we sailed with far less passengers, we had many discontented migrants, who just could not adjust to Australia, as well as the "wool people". In both directions, children were a very big and profitable part of our trade. I recall one voyage on the *Ellinis* where we needed one restaurant seating just for the younger passengers.'

The sailing pattern for the *Ellinis* was usually the same from year to year: from Southampton to Piraeus and Port Said (or via the South African Cape in later years), then onwards to Fremantle, Melbourne, Sydney and Auckland. Homebound, she used the Pacific route, travelling via Tahiti, the Panama Canal and then across the Atlantic to Southampton. Occasionally, she might put into New York for some transatlantic traffic.

Within a decade, by the mid-1970s, as the Australian migrant contract was being shifted to airlines, the *Ellinis* began to spend more time in cruise service. Often, she sailed from Southampton to the Atlantic Isles, West Africa and the Mediterranean. In a life-extension refit, in June 1974, she was drydocked at Rotterdam and a faulty turbine was replaced by one bought from her former sistership *Mariposa*, which had just been scrapped as the *Homeric*. Her other former Matson fleetmates were also still about: the former *Malolo*, then sailing as the *Queen Frederica*, had just been laid-up near Piraeus, and the ex-*Monterey* was now also in Chandris hands, trading as the *Britanis*.

The *Ellinis* was laid-up at Perama Bay in late 1978. She has been moored alongside or quite close to several other out-of-work Chandris passenger ships, including the former *America*. Rusting and neglected, it is doubtful that she will ever return to service. Now (1984), being well passed 50 years old, she has given superb service.

Gross tonnage: 18,021 (1933); 18,163 (1942); 18,564 (1948); 24,351 (1963)
Length overall: 631 feet (1933); 642 feet (1963)
Width: 79 feet
Machinery: Steam turbines, twin screw
Speed: 20 knots
Capacity: 550 first class and 250 cabin class (1933); 761 first class (1948); 1,642 all-tourist class (1963)
Built: Bethlehem Steel Co, Quincy, Massachusetts, 1932–33

Above *'She's waterborne'—*Lurline *shortly after launching, the beginning of an amazingly successful career.*

Right *A painting by Anton Refregier on a bulkhead in* Lurline's *first class smoking room before World War 2.*

Right *Entering San Francisco in December 1944 with wounded aboard and survivors of several ships sunk in the Battle of the Philippines.* Lurline *has quite a list!*

Lurline

Above *After being rebuilt for peacetime service, she again enters San Francisco.* **Below** *After another conversion, this time by Chandris Line, she was renamed* Ellinis. *Her reconstruction included a new bow, altered smokestacks and the elimination of her two tall masts. She was very popular on the Australian immigrant tourist route.*

Georgic

In the late 1920s, the renowned White Star Line was slipping deeper and deeper into financial trouble. Following the tragedy of the *Titanic* in 1912 and then the loss of another four-stacker, the *Britannic*, which was mined in 1916, the company never regained its supreme sparkle. After the First World War, White Star ships somehow seemed outstepped by the rival Cunarders. Then, as the depression neared and passenger figures began their decline, many of the White Star liners fell on hard times. There were reports that even the giant *Majestic* and *Olympic* were steaming into port scarred by rust and that onboard their crisp service was no longer quite as smart. However, company directors still thought of glory and distinction, and even of better times ahead on the North Atlantic. They ordered a superliner, their biggest yet, the 60,000-ton *Oceanic*, from their good friend and collaborator, the Harland & Wolff Yards at Belfast.

The new *Oceanic* was to be the transatlantic partner to Cunard's projected giant, a 75,000-tonner that would come from the Clyde. She would, of course, emerge as the *Queen Mary* in 1936. The White Star ship was beset with problems, however, and not the least of which were White Star's dwindling financial reserves and then the start of the sinister depression. Consequently, when less than one-fourth complete, the big liner was abandoned. The White Star board accurately—and quite sensibly—revised their building plans for a 27,000-ton motorliner, which would use the existing steel from the *Oceanic*, and then a near-sistership. The first of these, the *Britannic*, was commissioned in June 1930.

Deliberately delayed somewhat, the second ship was christened as the *Georgic* in November 1931 and then placed into service in the following June, some two years after the earlier ship. This ship would be, in fact, the last new liner for the great White Star Co. As their problems became more and more acute, and as the transatlantic trade slumped deeper each season, discussions began with the aim of seeking a profitable alliance. The British government suggested a merger with the stronger Cunard Co. It was the perfect match, two British-flag companies that could compete more effectively with their ocean liner rivals on the Continent. In April 1934, the coupling was formed as the Cunard–White Star Line, with the former firm having the dominant position.

The new *Britannic* and *Georgic* were then the most promising ships in the otherwise aged White Star fleet. Assigned to the Liverpool–New York run, they were often berthed at Manhattan alongside the likes of the old four-funnel *Olympic* or a four-master like the *Adriatic*, dating from 1907. The Cunard–White Star board began an immediate house-cleaning programme. By the mid-1930s, all of the original White Star ships were retired, with the obvious exception of the two new ships.

The *Britannic* and *Georgic*, while always thought of as exact sister-ships, were officially listed as Britain's largest motorliners. They were also considered among the finest contemporary examples of a new generation of 'cabin liners', medium-sized, practical and profitable, and where cabin class accommodation rated as the premier space. Aboard the *Georgic*, the berthing configuration was listed as 479 in cabin class, 557 in tourist class and 506 in third class. Being so pleased with these ships, Cunard–White Star actually thought of building two further sister-ships, possibly somewhat larger. The overall plan was for a four-ship team that would make weekly sailings from either New York or Liverpool. Unfortunately, the idea never left the board room.

The *Britannic* and *Georgic* were not identical in appearance. The front superstructure on the *Britannic* was squared, but on the *Georgic* it was rounded. The *Georgic* also had more enclosed superstructure on the decks than her sister. Both ships had a popular look of the time: long, low superstructures with twin squat stacks. The forward funnel on both ships was a dummy and aboard the *Georgic*, this space was used as the engineers' smoking room and the wireless room.

On the boat deck, there were nine lifeboats and one launch on each side. Six boats on each side were nested. There were also eight other boats on the aft decks. From the aft funnel, the decks receded to a well deck, which was B deck, and after which the promenade deck continued. A docking bridge was positioned just short of the cruiser stern. For colouring, Cunard wisely chose not to alter the twin funnels of buff with black tops. Because of their low height, they would not have been suited to Cunard's orange-red and black stripes.

Publicity material on the *Georgic* emphasised that she took only two years to build. Other details listed included her 200 miles of electric wiring, her electric consumption being enough for the nightly use of a town of 30,000 and that 650,000 rivets were driven into her hull. She had 12 miles of piping throughout her innards and a streamlined rudder, made of cast steel which weighed 40 tons.

Being something of Britain's 'pioneer' cabin liners on the North Atlantic, much was written about the comfort and style of their accommodation. While the *Britannic* used more traditional decorative themes, the *Georgic* was done in modernistic styling. With present day interest in the 1930s, she would be a grand example of the Art Deco era.

Most of the staterooms in cabin class had private facilities and there were two special suites, which consisted of a bedroom, sitting room and bathroom. Most of the public rooms were placed along the promenade deck. The *Georgic*'s verandah was enclosed and formed the outer portion of the smoking room. Being the ship's most original room, it was panelled in strips of black and red lacquer, in horizontal layers, interspaced with grey and suggestive of the steel plating of a modern ocean liner. Part of the walls were alcoved. Forward of this on the *Georgic*, surrounding a funnel casing along the starboard side, was a card room and a childrens' playroom. On the port side was a 90 foot long gallery, which led into the main lounge. The *Georgic*'s main lounge was called a 'compact room', with a central dance floor over which was a dome and from which indirect lighting diffused over the floor. Pillars surrounded the dome.

Forward of this was the 'Palm Court', a space formed by the enclosed space in the rounded superstructure. Decorated in jade green, blue and ivory, it had a dance floor and was lighted ingeniously with Chinese lanterns. Aft along the promenade deck was a well-equipped gymnasium. The restaurant on C deck extended the full width of the ship and rose two decks in height. Done in a modern motif, the main colour scheme was a blend of sealing-wax red, ebony and ivory. The columns were bound in genuine leather. Indirect lighting from the ceiling of the restaurant well illuminated the centre of the room while the lower sections had lights shining through opaque glass panels, which obtruded slightly from the ceiling. The indoor pool on E deck was again done in very contemporary decor. Other general amenities included a childrens' playroom in each class, a tennis court, passenger elevators, an altar for religious services in the cabin class lounge and hot and cold running water in every cabin.

The *Georgic* (and *Britannic*) were very popular ships and worked the transatlantic trade from April through November and then cruised for the remainder of the year. In spring 1935, in a Cunard—White Star fleet reshuffling, the twin motorliners were transferred to the London service, sailing to New York via Southampton, Le Havre and occasionally Cobh. At the time, they ranked as the largest passenger liners to regularly use the Port of London. In cruise service, the *Georgic* made a diverse range of sailings. There were four-day cruises to Halifax, Nova Scotia for $45, eight-day trips to Bermuda and Nassau for $100, 11-days to Bermuda, Port-au-Prince, Havana and Nassau for $132.50 and 18-day runs to St Thomas, La Guaira, Kingston and Havana for $210. Further afield, she also cruised to the Mediterranean for six weeks, with fares beginning at $660.

While the *Georgic*'s only other historic notation was a rapidly extinguished cargo hold fire while berthed at New York's Pier 61 in January 1935, she was not immediately called to military duty in the autumn of 1939. Instead, she continued on the Atlantic, in something of an 'evacuation' service between Liverpool and New York. Thousands were anxious to leave both Britain and Europe, fearing the impending war that would soon follow. In the spring of 1940, she was sent to the Clyde and then refitted as a government troopship. Painted over in drab greys, she was hardly recognisable, which was the intention for her new duties. Unfortunately, her important war services were to be all too brief.

On July 14 1941, while anchored at Port Tewfik, at the lower end of the Suez Canal, she was badly hit by a bomb during a Nazi air raid. Fire started and then the ship's blowers and fans sent smoke throughout the interior. Hideously burned and blistered, she was left in the local waters half-sunk and all but abandoned. Very few believed that she could be saved. Instead, with the very serious wartime needs for all available tonnage, the *Georgic* was pumped-out and temporarily patched. Three months later, on October 27, she was again afloat. On December 29, she began the very tender and slow tow, under the care of Clan Line's *Clan Campbell* and Ellerman's *City of Sydney*, bound for Port Sudan. More temporary repairs followed.

In the following spring, she was again put under tow, this time being guided by no less than three ships, the cargo vessels *Haresfield* and *Recorder*, and the tug *Pauline Moller*. She reached Karachi on March 31 1942. Still more temporary repairs followed. Maintained by a small, very patient and very loyal crew, she sat at the Pakistani port for months, until moved to Bombay that December. Then, with some final attention, she was prepared for the longest trip of all: through the Indian Ocean, around the South African Cape and then northward along the eastern Atlantic to her builder's yard at Belfast. Amazingly, she averaged 16 knots on that voyage.

Totally rebuilt at the Harland & Wolff yards, she reappeared in December 1944, at last able to again participate in the war effort. However, she was still very much a fire-damaged ship. Her interiors still included twisted and misshaped beams and steel panels. Thereafter, she was known to her crew members as 'the corrugated lung'. Even the forward dummy funnel and mainmast were gone and the forward mast stumped. There was very little to reflect her earlier days as a luxurious White Star liner.

After completing considerable military service, the *Georgic* was sent to the Tyne in 1948, to be rebuilt as a government austerity ship (she had been sold by Cunard–White Star in 1943) with a dual purpose: immigrant sailings and occasional peacetime trooping. Generally, her new assignment was to help on the booming resettlement programme to Australia, trading between Liverpool, Port Said, Aden, Fremantle, Melbourne and Sydney. However, within a year, she was back in her original owner's service. Chartered to Cunard for peak summer season sailings with budget tourists and migrants, she crossed between Liverpool or Southampton, Le Havre and Cobh to Halifax and New York. Although not listed as an ordinary Cunarder, she provided very useful and important work. During 1950, passenger loads were such that Cunard was forced to charter P&O's *Stratheden* for four trips to New York. In winter, the *Georgic* returned to the Australian trade.

Completing her final Cunard summer season charter in October 1954, she continued for a final year on the Australian trade. Faulty and tired, and with those lingering traces of her wartime bombing, she could not attract a buyer. At 24 years old, in February 1956, she went to the breakers at Faslane in Scotland. Her former sister, the *Britannic*, would finish at Inverkeithing just over four years later. They were the last of the once illustrious White Star fleet.

Gross tonnage: 27,759 (1932); 27,268 (1943); 27,469 (1948)
Length overall: 711 feet
Width: 82 feet
Machinery: Burmeister & Wain diesels, twin screw
Speed: 18 knots
Capacity: 479 cabin class, 557 tourist class and 506 third class (1932); 1,962 austerity class (1948)
Built: Harland & Wolff Ltd, Belfast, Northern Ireland, 1932
Demise: Scrapped at Faslane, Scotland, 1956

Left *Elegant sitting room with a fireplace in the* Georgic, *the last White Star Line ship ever built* (courtesy British Information Service).

Below *The new* Georgic *under tow. Her rounded forward superstructure was an improvement over the Britannic's flat forward design.*

Right *Striking view of the* Georgic *being docked by Moran tugs in bad ice conditions at New York* (courtesy of Moran Towing).

Right *The burnt-out remains of Cunard-White Star's* Georgic *at Port Tewfik, Egypt, in 1941* (courtesy of John Havers collection).

Right *Reconstructed after the war, the* Georgic *still looked sleek and modern even with only one stack.*

Santa Rosa

The American-flag Grace Line decided, in the early 1930s, to expand and modernise its Latin American passenger fleet with a quartet of very fine sister-ships. Based in New York City, the company had the ships built within the very confines of that great port, just 15 miles west at the Kearny, New Jersey yards of the Federal Shipbuilding & Drydock Company. Financed under the special US Merchant Marine Act of 1928, these new ships cost a very expensive $5 million each. They were completed in 1932–33, and named as the *Santa Rosa*, *Santa Paula*, *Santa Lucia* and *Santa Elena*. Surprisingly perhaps, the former *Santa Rosa* remains afloat at the time of writing.

Designed by William Francis Gibbs, the foremost American ship designer of his time and the man who later created the *America* of 1940 and the record-breaking *United States* of 1952, the Grace liners show a resemblance to these later transatlantic liners. The forward funnel was domed and given a smoke-deflecting fin, modified versions of which were used afterward on the two larger ships of the United States Lines. The *Santa Rosa* was the first of this new foursome, having been launched in March 1932 and then commissioned that November. The other ships followed in timed sequence. Their initial purpose was to work a rather extensive, intercoastal routing: sailing from

New York to Havana, La Guaira, Cartagena, passing through the Panama Canal and then travelling northward along the Pacific to ports in Costa Rica, El Salvador and Guatemala, then to Mazatlan in Mexico and finally to Los Angeles, San Francisco and Seattle before turning-around.

The government intention was to have them serve Cuba in three days, Panama in six, El Salvador in nine, Guatemala in ten, Mexico in 13 and Los Angeles in 16 days. Unfortunately, this extended service was not as successful as intended. In less than two years, by 1934, the Seattle call was eliminated and the ships terminated their sailings at San Francisco. Then, three years later, the West Coast ports were dropped entirely. Thereafter, the quartet sailed to the West Indies and South America only from New York.

Lloyd M. Stadum enthusiastically described the high standards of the *Santa Rosa* class: 'Although built in 1932, they introduced new standards of comfort and luxury, with accommodation that surpassed the large transatlantic liners. For instance, all first class cabins had private baths and were outside rooms with lower beds (some had Pullman berths for family groups). The dining room, situated amidships on the Promenade Deck, was more than two decks high with tall casement windows and a dome that rolled back giving the effect of a breeze-swept outdoor cafe. The galley was located aft and above on the Boat Deck. Waitresses did the serving.

'Departing from the usual practice, the social hall was called the "living room" and the former mostly masculine smoking room went coeducational and was renamed "the club." Other public rooms were the Palm Court, library and grill. Like the present-day cruise-ships, a large outdoor swimming pool, a well-equipped gymnasium, barber shop, beauty salon and gift shop were all installed for the passengers' enjoyment.'

Mr Stadum did raise some question about the new Grace liners, however. 'There were two minor mysteries concerning the *Santa Rosa* and her sister-ships. First, the earliest publicity mentioned that the four vessels were to run between New York and San Francisco and would maintain a fortnightly service. However, the extension to Seattle (and Victoria) and the short trip back to San Francisco were accomplished within the same time span. When San Francisco became the terminal port [1934], only three ships were required and the fourth [the *Santa Lucia*] was reassigned to the New York and West Coast of South America route. So it appeared that too many ships had been built. The other mystery was the lifeboat launching gear. The *Santa Rosa* class was fitted with an older type of luffing davits, when efficient modern gravity davits were available and had been used on three earlier Grace Line passenger vessels.'

Used in the two-week West Indies cruise service out of New York until December 1941, the *Santa Rosa* and her three sisters were called to duty soon after the attack on Pearl Harbor. They were especially useful as transports, with their combined passenger-troop capacities (increased to 2,426 from her pre-war capacity of 289) and 7,000 tons of cargo, which included 100 tons of refrigerated space and 850 tons of liquid tank provision. Hurriedly outfitted, the USS *Santa Rosa* was 'on duty' by late January. Her sailing patterns thereafter were diverse. On January 23 1942, she left New York for the Panama Canal, Melbourne and Noumea; in April, she steamed off to Suez, Massawa, Aden and Durban; in September, she went to the Clyde; and in November, to Casablanca. In early 1943, she made two further trips to Casablanca, one of which went via Bermuda. In April, she travelled to Casablanca, Gibraltar, then up to the Clyde before reversing course out to Algiers and Philippeville; in August, she had a transatlantic roundtrip to Oran from New York; and in October, she left Boston for Swansea, the Clyde, Palermo and then homeward via Newport in Monmouthshire. She completed that year with a round voyage to Bristol and Newport.

During 1944, there were trips to Belfast; then to Avonmouth and Cardiff; a voyage from Norfolk to Oran and Naples; and then other trips to Marseilles, Gibraltar and return visits to Swansea. For most of 1945, she sailed on the North Atlantic troop shuttle, to Le Havre and Southampton. Her final military voyages were two trips in the winter of 1945–46 out to Port Said and Karachi. Decommissioned in January 1946, a hardworked, well worn *Santa Rosa* was sent to the Newport News

Shipyard in Virginia for a government-sponsored face-lifting and renewal. Completed that October, she was then officially returned to the Grace Line.

While the *Santa Paula* also came through the war unharmed, the other two sister-ships were casualties. The *Santa Lucia*, which became the troop transport USS *Leedstown*, was torpedoed on November 9 1942, off Algiers, during the invasion of North Africa. All troops and crewmembers were saved. However, the ship was damaged badly and then beached and she was never refloated. The *Santa Elena* met her end in the same area, but a year later. On November 6, while off Philippeville, she was hit by an aerial torpedo. All of her 1,900 Canadian servicemen, 100 Canadian nurses and 123 crew were saved.

The *Santa Rosa* and *Santa Paula* were placed on a weekly post-war service, sailing from New York each Friday. They worked a 12-day itinerary that called at Curacao, La Guaira, Puerto Cabello (also in Venezuela) and Cartagena. Roundtrip fares began at $200.

As the two older ships neared their 25th years, the Grace Line was busily preparing for their replacements, a new *Santa Rosa* and *Santa Paula*. William Kooiman, who served aboard the original *Santa Rosa* in 1953, wrote a history of this ship and noted, 'In 1958, the two veteran *Santas* were replaced by two new vessels that were only slightly larger in size and passenger-cargo capacity. The general layout of the new ships was very similar to the vessels they replaced. In a unique ceremony, in August 1957, the *Santa Rosa* interrupted her 271st voyage to steam up the James River [to the Newport News Shipyards in Virginia] and salute her namesake on the day that she was launched.'

In that summer of 1958, there were some rather confusing name changes within the Grace fleet. As the new *Santa Rosa* came into service that June, the original *Santa Paula* was retired. Therefore, the older *Santa Rosa* had to be renamed. She became the *Santa Paula*, to keep the popular pair of names. Then, in September, when the new *Santa Paula* first arrived, the older ship, the former *Santa Rosa*, was retired. The veteran liners were laid-up for nearly three years at the north end of the Bethlehem Shipyards in Hoboken, nested together and both apparently named *Santa Paula*. Kept in near-operative condition, but with their twin stacks painted over in solid black, their twin sterns revealed another oddity: their homeports were shown as San Francisco. As all other Grace ships were registered at New York, this was no doubt a reflection of their earlier trade, from the 1930s, when they travelled to the West Coast.

Since the US government had little interest in retaining the elderly pair for possible emergency military use, they were 'cleared' for sale to overseas buyers, but with the contractual stipulation that they would be returned immediately should the need arise. In 1961, they were sold to the Typaldos Brothers of Greece, to become that growing firm's largest cruise-ships. The *Santa Paula* (ex-*Santa Rosa*) became the *Athinai*; the original *Paula* changed to *Acropolis*. Both were refitted prior to entering Greek-flag service.

The accommodation on the *Athinai* was extended to 240 in first class (using all of the original Grace Line berths), 180 in cabin class and 200 in tourist. The stern section was extended and a second outdoor pool was added. The public rooms were enlarged and a lido deck installed. All of the first and cabin class staterooms had private facilities; none of those in tourist class did. The ship was assigned to a two-week schedule, sailing in tandem with the former French Line *Colombie*, which had become the *Atlantica*, from Venice to Split, Piraeus, Limassol, Haifa, Larnaca, Rhodes, Piraeus and then return to Venice. She was used also for occasional cruises.

While the Typaldos fleet grew steadily and increased in popularity and reputation, it was ruined completely in 1966. The company ferry *Heraklion*, the onetime Bibby liner *Leicestershire*, sank during a storm in the Aegean, on December 8. There were some 241 casualties. In the inquest that followed, the vessel was found to have been loaded unsafely and therefore negligent. The Typaldos Brothers were sent to prison and their fleet disbanded. Ships such as the *Athinai* were seized by their mortgage-holder, the National Bank of Greece, and sent to the backwater anchorages of Perama Bay, near Piraeus. Despite continued rumour of reactivation, she and most others in that fleet would never sail again commercially. However, over a decade later, in 1978–79, the greatly neglected and rusted ship was leased to film producers. Their requirements had been for an older vessel, particularly useful for deck scenes in a fictional tale entitled *Raise the Titanic*.

Another idle liner, the *Queen Frederica*, was at first considered, but then the scrappers were already at work and the setting was therefore less acceptable. The *Athinai* was the second choice. Her original Grace Line owners could never have suspected that their ship would be used one day as the immortal, tragic *Titanic*. Towed out to the Aegan for some film sequences and then brought alongside the Ocean Terminal at Piraeus, to some film audiences she might have been a salvaged *Titanic*. A superb $6 million, 75-foot-long model of the White Star liner was used for the more specialised film segments, while floating in large tanks at the Mediterranean Film Studios on Malta.

When the film company lease expired, the *Athinai* was returned to her moorings in Perama Bay. While the *Acropolis*, the former *Santa Paula*, was broken-up in about 1972 (actual records concerning these idle Greek liners have been most difficult to obtain), the one-time *Santa Rosa* is the sole survivor of that very fine Grace quartet.

Gross tonnage: 9,135 (1932); 9,237 (1961)
Length overall: 508 feet
Width: 72 feet
Machinery: Steam turbines, twin screw
Speed: 19 knots (1932); 17.5 knots (1961)
Capacity: 225 first class and 64 third class (1932); 280 first class (1948); 240 first class, 180 cabin class and 200 tourist class (1961)
Built: Federal Shipbuilding & Drydock Co, Kearny, New Jersey, 1932

Above right Santa Rosa's *launching in March 1932, with two of her three sister ships shown on adjoining ways.*
Right *The start of her maiden voyage from New York on November 26 1932. Santa Rosa was beginning Grace Line's service to the West Coast.*

Notice the faces looking out of the ports on the lower deck as Santa Rosa *sails on a cruise. The roll-back dome over the superb dining saloon can be made out between the stacks.*

The Santa Rosa *as a troopship* (courtesy of US Army Signal Corps).

Her one time Grace Line owners could never have guessed that their former Santa Rosa *would one day be used as the* Titanic. *Briefly taken from her lay-up moorings, she served as a floating prop for the film 'Raise the Titanic'* (courtesy of Antonio Scrimali).

Manhattan

In the late 1920s and early 1930s, many of the big Atlantic passenger companies were thinking of pairs of ships. The Germans had their *Bremen* and *Europa* of 1929–30, the Italians had the *Rex* and *Conte Di Savoia*, White Star ordered the *Britannic* and *Georgic*, Cunard was talking of a team of speedy superliners and even Sweden had their *Gripsholm* and *Kungsholm*. The Americans were not to be left out.

By far the most dominant US-flag company on the North Atlantic, the United States Lines had a rather eclectic passenger fleet by 1930. It included the gigantic but unprofitable *Leviathan*, the former German flagship *Vaterland*; three aging four-masters, the *George Washington*, *America* and *Republic*, all of which were also former Germans; two cabin class ships, the *President Harding* and *President Roosevelt*, which were built in the early 1920s; and finally a series of seven 80-passenger combination passenger–cargo ships. Certainly, some new, more competitive and more economical tonnage was needed. However, the Americans were worried about the effects of the Depression. They did not foresee a booming transatlantic trade in the years ahead. In their caution, they selected two medium-sized 'cabin steamers' as their bid for a share of the trade. While certainly the biggest ocean liners (at 24,200 tons each) to be built to date in American shipyards, the new pair would not break any established records. They would be comfortable, conservative ships.

The building orders for both was given to the New York Shipbuilding Corporation at Camden, New Jersey, a yard located just across from the city of Philadelphia. The keel for the first, to be named *Manhattan*, was laid down on December 8 1930. She was launched a year later, on December 5th. Already, some earlier ships—the *George Washington*, *America* and *Republic*—were retired. The big *Leviathan* would finish very soon as well.

In the era of squat-stacked motorliners and decorative streamlining, the *Manhattan* and her subsequent sister-ship, the *Washington*, were designed with very short, stumpish funnels. They were totally unsuccessful, spilling smoke and soot all along the aft passenger decks. Quickly heigh-tened, they gave the ships a better overall appearance and used more vivid bands of red, white and blue.

The *Manhattan* was commissioned in August 1932, for a balanced service between New York, Cobh, Plymouth, Le Havre and Hamburg. She was joined by the *Washington* in the spring of the following year. United States Lines' advertising emphasised their American qualities: 'The *Manhattan* and *Washington* provide the living standards the world admires. These great ships were built in America to provide American luxury. The enormous decks, the huge public rooms, the air-conditioned dining rooms, the big, airy cabins typify American fondness for spaciousness. The American insistence on practical luxury finds expression in real beds, fine furnishings, private bathrooms and dexterous service. It is seen in the meals, as elaborate or as simple as desired, but always of quality beyond criticism. Yet the fares are low on America's largest, fastest ships. To make your voyage a real flight from worry, say to your travel agent, "I'll sail American".' Fares between New York and Plymouth for 1935 were listed as $172 in cabin class, $116 in tourist class and $84.50 in third class.

Although not a record, the *Manhattan*'s fastest passage was between New York and Cobh, taking 5 days, 4 hours and 55 minutes. Costing a very high $11 million, she was the epitome of

American marine engineering and design at the time. Her hull was divided into no less than 12 watertight compartments. The hatchcovers were made of steel and the lifeboats of copper, but bearing steel to avoid corrosion. The air-conditioning system in the dining rooms was then considered to be the finest afloat. The cabins had Punkah-Louvre ventilation as well as 12-inch oscillating fans. Almost all of the cabin class staterooms had private bathrooms and there were a dozen special deluxe suites. The public rooms included the cabin class smoking room, which was done in an American Indian theme and had a wood-burning open fireplace, the 'Palm Court' in Chinese Chippendale and a main lounge that could be converted into a sound cinema. An indoor pool and gymnasium were also provided.

Both the *Manhattan* and *Washington* were among the most popular liners on the Atlantic run by the mid-1930s. For example, in 1935, they each had a 72 per cent occupancy rate. They surpassed the 59 per cent for the magnificent *Normandie*, the 58 per cent for Germany's *Europa* and the 36 per cent for the Cunarder *Berengaria*. Such was the demand for the two United States liners that in the spring of 1936 Panama Pacific Line's *California* had to be chartered for extra service to Le Havre and Southampton. She even had her twin stacks repainted in the traditional red, white and blue for the single crossing.

The *Manhattan* maintained regular Atlantic service and some periodic cruises until the invasion of Poland, in September 1939. She had reached New York on August 31, the day before the Nazi attack and the same day as the launching at Newport News, Virginia of her new United States Lines fleetmate, the improved and larger *America*. The *Manhattan*'s schedule for the remainder of 1939 was abruptly cancelled. Instead, the ship had more urgent work. She ran four 'emergency evacuation' trips between New York and Bordeaux, taking as many as three times her normal passenger complement. Anxious and worried evacuees without actual stateroom accommodation slept on cots and sofas in the public rooms and even on mattresses placed on the carpeted floors. Huge identification markings, that included bright American flags and the ship's name, were painted along her sides. At night, she used illuminated

markings. While the United States was still neutral, her operators were most concerned about a possible attack, even if made in error, from a lurking Nazi submarine.

In December 1939, the *Manhattan* was sent into the Mediterranean for more evacuee service. She made a series of trips to Genoa and Naples and then a final roundtrip, in the following July, between New York and Lisbon. Thereafter, her safety on the Atlantic could no longer be guaranteed. Consequently since her owners wanted to avoid the possibility of lay-up, she was sent on a temporary cruise service, between New York, Havana, the Panama Canal, Acapulco, Los Angeles and San Francisco. Even the brand new *America*, which first appeared in that summer of 1940, was detoured to this trade as an alternative to her intended North Atlantic service. For some months, America's three largest liners—the *Manhattan*, *Washington* and *America*—were running Caribbean and intercoastal cruise services.

The *Manhattan* unexpectedly carried her last commercial passengers, 199 in all, in January 1941. While outbound on another cruise to California, she was off the Florida coast, near Palm Beach, when she was accidentally run aground. She became an extraordinary spectacle as she sat, stuck on a local sandbar. Local people, motorists and tourists lined the shore to see the towering ship. It took 22 days before she could be freed. Even at that, her twin propellers were bent badly and the ship had to be towed all the way to New York for full repairs. The entire affair cost a staggering $2 million. Immediately afterward, the ship was called to military duty. She would never see commercial service again.

Renamed as the USS *Wakefield*, after the Virginia birthplace of George Washington, she was outfitted completely as a 7,000-capacity trooper. Beginning her military duty in June 1941, she was on a transpacific voyage, steaming out to the Philippines, when the Japanese attacked Pearl Harbor on December 7. A month later, in January, she was hit during an air attack on Singapore. Although there were casualties and several fires, the ship was repaired, sent off to Bombay and then fully overhauled at the Philadelphia Naval Shipyard.

Returned to troop service, the *Wakefield* faced

more serious dangers on September 3 1942, with 950 evacuees aboard, during a westbound crossing from the Clyde. An otherwise small fire broke out in a storage closet on B deck. Initial firefighting was so ineffective that, within ten minutes, the blaze had reached A deck and then engulfed the forward funnel. Being part of a large North Atlantic convoy, three rescue ships—the warships *Brooklyn*, *Madison* and *Mayo*—were promptly alongside. The burning *Wakefield* was abandoned.

Seven days later, on September 10, the still-burning *Wakefield* was brought by ocean-going tugs to a cove near Halifax and deliberately beached. Once the final fires were extinguished or had burned themselves out, Navy crews inspected the scorched ship. Despite all, and even in view of her very sensitive stability, it was decided to tow the ship to Boston for further inspection and possible repairs. Among the earliest decisions, she was sold outright to the United States Navy. Once at the Boston Naval Shipyard, she was examined, declared a total constructive loss, but selected for massive rebuilding. Such was the vital need for big wartime troopships.

The *Wakefield* was not reactivated until April 1944, when full repairs were completed. Most noticeable among the alterations was the elimination of the entire promenade deck. Although still painted over in grey, she appeared especially sleek with that single deck now gone. Thereafter, the *Wakefield* was converted to a permanent troop transport and she began a series of 13 successive trips from either New York or Boston to Liverpool. These were followed by a round voyage between Newport News, Gibraltar and Naples, and then subsequent crossings to Marseilles, Taranto, Le Havre, Cherbourg and Antwerp. In December 1945, well after the war had ended, she returned to the Pacific, going from Boston via Hampton Roads in Virginia to the Panama Canal and then onwards to Taku and Tsingtao in China. The following voyage took her to Guam and Kwajalein. She returned to New York in May 1946.

She would not sail again. Shortly afterward, she was towed to the Hudson River 'mothball fleet', at Jones Point, New York, where she was nested among other wartime tonnage, including former passenger and troop ships and considerable numbers of standardised Liberty and Victory class freighters. Her twin, raked stacks always stood above the other ships. Years later, in 1953, she was joined by her former sister-ship *Washington*, which was used in transatlantic austerity service after the war. The sisters were moored together.

In 1964, during a government re-evaluation of laid-up tonnage, both the *Wakefield* and the *Washington* were considered unlikely for revival. They were cleared for sale and then bought by New York Harbor scrappers, the Union Metals & Alloys Corporation. A year or so passed before a group of Moran tugboats brought both ex-liners down river, past the United States Lines terminals in Manhattan and then to the backwaters of Kearny, New Jersey. The sisters were quietly broken-up at the former Federal Shipyards, in the same berths that had once been used by many brand new ships, including the four Grace Line *Santa Rosa* class sisters of 1932–33.

Gross tonnage: 24,289
Length overall: 705 feet
Width: 86 feet
Machinery: Steam turbines, twin screw
Speed: 20 knots
Capacity: 582 cabin class, 461 tourist class and 196 third class
Built: New York Shipbuilding Co, Camden, New Jersey, 1932
Demise: Scrapped at Kearny, New Jersey, 1965

Striking artist's impression of the Manhattan *to be.*

Left *With her original low stacks she starts her trials off the coast of Maine, USA, in July 1932.*

Left and below left *Artist's impressions of the cabin lounge and dining saloon on Manhattan. She and her sister ship Washington were so luxurious that they forced most of the other liners to be regarded as cabin liners.*

Right *Her stacks were raised giving less soot on the decks and a much better appearance.*

Right *October 1939, she is anchored at Quarantine in New York loaded with worried tourists and fortunate refugees from a tense Europe* (courtesy of Everett Viez collection).

Right *She was put on an intercoastal run and went aground off Florida. The photograph shows her passengers being removed by US Coast Guard, January 13 1941.*

Queen of Bermuda

Amidst a splendid wheelhouse of wood, brass and overhead tubing, Captain M. E. Musson bravely pronounced, 'All good things must come to an end'. Shortly thereafter, on Saturday afternoon, November 19 1966, the *Queen of Bermuda*'s steam chime whistles signalled with three booming blasts that her final sailing from New York to Bermuda and return was about to begin. That voyage also closed the curtain on the 46-year passenger history of the Furness Bermuda Line, a member of the giant Furness Withy Group. It was also the end for one of the world's most illustrious passenger ships.

The sentiment that was attached to the *Queen* by both ship buffs and the travelling public alike was almost doubled when Furness Bermuda announced that the majestic little lady was sold to ship-breakers at Faslane in Scotland. The regularity of Saturday afternoon sailings by the *Queen* (and her running-mate, the smaller *Ocean Monarch*) were a fixture of New York Harbor. Almost without fail, by 3:15 pm, both of the ships, or at least one of them, would be in the Hudson and steaming southbound for the Lower Bay and the open Atlantic.

The *Queen of Bermuda* had, apart from war service, been plying the six-day Bermuda cruise circuit since her completion and entry into service in March 1933. Built by the Vickers-Armstrong Yard at Barrow-in-Furness, she was a very close sister to the *Monarch of Bermuda*, completed two years earlier. The *Queen* was built as a replacement for the fire-wrecked *Bermuda*, a liner which saw only four years of service (1927–31). The two newer Furness Bermuda liners were elegantly decorated and instantly won for themselves the reputation of 'the millionaires' ships'. Together, they were capable of carrying 4,500 tourists to Bermuda every three weeks. Each had a well-balanced profile, with gradually reclining decks and three evenly slanted funnels (the third being a dummy). Considered generally to be all-first class ships (the *Queen* had, in fact, space for 31 second class passengers), every cabin had private facilities. This was an exceptional and very unique amenity for the early 1930s.

Like so many other ships, the *Queen* was abruptly pulled off commercial service in that tense September of 1939 and ordered to return to home waters. Being repainted in grey for the crossing, she was the first large liner to sail from New York in such, soon-to-be familiar colours. At the Harland & Wolff Yards at Belfast, she was stripped of her passenger fittings and then outfitted as an armed merchant cruiser. Nine guns were placed along her upper decks. Numerous empty barrels were jammed into her hatches for extra stability and special plating was added to the hull and superstructure for added protection. A year later, in 1940, the third funnel was temporarily removed, no doubt as a form of disguise. (In later years, when the *Queen* was rebuilt with a single stack, she gained the distinction of being the only liner to sail as a one-, two- and three-stacker.) She far exceeded her intended 40-hour, 600-mile runs to Bermuda—instead travelling 370,251 miles and carrying 110,365 wartime personnel. She visited such diverse ports as Gibraltar, Halifax, Toulon, Algiers, Naples, Taranto, Suez, Aden, Bombay, Colombo, Rangoon, Singapore, Fremantle, Freetown, Capetown, the Falkland Islands, St Helena and even Iceland.

Handed back to her owners in 1947, it had been Furness Bermuda's intention to restore both liners and resume Bermuda cruising. Unfortunately, while undergoing her refit, the *Monarch of Bermuda* was badly damaged by a fire in March 1947.

Queen of Bermuda *saluting as she comes through 'Two Rock Passage' into Hamilton, Bermuda* (courtesy of Bermuda News Bureau).

Thought to be unworthy of further repairs, she was laid-up for a time and then sold to the British government, who rebuilt her as the Australian migrant ship *New Australia*. Years later, in 1958, she was improved even further and appeared in transatlantic service as the *Arkadia* of the Greek Line. To Furness, it seemed that the *Queen* would resume service alone, at least in the beginning. She left on her first post-war Bermuda run in February 1949. The replacement for the original *Monarch of Bermuda* appeared two years later, in May 1951, in the form of the yacht-like 13,500-ton *Ocean Monarch*. Unlike the two earlier ships, she was intended to periodically cruise off the Bermuda trade, to go deeper into the Caribbean or in summer to the St Lawrence River region and Canadian Maritime Provinces.

Because of their Saturday afternoon sailings, the *Queen* (and the *Ocean Monarch*) were especially popular with the 'just married' set. In fact, the team was known as the 'honeymoon ships'. After leaving New York, all of Sunday was spent at sea. They would reach Bermuda early on Monday morning, with the *Queen* usually going to the preferred berth alongside Front Street in Hamilton. Alternately, the *Ocean Monarch* went mostly to St Georges. They would remain at Bermuda for nearly three full days, leaving on Wednesday afternoons. There would be another full day at sea on Thursday and then arrival at New York's Pier 95 by early Friday morning. It was a convenient pattern that lured tens of thousands of passengers, among them former President Harry S. Truman of the United States. Minimum six-day fares began at $150 by the late 1950s.

Mr Ian Denton of Tavistock in Devon was a staff-member in those years aboard the *Queen of Bermuda*. He has fond memories of the beloved liner: 'We were the first outbound ship to pass under the Verrazano-Narrows Bridge in New York Harbor after its official opening in April 1964. We had a special cattle deck onboard, which was often used to carry race horses between New York and Bermuda. We actually carried very few cattle. Usually, one of our most important pieces of cargo was fresh water. We would carry more than needed in the tanks so as to have a surplus to pump ashore in Bermuda. Bermudians were always short of fresh water and the Hamilton Fire Brigade would transport the water from the *Queen* to individual bungalows, for storage in special tanks.'

In the autumn of 1961, it was decided that the *Queen* needed some face-lifting. Little was actually done to the interiors or her accommodation, but instead attention was given to the exterior details. At the Harland & Wolff Yards at Belfast, her bow was raked and extended by 8 feet (increasing her length overall to 588 feet). More importantly, her three funnels were removed and replaced by one, positioned in place of the original second stack.

The new funnel was tall, tapered and certainly did not detract from the ship's overall appearance. Admittedly, at first, it was rather difficult to imagine a three-stacker becoming a single-stacker. It is most unlikely that the *Queen Mary* could have ever endured such a transformation. However, because of her much smaller size, the 'surgery' worked for the *Queen of Bermuda*. She returned to service—and more praises—in April 1962.

However, several years later, the ageing *Queen of Bermuda* was facing some serious new competiton, namely the ultra-modern, 39,200-ton *Oceanic*, commissioned in April 1965 for rival seven-day cruises to Nassau. Even some Furness Bermuda loyalists were hardpressed to reject the lures of such a trendy new generation of ocean liners. Indeed, the *Queen* became more and more of the 'distant, old relative' on the New York cruise run. Then, as if to complicate matters further, there were more problems in the form of the US Coast Guard. Prompted by several disasters involving elderly passenger ships, new safety regulations were to be enforced. The *Queen* would need another expensive refit just to pass inspection. At Furness

headquarters in London, it seemed impractical. Quite suddenly the owners decided to terminate Bermuda cruising entirely. The *Ocean Monarch* left service first, in August 1966, and was soon sold to the Bulgarians, becoming the Black Sea cruise-ship *Varna*. Alone, the *Queen* continued for several months, until November. On the 26th, making a rare morning departure, she left New York for the very last time and went direct to the breakers at Faslane. She was finished-off that winter. Strange are the fates: the Greek *Arkadia*, the former *Monarch of Bermuda*, was being scrapped at the same time, in Spain.

Gross tonnage: 22,575 (1933); 22,501 (1949); 22,552 (1962)
Length overall: 580 feet (1933); 588 feet (1962)
Width: 76 feet
Machinery: Steam turbo-electric, quadruple screw
Speed: 19 knots
Capacity: 700 first class, 31 second class (1933); 733 first class (1949)
Built: Vickers-Armstrong Shipbuilders Ltd, Barrow-in-Furness, England, 1933
Demise: Scrapped at Faslane, Scotland, late 1966

Left *Alongside at Hamilton* (courtesy of Bermuda News Bureau).
Right *Voyage repairs are made in drydock at Brooklyn. Note that she had four screws.*

Queen of Bermuda

Queen of Bermuda *(left) and* Monarch of Bermuda *at New York.*

With her third stack removed, the Queen of Bermuda *served with distinction throughout World War 2 (courtesy of US Coast Guard).*

After 1962 she was reduced to only one stack. Her whistle blows one blast to let everyone know she is reversing out of New York pier (courtesy of Moran Towing).

Dunnottar Castle

One of the more outstanding accomplishments of the modern shipbuilder has been the ingenuity applied to transforming the aged vessel into an ultra-modern 'glamour ship'. These face-liftings usually began with the junking of most of the original facilities, equipment and overall design, and then culminate in a thorough transformation and rejuvenation. Union-Castle's *Dunnottar Castle* is a classic example of such a revived liner. In mid-life, just after the age of 20, she was totally rebuilt as a tropical cruise-ship. Union-Castle designers and management could not have guessed that their original ship would remain sailing close to her 50th year (1986).

The *Dunnottar Castle* was commissioned by the famed Union-Castle Mail Steamship Company Limited in July 1936. Little noticed, it was an era of brisk ocean liner creation, with the giant new *Normandie* and *Queen Mary* as well as new flagships for such firms as the Ellerman, Orient and P&O Lines. Design firms were equally busy. The biggest passenger ships yet were being planned for the likes of Blue Funnel, Cunard, Royal Mail and Shaw Savill. Union-Castle had just commissioned their largest liners, the 25,500-ton sisters *Athlone Castle* and *Stirling Castle*. Within a year, an even bigger liner, the 27,000-ton *Capetown Castle*, was to come off the ways.

The *Dunnottar Castle* and her identical sister-ship *Dunvegan Castle* (which was sunk off western Ireland in August 1940) were products of the famed Harland & Wolff Yards at Belfast in Northern Ireland. The general design and silhouette followed the Union Castle pattern of the day: twin masts, a wide, flattish funnel and a neatly balanced superstructure. There was nothing pretentious about the *Dunnottar Castle*. She was clearly a member of the Union-Castle Line and an obvious descendant of the company's larger, more famous liners. The accommodation was quite moderate— a mere 220 in first class and 240 in tourist—but offset by five holds for valuable cargos.

The *Dunnottar Castle* was designed especially for the round-Africa service, but was initially used on the Southampton–Cape mail express run while several of the larger liners were re-engined. Later, she entered her intended trade, sailing from the London Docks to Gibraltar, Port Said, Suez, Aden, Mombasa, Zanzibar, Dar-es-Salaam, Beira, Louerenco Marques, Durban, East London, Port Elizabeth, Capetown, Walvis Bay, St Helena, Ascension and Las Palmas.

Even before the Second World War erupted, the *Dunnottar Castle* was called to duty. She was officially requisitioned several days before the actual declaration of hostilities, on August 28 1939. Sent to a drydock, she reappeared in October as a fully outfitted armed merchant cruiser. Her sailing patterns thereafter became quite diverse and highly secret. Her most notable voyage was in May 1942, when, under even greater secrecy, she carried British Army engineers and their assistants to Tristan de Cunha for the construction of an important wartime meteorological and wireless station.

In June 1942, she went back to drydock for a six-month conversion to a troop transport. Subsequent sailings were varied: the Mediterranean, Egypt, India, Australia and New Zealand. During 1944, she was used as part of the enormous 'ferry

service' between Southampton and the shores of Normandy, in preparation for and during the resulting invasion of western Europe. Thereafter, she returned to long-distance trooping. With a steaming record of over 264,000 miles, the *Dunnottar Castle* was not officially decommissioned until March 1948. Her wartime passenger total had reached 259,000.

Stripped of wartime fittings and then refitted to much the same condition as in the pre-war years, the liner resumed sailings for Union-Castle in February 1949. Her passenger capacity had declined even further, however. The new berthing arrangement was for 105 in first class and 263 in tourist, a total of 368 in a 15,000-ton passenger ship. Certainly, there must have been something of the 'private yacht' about her onboard atmosphere. All of the Union-Castle liners have had relatively small passenger capacities when compared to their overall sizes. While a large area of open-air deck space was assuredly an important element on 'sunshine sailings' to Africa, these ships derived at least 50 per cent of their incomes from cargo. Accurately, even the biggest Castle liners were actually combination passenger–cargo ships.

By the mid-1950s, Union-Castle began to streamline and modernise its extensive passenger fleet. Furthermore, there was some decline in general passenger trading. Three new mail liners were on the boards—the *Pendennis Castle* for 1958, the *Windsor Castle* for 1960 and then the *Transvaal Castle* for 1961. Gradually, the pre-war liners were to be retired. On the round-Africa route, the company forecast was that the newer post-war trio—the *Braemar Castle*, *Kenya Castle* and *Rhodesia Castle*—would be adequate to projected demands. Again, all of the pre-war tonnage was to be phased-out. The *Dunnottar Castle*, by then (1958) 22 years old, was among the first to go. Because of very sound construction and high maintenance over the years, she found a new owner almost immediately. In January 1959, she was towed from London to Schiedam in Holland, to begin a new life.

The Incres Line—based at New York, flying Liberian colours and with mostly Italian staff— was created in the early 1950s. After a brief stint in transatlantic service, they turned to a highly limited operation for the time: full-time cruising from New York. P&O's old *Mongolia*, having been extensively refitted as the cruise-ship *Nassau*, was a sweeping success. With the *Dunnottar Castle*, Incres wanted to reach for the more luxurious cruise market as well as for longer trips into the Caribbean (mostly 12–16 days).

The *Dunnottar Castle* was given over to the Wilton-Fijenoord Shipyards, who gutted and removed all the original accommodation and fittings: passenger and crew areas, engine spaces, masts, cargo equipment and even the bow and stern sections. A new ship then emerged. Modern passenger decks were constructed and included strikingly modern public rooms and staterooms, a complete cinema and a large outdoor lido area surrounding twin swimming pools. The original Burmeister & Wain diesels were replaced by twin Italian-built Fiat types, which rendered an adequate cruising service speed of 18 knots. The outward appearance of the ship was greatly altered by attaching a single mast to a new, tapered funnel. The vessel was given a 'tropical colouring' scheme of white hull and superstructure balanced by a dark blue waterline. Overall, in her new configuration, the former *Dunnottar Castle* could accommodate 600 all-first class passengers, nearly doubling her Union-Castle capacity.

At completion in December 1959, the ship was officially rechristened *Victoria*. She entered service with a brief, 'show off' Mediterranean cruise. In January, she first crossed to New York to begin her first cruise series to the Caribbean. That summer, she also ran two luxury cruises, long-distance jaunts to Scandinavia and the Mediterranean. Highly appraised and quickly developing a devoted following, the *Victoria* was a great success.

The Incres operation changed hands in October 1964. Bought out by the Swedish-flag Clipper Line, owner of the cruising yacht *Stella Polaris*, they created a special Liberian holding firm for the *Victoria*. Registered to the Victoria Steamship Company of Monrovia, the well-known Incres name was continued in North America. Outwardly, there seemed to be little alteration in the operation of what was by then one of North America's highest rated cruise-ships.

One subsequent change, however, was the summer programme for the liner. Each June, she would sail from New York on a transatlantic crossing, usually to Southampton and Amsterdam. Until early autumn, she was used for European cruising, mostly to Scandinavia from Copenhagen. Again, the ship gained a strong following. Unfortunately, soon after the dramatic fuel oil price increases of 1973, the single-ship operation of the Incres Line began to run head-on into financial trouble. General costs were rising, fares had to be increased and all the while her passenger loads began to decrease. Suddenly and most surprisingly to the general public, Incres declared bankruptcy and closed in the summer of 1975. The *Victoria* was sent to an unused berth at the old Brooklyn Army Terminal in New York Harbor. For some time, she sat—lifeless, rusting and listing noticeably against the terminal shed. Her future was the subject of considerable rumour.

The initial news was that she would to go the Amazon River area to become a hotel-ship. In November, however, she was rather abruptly sold to the Phaidon Navigation Company, a subsidiary of the large Chandris Group. Placed under the Greek flag, she was towed across the Atlantic to Piraeus by the tug *Heidi Moran*. A general overhaul and rejuvenation followed. She resumed cruising in June 1976, mostly from Venice and Piraeus to the Aegean, Eastern Mediterranean and Black Sea. A year later, in something of a fleet reshuffling, her registry was changed to Panama and her name altered slightly to *The Victoria*. Still popular and maintaining that revised appearance that defies her actual age, this former Union-Castle liner has, remarkably, outlived many of her former African fleetmates.

Gross tonnage: 15,007 (1936); 15,054 (1948); 14,917 (1959)
Length overall: 560 feet (1936); 573 feet (1959)
Width: 72 feet
Machinery: Burmeister & Wain diesels, twin screw (1936); Fiat diesels, twin screw (1959)
Speed: 17 knots (1936); 18 knots (1959)
Capacity: 258 first, 250 tourist (1936); 105 first, 263 tourist (1948); 600 first (1960)
Built: Harland & Wolff Ltd, Belfast, Northern Ireland, 1936

Dunnottar Castle *(foreground) at the T Jetty, Durban Harbour, South Africa.*

Above *Union-Castle's* Dunnottar Castle *as built in the mid-1930s* (courtesy of Roger Sherlock).

Left *Undergoing conversion into a cruise ship at Rotterdam. She became the* Victoria *(courtesy of Incres Lines).*

Below *With a strikingly new profile she enters New York Harbor to commence her new cruising career.*

Bremen

In September 1957, several members of the French National Assembly bitterly reacted to a rumour that the big troopship *Pasteur*, France's third largest passenger ship, was to be offered for sale. It was a particular, yet restricted, viewpoint that the 18-year-old ship should remain under the Tricolour. Various schemes were presented, including renovating the ship for the French Line's transatlantic service, but none of these seemed entirely feasible. Even further protest was aroused when word leaked that the ship was to be sold to the North German Lloyd and in direct competition with the French Line itself. Indeed, in rather quick time, terms were reached and the idle *Pasteur* was moved from Brest to Bremen. The ship changed hands for $5 million.

The *Pasteur* had been built in the late 1930s at the famed Penhoet Shipyards at St Nazaire. Named in honour of the brilliant scientist, she was designed to be the most luxurious and fastest liner on the Europe–South America trade. The French, in the form of the Compagnie Sud-Atlantique, were keenly interested in outstepping all of the existing competition, namely Germany's *Cap Arcona* and a new British entry, the *Andes* of the Royal Mail Lines. The new French ship was, in the end, the slightly larger and more powerful. She was sure to be 'the crack ship' to South America.

At nearly 30,000 tons, the new ship was of rather unique, eye-catching design. Her foremost feature was a mammoth, almost overpowering single stack, which was positioned far forward. This funnel was indeed the ship's most distinguishing mark and left a distinct impression on any observer of ships and ship design. Shipowners have often tried to create or add some design feature that might help with overall publicity and public relations. A decade later, Cunard had its *Caronia* painted in four shades of green. Promptly dubbed the 'Green Goddess', such an unusual colour scheme made the liner far more recognisable and memorable. The owners of the *Pasteur* might well have had similar thoughts when they first approved such a huge stack.

In addition, the French liner's bow had a squared-off appearance, contrary to the customary rounded design. Twin steel reinforcements in the bow section created this unusual proportion. The promenade deck was deliberately 'broken', with one section rising a full three decks above the other. Consequently, the lifeboats were separated as well into two groups, four in the forward, upper portion and the remainders aft.

Aside from her size, speed and acclaimed French decorative touches, the *Pasteur* also represented, particularly to the Compagnie Sud-Atlantique, the long-awaited replacement for the giant 42,000-ton *L'Atlantique*, an ill-fated ship that was commissioned in 1931, burnt out two years later and then scrapped in 1936. Often called a 'first cousin' to the luxurious *Ile De France* of transatlantic fame, this latter ship was briefly the ultimate liner on the Latin American run. Although smaller in dimensions, the *Pasteur* was her successor. She was moved to a fitting-out berth in early 1939 and was intended to be commissioned by late summer.

During her trial runs, the steam turbines produced a highly satisfying 26 knots. Her maiden sailing was set for September, from Bordeaux to Rio de Janeiro, Santos, Montevideo and Buenos Aires. But, quite suddenly, the Second World War erupted and all plans were shelved. Without having had any form of commercial maiden trip, the *Pasteur* was ordered to Brest, supposedly for temporary lay-up. The French government saw only the greatest risks in sending their newest liner out to sea.

Bremen

The war has ended and the Pasteur, *now called* Bremen, *is outbound and is passing the* United States. *The year is 1959* (courtesy of Moran Towing).

Eleven months later, in June 1940, with the Nazi armies close at hand, the *Pasteur* was ordered to Halifax. With a limited crew and no passengers, she carried a very valuable cargo: a large shipment of gold from the French National Reserves bound for wartime storage in Canada. Upon arrival, she was transferred to the British Ministry of War Transport and then assigned to the operational expertise of Cunard-White Star. Hereafter, she was to be an important military trooper, in fact for her entire French career.

Captain Eric Ashton-Irvine, then just hired by Cunard, served aboard the *Pasteur* in the early 1940s. 'Nazi sympathisers had actually tried to sink her at Halifax when she first arrived there. Unfortunately, my recollections of this mighty Frenchman are not terribly favourable. She was not a good sea boat. She had a rather shallow draft [27 Feet], rolled enormously and that huge funnel always gave us wind problems. Internally, she was equally displeasing. There seemed to be an endless series of interconnecting cabins, the ceilings were too low and the heavily mirrored bathrooms always confusing.'

At first, the *Pasteur* sailed the Atlantic, carrying British troops, who were relayed in American ships out of US ports to Singapore. Her travels were, however, always secret and quite diverse. By the autumn of 1943, she had visited such ports as Liverpool, Rio de Janeiro, Freetown, Capetown, Durban, Aden and Port Suez. During the winter of 1943–44, she was given a thorough overhaul at Liverpool. A year later, more extensive work was carried out at New York, divided between ship-

yards in Brooklyn and Hoboken. In the final year of the war, the *Pasteur* sailed almost regularly on the North Atlantic, mostly in company with the famed *Ile De France*.

By the spring of 1945, just as Nazi Germany collapsed, the *Pasteur* had carried some 300,000 personnel, of which 220,000 were troops and 30,000 wounded. She was pulled off the Atlantic that June and was urgently sent from France out to Indo-China. Carrying members of the noted Leclerc Division, her mission was to help restore order to those troubled Asian colonies. In fact, this task was to be her employment for over a decade.

Although some consideration was given to restoring the ship for luxury service, the French government retained the *Pasteur* as a 'giant ferry' for national troops. She was, however, repainted in her commercial livery and managed by her original owners. With a peacetime capacity listed at 4,500, she was for some time the world's largest troopship.

By 1956, the *Pasteur* had become superfluous to even the troop requirements. In January of the following year, she was 'mothballed' at Brest, supposedly awaiting reassignment under the Tricolour. In fact, in the autumn of 1957, she was sold to the North German Lloyd and moved to the Bremen-Vegesack Shipyards for thorough gutting and then rebuilding.

The Lloyd had not resumed Atlantic liner trading until early 1955, when the Swedish *Gripsholm* was purchased. Renamed *Berlin*, she quickly became a popular and profitable ship, once again allowing Germans to travel in a national liner.

However, the Lloyd directors wanted a more striking and faster ship. They were more than excited when anticipating the rebuilt *Pasteur*. With a strong sense of tradition, she was named *Bremen*, long considered Germany's most popular and distinguished sea name.

Costing over £4 million, the rebuilding was an extensive project. The previous interiors were scrapped along with the original French turbines and that once notable funnel. The *Pasteur* had been reduced to a bare hulk. In creating the *Bremen*, however, materials and furnishings were of the highest quality and most contemporary style, ingredients certainly fitting for the new flagship of the West German merchant marine. New turbines were fitted, improved wiring and plumbing was installed and the passenger accommodation built anew with berths for 1,122 passengers. A new, far less pronounced funnel was added.

Enthusiastically received from the start, the *Bremen* first crossed to New York in July 1959. While the older and smaller *Berlin* remained in service, the larger ship maintained an independent schedule, sailing for most of the year between Bremerhaven, Southampton, Cherbourg and New York. In the cold winter months, she sailed southwards to the Caribbean, mostly on two-week cruises. The *Bremen* was a highly profitable investment for the North German Lloyd.

By the early 1970s, however, the situation had changed. The economics of shipping were far more competitive and cost-conscious. Another, more specific development was the enormous transition in the passenger ship business, shifting from pure transportation to pure luxury vacation. In response to these conditions, the North German Lloyd merged with an old rival, the Hamburg American Line, and in turn became known as Hapag-Lloyd. Among the new firm's first decisions was to eliminate the dwindling, money-losing transatlantic service. Aeroplanes had secured a huge portion of the Atlantic trade. The *Bremen* (and her fleetmate, the *Europa*, the former *Kungsholm* of 1953) were shifted to fulltime cruising—both from New York as well as European ports. Unfortunately, there were further problems for the former French ship. Her machinery turned difficult and troublesome. There were a string of delayed and cancelled cruises. To the impeccable Hapag-Lloyd, this was a deep tarnish to their otherwise sterling record. The accountants advised that repairs were uneconomic. The ship was simply too old.

In December 1971, the *Bremen* departed from New York for the last time and therein closed out her owner's historic transatlantic service. Soon after reaching Bremerhaven, she was sold to the Greek-flag Chandris Group. Then, after some dry-docking and mechanical repairs, she reappeared in the spring of 1972 as the *Regina Magna*. Her purpose was cruising: from Amsterdam and London to Scandinavia, from Genoa within the Mediterranean and to West Africa, and later within the Caribbean. However, there were more problems ahead. With a swift increase in the cost of fuel oils, the ship's consumption proved to be enormous and therefore quite uneconomic. In October 1974, she was laid-up in Perama Bay, near Piraeus, secured to a series of equally unwanted tankers and freighters.

The rusting ship managed, however, to find yet another buyer, the Philippine–Singapore Ports Corporation, in 1977. She was moved to Jeddah, Saudi Arabia, for use as a workers' accommodation centre, with a total capacity placed at 3,600. First renamed *Saudi Phil I*, she later became the *Filipinas Saudi I*. When this assignment ended, her only alternative—with an age of 41, those faulty engines and a greatly neglected condition—was the scrapyards of Taiwan. Placed under tow and otherwise empty, she never completed the voyage. On June 6 1980, she heeled over and sank, rising by the bow in a scene reminiscent of some wartime tragedy. Within minutes, the long career of the original *Pasteur* had finished.

Gross tonnage: 29,253 (1939); 30,447 (1948); 32,336 (1959); 32,360 (1966); 23,801 (1972)
Length overall: 697 feet
Width: 88 feet
Machinery: Steam turbines, quadruple screw
Speed: 23 knots
Capacity: 287 first, 126 second, 338 third (as designed, 1939); 4,500 troops (1945); 216 first, 906 tourist (1959); 1,100 first (1972)
Built: Chantiers de L'Atlantique, St Nazaire, France, 1939
Demise: Sunk while under tow, June 6 1980

Left *Just before the* Pasteur *sailed from New York for war service. This picture shows both* Normandie *and* Queen Elizabeth *in slip above her.*

Left *An unusual view of* Bremen *being manoeuvred at Bremerhaven. North German Lloyd and Ellerman Lines' freighters are to the right* (courtesy of North German Lloyd).

Below *Wearing the familiar white X of the Chandris group of companies, the former* Bremen, *now the* Regina Magna, *was painted with a white hull and operated at a reduced speed to conserve fuel* (courtesy of Alex Duncan).

Mauretania

On July 1 1935, the illustrious four-stacker, the first *Mauretania*, which was the unrivalled speed queen of the North Atlantic for 22 years (1907–29), sailed from Southampton to Rosyth in Scotland for scrapping. It was a sad occasion, marking the death of one of the world's greatest liners. Although the world was still caught in the clutches of the sinister Depression, it seems a great pity, at least at this distance in time, that she could not have been saved and preserved, perhaps in similar manner to the *Queen Mary* in Southern California. Surely, the chance to see and explore one of the grand four-stackers would be well appreciated a half-century later. The Cunard–White Star Company, as it was then known, had arranged for a Southampton-based company to rename one of its small paddle steamers as *Mauretania* until such time came when a new liner could bear the distinctive name.

The magnificent 81,000-ton *Queen Mary* was commissioned in May 1936, and plans for an equally sized running-mate were well underway. Cunard's plans also called for a somewhat smaller liner, smaller only in comparison to the giant *Queens*, but one that could serve as a relief ship. This new vessel was designed at the same time as the new twin-funnel *Queen Elizabeth* and consequently there would be a marked similarity between the two ships. They would rank as two of the most handsome liners of their day.

The keel for this new liner was first laid down on May 24 1937, at the Cammell Laird Shipyards at Birkenhead, just across from Liverpool and the Cunard home office. She would be named *Mauretania*. A year later, on July 28, she was named and launched by Lady Bates, the wife of the Cunard–White Star chairman. While shipyard crews and then the decorators finished their tasks, the publicity and press people had a special problem. They felt that the new *Mauretania* could easily be overshadowed by the fame and popularity of her distinguished predecessor. Therefore, a special campaign was arranged to make the new vessel as distinctive in her own right as possible. The interested public was flooded with promotional material on the new *Mauretania*. Because she would provide the greatest amount of daylight and fresh air to fill her inner accommodation, she was dubbed the 'Sunshine Ship'. This projected a special, innovative image for the new liner.

The *Mauretania* had yet another distinction. At over 35,000 tons, she might have been rather medium-sized to Cunard, but, in fact, she was outranked by only ten or so other liners then afloat. She was larger than the new Dutch flagship *Nieuw Amsterdam*. Larger too than the *America*, the new flagship of the US Merchant Marine. She also surpassed the flagships of several other mighty British shipping lines, namely the P&O, Orient and Union-Castle lines. More specifically, the *Mauretania* was the largest liner yet to be built in England, since all previous larger British liners were constructed in either Northern Ireland or Scotland. This somewhat incidental distinction was later given to the 41,000-ton *Oriana* (completed at Barrow-in-Furness in 1960).

The *Mauretania* sailed from Liverpool, although Cunard's big ship terminal was at Southampton, for her first crossing to New York, on June 17 1939. Subsequent sailings were from London (Tilbury), Southampton and Le Havre, joining the motorliners *Britannic* and *Georgic* as an operative

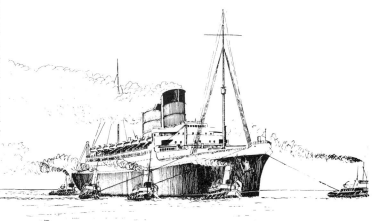

team. The new *Mauretania* was, in fact, the largest liner to use the London Docks. Unfortunately, within less than three months, such distinctions seemed to have little significance. The world was again at war.

The *Mauretania* was one of the first liners to be outfitted for military service. She was completely repainted in grey and armed with two six-inch guns, three twelve-pounders, three single 40 mm guns, 22 20 mm guns and two rocket projectors. Following a voyage to New York, she was laid-up at Liverpool, a rather dangerous choice due to the threat of an air attack. Rather quickly, the decision was revised and the liner moved to New York. At first, she was berthed at the famed luxury piers, silently sitting in company with two other noted ships, the *Queen Mary* and the French *Normandie.* Months passed before a decision was made on just how to best use such large liners.

On a rainy day in March 1940, the *Mauretania* slipped off to war (and was followed by the *Queen Mary* a day later). Unlike the gala departures of the peacetime days, secrecy now surrounded these ships. All were potential targets for possible sabotage. Certainly, enemy agents tried to keep abreast of their movements. Comparatively few even saw the *Mauretania* or *Queen Mary* depart.

While the larger and faster *Mary* sped for the South African Cape and then Australia, the *Mauretania* used an alternative route: via Panama, then San Francisco (to store her passenger fittings), Honolulu and finally full conversion to a troopship at Sydney. She was a most unexpected sight in such a distant port. Initially, she was paired with two other equivalent liners, the French *Ile De France* and the Dutch *Nieuw Amsterdam.* They worked the Indian Ocean troop shuttle, carrying Australians outwards to Suez and returning with prisoners, evacuees and the wounded. Of course, there were occasions when the *Mauretania* was in company of some of the world's largest ocean liners, namely both Cunard *Queens* and the four-funnel *Aquitania.* Toward the latter years of the war, she shifted to the more pressing North Atlantic, in preparation for the European invasion. In total, her wartime loggings amounted to over 538,000 miles, which included her longest trooping voyage in which she circled the globe in 81 days, 16 hours. She was not overhauled completely throughout the war years

yet she was known to have a maximum speed in excess of 25 knots at times.

The *Mauretania* had but one mishap during the war. On January 8 1944, while fully loaded with troops, in New York Harbor's Lower Bay, she collided with the American tanker *Hat Creek.* Damages to the Cunarder forced her to return to port, to a Brooklyn shipyard. Astonishingly, the repairs were completed within 12 hours, a task that would have normally taken three days.

On September 2 1946, the *Mauretania* arrived at Liverpool (from India) and finished her war service. She was sent to her builder's yard for an eight-month reconversion. She resumed commercial service in April 1947, first sailing from Liverpool and later from Southampton via Le Havre and Cobh to New York. In the winter months, with her capacity specially reduced to 600 all-first class, she cruised to the Caribbean, mostly on 12–18 day voyages.

While always a popular and special ship in her own right, the *Mauretania* did understudy for one of the giant *Queens* each summer on the Southampton–New York express service. Since the *Queens* were always scheduled for a major overhaul in winter as well as for a short turn in drydock in late July or early August, the latter time was, in fact, peak summer season. Each voyage was filled to capacity. That one of the *Queens* was missing a round voyage seemed to have little effect. Most passengers found the *Mauretania* to be a miniature version of the big *Elizabeth.*

In late 1957, the *Mauretania* was upgraded and given full air-conditioning. While Cunard was still the most dominant passenger firm on the North Atlantic, they would soon be facing more startling competition, namely rivalry from the new Dutch *Rotterdam,* Italy's *Leonardo Da Vinci,* West Germany's *Bremen* and, even more dramatically, from the French super-liner *France.* However, there was an even more potent rival: jet aircraft. Soon after the first commercial jet flights to London, in the autumn of 1958, ships like the *Mauretania* began to lose clientele and therefore revenue. She was, most unfortunately, among the first Cunarders to slip into the red.

In rather desperate efforts to keep her in service, she was repainted in Cunard's 'cruising green' in late 1962. Supposedly, she was to spend more and more time on the leisure circuit, sailing to tropic isles and exotic ports. More clearly, she was, by the early 1960s, an ageing ship. Her oversized stuffed chairs and glossy veneers contrasted sharply with a new generation of liners, 'floating pleasure palaces' of vast lido decks, pools, casinos, discos and shopping arcades. In 1963, in another survival tactic, she was placed on a Mediterranean service, sailing between Naples, Genoa, Cannes, Gibraltar and New York. Dominated by the sleek American Export and Italian liners, the old Cunarder barely made a trip more than half-full. It was becoming more and more discouraging.

A year later, there were further cruises—from New York as well as from Southampton, to the Caribbean, Bermuda, the Bahamas, West Africa and the Mediterranean. Having become even less profitable, the *Mauretania*'s last trip was, in fact, a cruise. She left New York on September 15 1965, on a 61-day trip to the Mediterranean, that terminated at Southampton. Passage fares included first class return on any other Cunarder, including the two *Queens*. Laid-up for a brief ten days and stripped of a few corporate keepsakes, the ship then set course for Inverkeithing in Scotland. Her final berth was the scrapyards.

Occasionally, in discussions of ocean liner history, she is still referred to as the 'new' *Mauretania*. The name *Mauretania* is still very well known and the two, quite different ships of the name still very well remembered.

Gross tonnage: 35,738 (1939); 35,677 (1947); 35,655 (1958)
Length overall: 772 feet
Width: 89 feet
Machinery: Steam turbines, twin screw
Speed: 23 knots
Capacity: 440 cabin, 450 tourist, 470 third (1939); 470 first, 370 cabin, 300 tourist (1947)
Built: Cammell Laird & Co Ltd, Birkenhead, England, 1939
Demise: Scrapped at Inverkeithing, Scotland, late 1965

Above right *Cabin class lounge aboard* Mauretania.
Right *From the crow's nest looking at the forward superstructure.*

Mauretania

Above *Finishing touches being put to* Mauretania—*April 11 1939.* **Below** *Painted with a green hull in 1963,* Mauretania *is on a run from Naples to New York* (courtesy of Cunard Line).

Cristobal

In the summer of 1939, three American-flag sister-ships—the *Ancon*, *Cristobal* and *Panama*—put into New York Harbor and won instant high praises for their degree of sleek modernity. They were the very essence of the 1930s streamlining. More recently, in early 1982, the *Cristobal* was scrapped at Brownsville, Texas, the last survivor of that old trio still under the Stars and Stripes.

The *Cristobal* was given a cheerful harbour welcome at New York in that otherwise tense summer of 1939. She berthed at Pier 64, at the foot of West 24th Street, which had been specially built for the three new sisters. Their owners, the Panama Railroad Company, would have a weekly sailing from Manhattan to the Canal Zone and relied not only on passengers, but on a substantial amount of cargo as well.

The *Cristobal* was designed by noted American marine architect George Sharp. He artificially eliminated the sheer (that sense of 'drooping' in a vessel's middle section), but instead created a well-balanced flow of decks, public lounges and cabins that gave the ship the ambiance of a shoreside hotel. The concept was, to some degree, an effort to have passengers forget that they were aboard a steamer, but instead remind them as closely as possible of land-side pleasures. Every cabin was convertible to a daytime sitting room, which was quite a novelty for 1939. All of them had private bathrooms while some even had private or semi-private verandahs overlooking the sea. The dining room was air-conditioned and an open-air tiled pool was on one of the aft decks. The decorations were done in strikingly modern styles, with a good use of metallic touches and balances. There were absolutely no heavy woods or dark furniture. In all, 216 passengers had full run of the first class spaces. Success seemed assured.

Commercial sailings were shunted aside by the end of 1941, when the *Cristobal* was recomissioned as a US Army transport. Her capacity jumped to over 2,000, with 'Standee' berths positioned throughout—even in the drained swimming pool! Her travels were suddenly diverse: the Pacific, Australia, transatlantic to Ireland and England, and troop landings at Casablanca and Normandy.

Cristobal

Then, with five years of heavy-duty military sailings behind her, she was converted in January 1946, at the Newport News Shipyard in Virginia, to carry 119 war brides and 101 dependent children. More military sailings followed. When finally decommissioned, she went directly to her builder's yard at Quincy, Massachusetts, to be refitted to her original luxurious self. Furniture came out of storage, a fresh crew was assembled and a new coat of commercial colours applied.

The Panama Line trio was as successful as intended. Sailings were on a 14-day schedule, either on Tuesday or Friday afternoon from New York to Cristobal with a stop at Port-au-Prince in each direction. Business was brisk not only with one-way passengers, but also with round-trip cruise travellers. However, one unusual aspect for American-based cruise-ships was that all passengers had to use shoreside hotels during stays in port due to the continuous loading and unloading of cargo By 1960, a fortnight's voyage on the *Cristobal* had a minimum fare of $350.

When aircraft and economic problems began to intrude by 1957, the *Panama* was the first to go. She was sold to the American President Lines and became their *President Hoover* for transpacific service from San Francisco and Los Angeles. Later, in 1965, she was transferred to the Greek flag for Chandris Cruises as the *Regina*. She spent some years in Mediterranean and Caribbean cruising

before finally being laid-up (in 1978) in an anchorage at Perama, near Piraeus in Greece, where she remains to this day.

The *Ancon* and *Cristobal* had four more years of service before being phased-out in 1961. The Grace Line thought briefly of taking the ships, but in the end found them incompatible with their then brand new *Santa Rosa* and *Santa Paula*. The *Ancon* was handed over to the Maine Maritime Academy and became their cadet training ship *State of Maine*. She was ultimately scrapped in New Jersey in 1973.

The *Cristobal* remained with the Panama Canal Company, although on a new 'government only' service between New Orleans and Cristobal. Her sailings were no longer advertised to the public. All but two of her lifeboats were removed, the public rooms and cabins stripped of furnishings and her certificate downgraded to a mere dozen passengers (more than 12 passengers onboard requires a doctor under International Maritime Law).

In July 1977, I [WHM] had the good fortune to visit the *Cristobal*, while loading Army cargo at Cristobal. She was, in few ways, the same liner of 20 or so years before. The main ballroom was completely bare except for the white walls and lino floor. Two smaller lounges remained, but were decorated in a hodge-podge of pre-war, post-war and contemporary pieces. Interestingly, the ashtrays were miniature smokestacks secured to the bulkheads. The bridge was museum stock: wooden wheel, overhead brass tubes, a mass of heavily-painted wires and portholes rather than windows overlooking the bow section. The former suites and adjoining verandahs were empty. The space for the 12 government-affiliated passengers was in six double-berth cabins, then recently modernised in formica, shag carpet and plastic lamps. The government of the Canal Zone was to use one of these rooms on the next sailing to New Orleans. The dining room, still in its original tiered design, was halved by an artificial wall. The *Cristobal* seemed to be more of a freighter than combination liner of the past.

During 1981, her final year of service, the *Cristobal* ranked as the oldest active vessel in the American Merchant Marine. Soon after, she finished her long career.

Gross tonnage: 10,021 (1939); 9,978 (1948)
Length overall: 493 feet
Width: 64 feet
Machinery: Steam turbines, twin screw
Speed: 17 knots
Capacity: 202 first (1939); 216 first (1948); 12 first (1961)
Built: Bethlehem Steel Co, Quincy, Massachusetts, 1939
Demise: Scrapped at Brownsville, Texas, early 1982

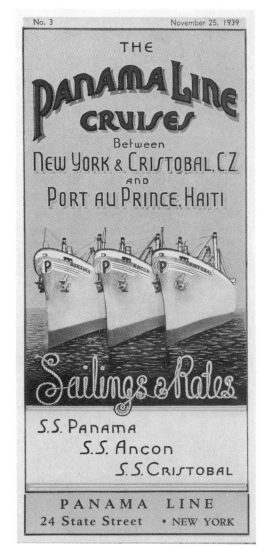

The cover of brochure No. 3 of the Panama Line, dated November 25 1939.

Right *Entering New York Harbor on her maiden voyage, August 12 1939.*

Right *During the war* Cristobal *was operated by the US Army* (courtesy US Army Signal Corps).

Right *Sailing with the aid of Moran tugs after being restored to peacetime dress after World War 2* (courtesy of Moran Towing).

La Guardia

In February 1983, Captail Daniel Zenicazelaya remarked, 'We expect the *Emerald Seas* [the one-time *La Guardia*] to last until 50. Her original American troopship construction, hull and engines blended with constant high maintenance will make this possible. Furthermore, the ship is now in the most profitable phase of her entire career—short-sea voyages with high passenger loads'. The *Emerald Seas* is presently one of the world's veteran passenger ships, now in her sixth life, sailing for an equal number of owner-operators. She ranks as the sole enduring American-built trooper from the Second World War.

The *General W. P. Richardson* was the ninth of 11 specially built wartime troopships, built between 1943 and 1945. At 17,900 gross tons each, they were given 'strong and powerful' appearances with two very large funnels placed rather close together, flared bows and very high hull formations. Without portholes for security reasons, they were among the earliest ships to be fully air-conditioned. The *Richardson* and her sisters were designed to take 5,200 troops each as well as 144,000 cubic feet of military cargo. The group—distinguished as the P2S2R2 type—were built practically in the confines of New York Harbor, at the Federal Shipbuilding & Drydock Yard at Kearny, New Jersey (located some 15 miles west of Manhattan Island and a facility that is now a scrapyard).

The *Richardson* was commissioned in November 1944, and assigned to the US Navy for trooping duties. She sailed mostly from the American East Coast, either to British or Continental ports, or to the Pacific via Panama. A native of Bilbao in Spain and the most recent Master of this vessel, Captain Zenicazelaya also mentioned, 'Occasionally, we have passengers on the present day *Emerald Seas*, who sailed aboard her as the *General Richardson*. Despite nearly 40 years, many memories are sparked.'

In February 1946, the *Richardson* was released from more pressing war duty, transferred to the US Army and given somewhat more comfortable accommodation during a 2½-month refit at the Todd Shipyards in Hoboken. Thereafter, she was assigned mostly to Mediterranean service, sailing not only with troops but with dependants, refugees and even some civilian passengers. The demands of the time were still quite strong. With a shortage of both Italian commercial tonnage and the virtual non-existence of American passenger ships on this run, the US government saw the important need for a more specific passenger operation between New York and 'the Med'. The *Richardson* was aptly selected for conversion—if not to a luxurious passenger vessel, then at least to a higher standard than as a troopship. Actually, this was to be a test case. It had been intended from their construction that several of the P2 class troopers be given over to commercial operators after the war. Among the plans were to have at least three converted for the United States Lines and possibly others for the Grace and Moore-McCormack Lines. In the end, however, no such plans ever came to pass. Only one other, the *General Gordon*, was partially modernised for civilian work, but then never to an active extent.

The *Richardson* was sent to the Ingalls Shipyard at Pascagoula, Mississippi. She was converted, at a cost of $5 million, to carry 609 commercial passengers, divided between 157 in first class and

452 in tourist. She was ready for service in May 1949. Quite sensibly, she was chartered (by the American government) to the American Export Lines, which had considerable experience in the Mediterranean. Prior to her inaugural run, she was given a new name: *La Guardia*, honouring New York City's beloved mayor, Fiorello H. La Guardia. At first, she sailed directly to Naples and Genoa, but later her travels were extended to include Gibraltar, Palermo, Piraeus and Haifa as well. She was considered a prelude to the new twin-liner express service that was being planned by American Export, using the 29,000-ton sisters *Independence* and *Constitution*, which were to be delivered in 1951.

However, while the *La Guardia* sailed with capacity loads of passengers in both directions, she was found to be impractical, simply too costly for commercial service. Her original design and operation had been created from the start with a military budget in mind. With double engine rooms and extra hull plating that caused additional drag, she consumed far too much fuel, even in the late 1940s. Within three years, *La Guardia* was returned to the government.

In December 1951, due to the Korean conflict, she was chartered to the Military Sea Transportation Service—the MSTS, for short—for further trooping. It appears that she was managed for a time by the American President Lines and wore their funnel colours. Also, she made several North Atlantic military runs, mostly to Southampton and Bremerhaven, but with United States Lines' colours. Then, with this phase of duty complete, she was laid-up in November 1952, in the James River Reserve Fleet in Virginia.

Two years later, the Hawaiian Steamship Company of Seattle expressed an interest in acquiring the idle vessel for California–Hawaii cruise service, offering direct competition to the very popular Matson liners on that run. Once the final arrangements were completed, the *La Guardia* was actually sold outright to Textron Incorporated and then chartered to Hawaiian Steamship. She was sent to the New York Shipbuilding Yards at Camden, New Jersey, and given another refit— this one costing $4 million—with all-tourist class accommodation for 650 passengers.

Renamed *Leilani* ('Lovely Flower'), her maiden voyage was set for January 1957, sailing from New York, via Panama, to her new base in California. The affair proved to be a near-catastrophe: the plumbing failed, some passenger cabins were flooded and then there was an outbreak of food poisoning among the passengers. The press reports were extremely damaging, such that the ship and her new service never fully recovered.

The *Leilani* worked the Hawaiian cruise trade for nearly two years, but again proved to be an expensive, uneconomic ship. In the end, she was operating for the Hawaiian-Textron Lines, with the Pacific Far East Line of San Francisco acting as general agents. Later, there was a rumour that she would be transferred to Mr Arnold Bernstein for his new American Banner Line service between New York, Zeebrugge and Amsterdam. It was planned that she would operate as a team with the 18,000-ton *Atlantic*, a converted Mariner Class freighter and with almost all tourist class accommodations. However, this scheme never materialised. The financially-ailing *Leilani* was laid-up at San Francisco in January 1959.

Offered for sale once again, she went to the American President Lines a year later as the perfect 'new' companion ship for the trans-Pacific services of the 19,900-ton *President Cleveland* and *President Wilson*. Specifically, she would replace the smaller and slower *President Hoover*, the former *Panama* of 1939, which had proved unsuitable to American President's needs.

The *Leilani*—now renamed *President Roosevelt*, in honour of both presidents, Theodore and Franklin—was sent to the Puget Sound Bridge and Drydock Company of Seattle for an $8 million refit. She was made into a luxurious, all first class liner—with high standard accommodation for only 456 passengers. She entered American President passenger service in May 1962, sailing between San Francisco, Los Angeles, Honolulu, Yokohama, Kobe, Hong Kong and Manila. From the start, she was very popular and received high praises on the standard of her decor and service. Later, she was detoured to considerable cruising— from three-day California coastal trips to two-weeks to the Mexican Riviera to 95 days around-the-world, which included periodic visits to New York. But, then once again, by the late 1960s, as the cost of passenger ship operations greatly increased, the *President Roosevelt* became a money-losing, expensive ship. Once again, she went to the auction block.

The Greek-flag Chandris Group were then keenly buying almost all adequate passenger tonnage, with a particular eye towards American hulls. The *President Roosevelt* was the perfect candidate. Sold for $1.8 million, she was registered to a Chandris holding company, Solon Navigation SA, but would be operated by the Chandris–America Lines for cruising in US waters. Renamed *Atlantis*, she was sent to Perama, near Piraeus in Greece, and was given yet another refit, this one costing $8.5 million. She was transformed into a very modern cruise liner. At the time, part of the Chandris success theory was to convert such ships at the company's own facilities at Perama, using Chandris staff and technicians, a rented warehouse, barges, portable generators and then limiting work and office spaces to the ship itself. In fact, the Chandris facility was nothing more than an anchorage. With such a self-contained operation, Chandris saved nearly 50 per cent of the ordinary conversion costs.

The vastly altered *Atlantis* re-entered service in June 1971. With a revised capacity of 1,092 maximum berths, she was assigned to a weekly cruise service between New York, Freeport (on Grand Bahama Island) and Nassau. During the winter, she would make fly-sail runs out of Freeport to ports in the Caribbean. However, neither operation was wildly successful, one of the first major blows to the otherwise contented Chandris empire. Again, now for the fourth time, the ship was on the sales lists.

Although there was the possibility of being chartered to Cunard for their seasonal New York–Bermuda run, she was, in fact, sold to the Eastern Steamship Lines of Miami. Eastern paid £13 million for the ship and included their 6,600-ton *Ariadne* in the trade. The *Atlantis* became the *Emerald Seas* under the Panamanian flag for Eastern; the *Ariadne* changed to Greek registry for Chandris and became the *Ariane*.

With her fuel-hungry engines still a nagging problem, the *Emerald Seas* was placed on the short-distance, overnight three- and four-day cruise trade between Miami and the Bahamas. The three-day cruises sail on Friday afternoons and call at Nassau; the four-day trips depart on Mondays for both Nassau and Freeport. More recently, a call at remote Little Stirrup Cay has been added.

Now, after over a decade on the Bahamas trade, the *Emerald Seas* seems to have at long last made great profits. To minimise her expenses, she sails at only 14–15 knots. Her capacity is limited to 960. Among her 380 crewmembers, there is representation from over 30 nations—including such diversities as Yugoslavian, Colombian, Canadian, Indonesian, Korean and Chilean. Greeks tend to fill out the deck and engine departments. Captain Zenicazelaya feels quite confident about the next decade of service, as the ship nears 50: 'She was built originally with very high standards, with excellent fireproofing and very, very strong hull plating. The one-inch thick plates are still almost like new.'

In early 1984, Eastern invested yet another $2 million in the ship. Assuredly, she has earned the distinction of having had more money spent in conversions and refits than any other passenger liner. The former *La Guardia* has a distinct place in ocean liner history.

Gross tonnage: 17,951 (1949); 18,920 (1962); 24,458 (1971)
Length overall: 622 feet
Width: 76 feet
Machinery: Steam turbines, twin screw
Speed: 20 knots
Capacity: 609 (1949); 650 (1956); 456 (1962); 1,092 (1971); 960 (1972)
Built: Federal Shipbuilding & Drydock Co, Kearny, New Jersey, 1944

Top right *As the troopship* General W. P. Richardson, *the first of six names, February 28 1945.*
Centre right *As* La Guardia *she boasted a large E for Export Line on each of her stacks and was chartered to American Export for their service between Italy and New York.*
Right *Sold to American President Lines for use in the Pacific, she was christened* President Roosevelt. *She is shown here entering New York on March 30 1966 during a world cruise.*

Left *An example of the simple, rather functional American shipboard decor of the 1950s and 1960s—the main lounge on* President Roosevelt *(courtesy of American President Lines).*

Left *The bedroom of one of the expensive* Lanai Suites *on* President Roosevelt *(courtesy of American President Lines).*

Below *Her sixth name is* Emerald Seas *and she is still in service at the time of writing* (courtesy of Eastern Steamship Lines).

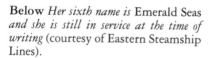

Caronia

In the immediate post-war years, the great Cunard Company laid plans to build a revolutionary liner, a ship designed almost exclusively for a relatively untapped passenger market—cruising. From the Liverpool headquarters, a large team of designers, decorators and technicians worked together to create yet another innovator to the mighty Cunard fleet. Officially, the new ship was said to be a transatlantic liner that would 'occasionally turn to cruising'. In fact, it was the reverse. Atlantic crossings would be at most periodic. However, the decorative staffs used a traditional ocean liner style (in fact, a late example of Art Deco), which was very much copied after the big *Queen Elizabeth*.

The new liner was named *Caronia*, a name taken from one of two very popular sisters, the *Carmania* and *Caronia* of 1905, which were scrapped in the early 1930s. The first hull plates were put down on February 13 1946, less than a year following the end of the Second World War, at the famed John Brown Yards at Scotland's Clydebank. Certainly, the John Brown Co was quite familiar with Cunard, having built not only the highly successful *Aquitania* of 1914, but both mighty *Queens* as well. Furthermore, in 1931, they created the brilliant *Empress of Britain* for Canadian Pacific, a dual-purpose ship that spent part of her year on long-distance, deluxe cruises. The new Cunarder copied this dual-purpose to some extent.

A young Princess Elizabeth and the Duke of Edinburgh travelled to the Clyde on October 30 1947 for the launching. Considerable publicity attended this new ship and there was assuredly a goodly amount of distinction and innovation. Primarily, the *Caronia* was Britain's biggest post-war liner, a luxurious symbol to an otherwise hardpressed, war-weary nation. (Realistically, while another smart creation of British shipbuilding genius, she was, in fact, aimed primarily at the American millionaire market.)

While Cunard might have painted her overall in tropical white, they again sought distinction. She was finished in four shades of green. It suited her design and unquestionably made for easy identification. In short time, she was nicknamed the 'Green Goddess'. She was also notable as the largest single-stack liner then afloat. Even her tripod mast was worthy of a mention. It was the tallest yet fitted to a ship. The aforementioned dual-purpose was a most practical development in ship design and soon to be copied by most major steamship firms. Incorporated into the *Caronia* was every possible luxury and amenity.

She was the first Cunarder to have a permanent deck swimming pool. This was a highly cherished facility, especially during her tropic cruises. Every passenger cabin had private bathroom facilities, another first within the Cunard fleet. Even first class in the *Queens* could not boast of such a distinction. Consequently, on those occasions when the *Caronia* ran two-class transatlantic sailings, every stateroom in both classes had full facilities. Furthermore, when she was divided into classes, according to regulation rules at the time, it was for first and cabin class. There was no tourist class. She was purely a high-grade liner, aimed at the 'upmarket' in sea travel.

The *Caronia* first left Southampton for New York, on January 4 1949. Soon after, she began cruising—first to the Caribbean and later on her intended long-distance voyages. She soon earned further nicknames: 'the millionaires' yacht' and 'the mink and diamonds cruise-ship'. Her sailings were consistent year after year. In January, she left New York on a three-month winter cruise, either to the Pacific, around Africa or completely around-the-world. Returning in May, she would then set off on a six-week Mediterranean–Black Sea cruise. In late June, she started a six-week Scandinavian

Caronia

voyage, which included the Norwegian fjord-lands, the Baltic and the northern capitals. This cruise usually terminated at Southampton, but fares included return first class passage in any Cunarder. Many loyalists preferred to wait for the *Caronia*. A month or so later, in September, she would cross to New York in preparation for two further Mediterranean cruises, one of about four weeks and the other of some two months. In December, she was back at Southampton, just in time for her annual overhaul. In January, the pattern began to repeat itself, beginning with a special Atlantic crossing via ports in the Caribbean.

1958 provides an example of the *Caronia*'s varied itineraries. She left New York on January 21, on a 108-day voyage that touched 23 ports in 17 countries and steamed over 34,000 miles. Minimum fares began at $3,200. She went south first to Trinidad, Bahia and Rio, and then crossed the South Atlantic via Tristan Da Cunha to Cape-town and Durban. From Zanzibar, she then set out across the Indian Ocean to Port Victoria, Bombay, Colombo, Singapore, Bangkok and Bali. In the Far East, she called at Manila, Hong Kong, Nagasaki, Kobe and Yokohama, and then sailed across the Pacific via Honolulu to Los Angeles and Acapulco. Following a transit of the Panama Canal, she went directly home to New York.

A spring-time Mediterranean cruise followed. Leaving New York on May 13, she set out for 38 days to Madeira, Gibraltar, Tangier, Malta, Piraeus, Dubrovnik, Venice, Catania, Messina, Naples, Villefranche, Barcelona, Palma de Majorca, Lisbon and then up to Cherbourg and Southampton (again, return to New York was included in the fare). Rates for this trip began at $975. On July 3, she departed for a 13,000-mile journey to Scandinavia. In 42 days, she called at Reykjavik, Hammerfest, the North Cape, Lyngseidet, Trondheim, Aandalsnes, Hellesylt, Merok, Bergen, Stavanger, Oslo, Stockholm, Helsinki, Visby, Zoppot, Copenhagen, Hamburg, Queensferry, Oban, Dun Laoghaire, Glengarriff, Le Havre and finally Southampton. Fares started at $1,100. The year's programme concluded with an autumn Mediterranean cruise to Madeira, Casablanca, Malta, Alexandria, Haifa, the Dardanelles, Istanbul, Piraeus, Dubrovnik, Venice, Catania, Messina, Naples, Villefranche,

Barcelona, Malaga, Gibraltar, Lisbon, Cherbourg and Southampton. Rates for this 52–day sailing began at $1,000.

The *Caronia* seemed to be nearly everyone's dream ship. She was very popular and especially distinguished as the most deluxe cruise liner afloat, although her image was slightly tarnished in April 1958. While outbound from Yokohama during her world cruise, she rammed a lighthouse on a local harbour breakwater and pushed it into the sea. Fortunately, there were no casualties, but the Cunarder's bow plates were twisted and she was forced into the American Naval Dockyard at Yokosuka for emergency repairs. Furthermore, although not revealed until later years, the *Caronia* was the first big Cunard liner to slip into the red (in the late 1950s). Her operational and housekeeping expenses were enormous and obviously exceeded her income. Often, she averaged only 400 passengers per cruise, but with a staff of over 600 and all of it aboard a fuel-hungry 34,000-tonner. Cunard did, however, subsidise her. She was still a prestigious name and the corporate image then counted at almost any expense.

Problems for the *Caronia* began to mount. In 1965, in an effort to glamorise the ageing ship, she was sent to the Harland & Wolff Yards at Belfast for a major refit. Parts of the passenger accommodation were redecorated and a more contemporary lido deck and pool built in the stern. The once unique Cunarder was now competing with a new generation of luxurious long-distance cruise-ships, which included the Dutch *Rotterdam*, Italy's *Leonardo Da Vinci*, Norway's *Sagafjord* and the Swedish *Gripsholm* and *Kungsholm*. Even some of the old loyalists, 'the *Caronia* set' as one passenger called them, deserted her for some of the newer ships. The situation was complicated by Cunard's very serious and worsening financial state. The transatlantic trade was steadily collapsing and a secure future seemed to be mostly in one and two-week Caribbean trips out of American ports. Could the 'queen of cruise-ships' make the transition and survive? Most likely not. With the flashy likes of the new 39,000-ton *Oceanic* of the Home Lines, the Norwegians, in particular, were planning a new, large fleet of ultra-modern cruise-ships—with saunas and discos, vast lido and several pools, and even some with cocktail bars fitted in their smokestacks! Along with the *Queen Mary*, Cunard directors decided to withdraw the *Caronia* in the autumn of 1967. On her last trip, from New York to Southampton, she crossed without passengers.

Offered for sale, her first buyers were Yugoslavian interests, who wanted to make her a hotel-ship along the Dalmatian Coast. The plan never quite materialised. The next bidders were Greeks, but with Panamanian registry, that were identified first as the Star Line and then the Universal Line. Monies were transferred to a rather depleted Cunard treasury in July 1968.

Renamed *Columbia* and then quickly changed to *Caribia*, she was sent to Piraeus and then Naples for improvements and repairs. In the following winter, she reappeared at New York, heavily advertised as being the former *Caronia*. The initial schedule called for two-week trips to the Caribbean. On the second of these, there was a serious engine room explosion off Martinique. The passengers had to be flown home and the stricken ship slowly towed back to New York. Therein began her sad, painful decline.

Her new Greek owners had their own financial woes. After some brief repairs at the Todd Shipyards in Brooklyn, the liner was laid-up, first in the Lower Bay, then at New York's Pier 86 (formerly the United States Lines' berth) and then finally at Pier 56 (a Cunard terminal until 1950). For several years, the former prestige Cunarder sat lifeless, rusting, seemingly abandoned. By day, there was hardly a sign of life or by night barely a light. A new generation of cruise-ships, such as the *Oceanic* and *Rotterdam*, sped past on their weekly relays to the tropics. There was, in fact, little hope for reviving the *Caribia*.

In February 1974, on a bitter winter afternoon, the innards of the otherwise unheated ship were opened to a curious and nostalgic public. Everything onboard that was even remotely removable was price-tagged and offered for sale. There were large pieces of wood panelling, dining tables and chairs, battered stainless steel utensils from the kitchens, even foot-stools and telephones. The sales were, in fact, quite brisk. The old *Caronia* was practically stripped bare. The unsold items were brought ashore and stored in Pier 56 (and then sold off at a later time).

Working on the bedroom of a main deck suite (courtesy of Cunard-White Star Line).

Two months later, in April, the ship was towed out of New York and bound for Panama en route to the ever-hungry scrappers of Taiwan. Her final months were not uncomplicated, however. At Honolulu, during the long, sluggish tow, leaks were reported. But it was at Guam that the *Caronia*'s final chapter was written. Seeking safety from a Pacific typhoon, she was being brought into the inner harbour waters for safety when high winds pushed her onto the local breakwater. Battered and lashed, she broke in three. Abandoned and empty, she began to sink. The scrappers of Taiwan would never see the *Caribia*. To the local authorities at Guam, namely the US Coast Guard, the wreckage was a menace. Quickly, salvage teams were brought in and removed the last pieces of the liner.

The legend of the *Caronia* as an innovative and distinguished cruise-ship remains. Many former passengers still recall her, often with a cozy fondness of a large private yacht. Indeed, she was one of the finest Cunarders of all.

Gross tonnage: 34,172
Length overall: 715 feet
Width: 91 feet
Machinery: Steam turbines, twin screw
Speed: 22 knots
Capacity: 581 first class and 351 cabin class; 600 first class for cruising
Built: John Brown & Co Ltd, Clydebank, Scotland, 1948
Demise: Wrecked on Guam, August 12 1974; remains later scrapped on the spot

Left Caronia *under construction* (courtesy of Cunard-White Star Line).

Below left *Escorted by Moran tugs she makes her maiden arrival at New York in 1949. She will dock at Pier 90 at the foot of West 50th Street, along 'Luxury Liner Row'* (courtesy of Captain Eric Ashton-Irvine collection).

Right *After running into a lighthouse in Japan,* Caronia *had temporary repairs made to her stem below the waterline—note the strange bend below the boot topping* (courtesy of Moran Towing).

Right *The Captain and his senior officers aboard* Caronia *in the late 1950s. Captain Eric Ashton-Irvine is seated, second from the right* (courtesy of Captain Eric Ashton-Irvine collection).

Below *Lashed by heavy seas and high winds, the former* Caronia *was thrown onto the breakwater at Guam and broke in three. Her remains had to be scrapped on the spot* (courtesy of US Coast Guard).

Himalaya

During the Second World War, the Peninsular & Oriental Steam Navigation Company Limited—the legendary P&O—lost several major liners. The relatively new *Strathallan*, one of the company's two largest liners, was gone. The very popular *Viceroy of India* was also sunk, along with two of the Bombay express liners, the *Rawalpindi* and *Rajputana*. Added to the casualty list of passenger ships were the *Cathay*, *Comorin* and the *Narkunda*. Consequently, the immediate post-war years saw an urgency for rebuilding. It was a new era with new demands for P&O.

The company had achieved enormous success with their 'white ships', the *Strathnaver* and *Strathaird* of 1931–32, the *Strathmore* of 1935 and then the final pair of sisters, the *Stratheden* and *Strathallan* of 1938. They were beautifully designed liners, with yelow-coloured stacks and all-white hulls (which supposedly lowered the onboard temperatures by as much as 10 degrees). They were all innovative and progressive. Each of the three designs had increased open-air deck spaces, which was so desirable on the steamy runs in the Mediterranean, Red Sea and Indian Ocean. The *Strathnaver* and *Strathaird* were, in fact, the first P&O liners to feature running water in every cabin. Sensibly, P&O directors and designers turned to the plans of these ships when thinking of a new post-war generation of liners.

There were other considerations and changes as well. The lucrative mail contracts of earlier days were gone by the late 1940s, secured by long-distance airliners. The once-important link to India, especially to Bombay, had also disappeared. In view of Indian independence, a special service between London and Bombay was no longer a necessity. Instead, the Australian liners would call at Bombay on their runs to Fremantle, Melbourne and Sydney. Furthermore, the war had brought about new technology, strides and a new sense of direction in passenger shipping. With the appearance of the aeroplane as something of a competitor, liners would need to be faster, to offer more frequent and efficient services. Onboard comfort and convenience had to be improved as well. The blueprints for the first post-war P&O liner therefore had to include the best concepts of the earlier 'Straths' as well as some innovations.

This new ship was launched as the *Himalaya* from the Vickers-Armstrong Yards at Barrow-in-Furness, on October 5 1948. P&O decided to give this new liner her own identity and therefore abandoned the continuation of the 'Strath' names. The design would be modified as well. There would not be a main-mast. This design balance had been used just before the war, in 1939, in two sizeable liners, Nederland Line's *Oranje* and Shaw Savill's *Dominion Monarch*. Statistically, the *Himalaya* would be larger than the largest of the *Straths*, the 23,700-ton *Stratheden*. The biggest P&O liner yet built, she would be nearly 28,000 tons.

Her passenger accommodations would not only be larger but represent some fresh ideas on configuration. Compared to the 530 first class and 480 tourist class berths in the *Stratheden*, she would carry 758 in first class as compared to only 401 in tourist. Obviously, P&O envisioned a rise of first class traffic, namely wealthy tourists, merchants and business people, successful Australians and those quite familiar upper-level civil servants. Tourist class was left for the budget tourists and some migrants. The bulk of the migrant trade would, in fact, be handled by some of the older liners, some of which were only moderately converted from wartime troop service.

The *Himalaya* left the London Docks on October 6 1949, bound for her four-week maiden voyage to Sydney. She used the traditional routing: London, Gibraltar, Port Said, Aden, Bombay, Colombo, Fremantle, Melbourne and Sydney. There was considerable press attention for this new P&O flagship. She had reached a rather astounding 25.18 knots on her trials, an impressive figure over her intended 22 knot service speed. She was also the first company liner to have air-conditioned cabins, although this was limited to the deluxe suites and some inside first class rooms. She followed the introduction made by the pre-war *Straths* of having air-conditioned restaurants in both classes. Even her cargo capacity was noteworthy. Being just short of 450,000 cubic feet, it was the largest ever fitted to a P&O liner and remained so to the very end of her days.

In Peter Padfield's fine *Beneath the House-flag of the P&O*, published by Hutchinson & Company of London in 1981, he quotes Captain D. G. H. O. Baillie: 'The first thing to strike me about the *Himalaya* was her size. There was a sports deck as large as a field, a midship lounge filled with acres of sofas, chairs and tables, a vast air-conditioned dining saloon which reminded me irresistibly, in the hush between meals, of a low-ceilinged cathedral, about which the white-coated stewards flitted like devoted acolytes. There were vistas of gleaming alleyways, stretching into apparent infinity.'

Captain Baillie had very special feelings for the *Himalaya*: 'My next strong impression was the *Himalaya*'s undoubted atmosphere—a quality produced more tangibly to the cubic foot in a ship than in any other object constructed by the hands of man. The *Himalaya* was always very special. Being the first P&O liner to be built after the war and therefore a symbol to us all of returning luxury and normality, there had always been lavished on her a very great deal of care, attention and affection.'

Ocean liner connoisseur C. M. Squarey was aboard a special introductory mini-cruise in the English Channel, in October 1949, and was also delighted with this new P&O liner: 'In designing and decorating this ship, her owners have, seemingly, studiously avoided producing anything sensational (realising, obviously, that one doesn't have to be sensational to progress) preferring instead to create a ship of which it can justly and proudly be said that she is thoroughly good throughout, and in the process of being that is also beautiful. Just as "good wine needs no bush", so this ship will need no fanfares to sell her—her merits will make her. I feel she fits rather aptly these words of Sally Bruce Kinsolving:

Ships, young ships,
I do not wonder men see you as women,
You in the white length of your loveliness
Reclining on the sea.

The first class accommodation, all of it, is delightful: the main lounge, a room of beautiful propor-

tions, taking my fancy in particular. The adjoining rooms, the library on the starboard side, the Australia room on the port side, are charming; the paintings of Australian scenes in the latter room should come in for much admiration, and there will be many who covet them. The tourist class accommodation sets a standard that will, I think, score a lot of marks amongst Australian travellers and, indeed, make some people wonder whether first class is worth the difference—in other words, it is very good. Another distinct feature of the ship is her sports area on the top deck where there are nine deck tennis courts, well spaced out, as well as ample room for every other form of deck game; it will certainly be the scene of many good tournaments and a great joy to others who play for the sheer fun of the game. There is also an elaborate telephone service throughout the ship, with every first class cabin having its own 'phone, and if the switchboard operator is efficient (she was) and has a pleasant voice withal (she had), it should make for distinctly good service.'

The *Himalaya* settled down to a highly popular, profitable life. She was the model for the next three P&O liners: the 24,200-ton *Chusan* of 1950, but which returned to having a main-mast, and then a pair of near-sisters, the 29,700-ton *Arcadia* and *Iberia* of 1954. Along with the *Straths*, these ships provided excellent service to Australia as well as

considerable cruising. Some sample cruise itineraries and fares for 1959 included: the *Iberia* for 24 days on May 30, from London to Teneriffe, Havana and New York, with two-class fares starting at £81; the *Himalaya* for 17 days on June 12, from London to Gibraltar, Venice, Palma and Lisbon, with fares from £71; and the *Chusan* for 13 days on August 22, from London to Leghorn, Malta and Lisbon, starting at £54.

In the mid-1950s, P&O—along with the affiliate Orient Line passenger ships — began to extend their service operations to the entire Pacific. This area was thought to be a new, untapped, highly profitable market by the P&O management. In 1958, the *Himalaya* inaugurated a new service from Melbourne, Sydney, Auckland and Wellington via other Pacific ports to Vancouver, San Francisco and Los Angeles. A year later, she began another new P&O link, from the North American West Coast via Honolulu to Yokohama, Kobe, Hong Kong and Manila. By 1960, as the new P&O flagship, the 45,700-ton *Canberra*, was being readied, P&O spanned the world. Liners such as the *Himalaya* touched at over 100 ports on five continents, and regularly used both the Panama and Suez Canals.

There were some specific changes for the *Himalaya*. In 1959–60, during a major refit at Flushing in Holland, she was made fully air-conditioned. All of the other P&O liners were undergoing similar alterations. At the end of 1963, when she was rapidly becoming one of the oldest members of the combined P&O–Orient fleet, the *Himalaya* was made all one-class with a total of 1,416 berths. In October 1969, she made the last P&O liner sailing from the London Docks. Thereafter, all of the ships would use Southampton. It was the break of a long, historic link between the Port of London and the traditional ports east of the Suez. It was, however, merely another of the rapid changes then affecting world shipping and the major sea ports. Increased economies in operation became more and more essential. There were further changes ahead.

Captain Philip Jackson, who served aboard the *Himalaya*, recalled, 'By the early 1970s, we were faced with some major decisions. Ships like the big *Oriana* and *Canberra* of 1960–61 were built primarily for the fast UK–Australia emigrant service. Then, quite suddenly and most dramatically, Mr Boeing's jumbo jet appeared in regions like Australia, the South Pacific and the Far East. We abruptly lost the bulk of our trade. Our passenger ships, including the ageing *Himalaya*, were sent roving around the world (including more frequent trips to North American shores) looking for business. In fact, it was rather quickly apparent that the older liners would have to go. Their good life's work, their economic well being, had ended. The original P&O–Orient Lines became P&O Cruises in 1973.'

The *Himalaya* followed the *Iberia*, *Chusan* and *Orcades* to the scrappers at Kaohsiung, Taiwan, in November 1974. The *Orsova* arrived a month later. The ships were stripped, run aground deliberately on local shores and then signed-over to the dismantling firm. Within months, they would be chopped-up and their remains recycled, often into the likes of razor blades and Japanese motor cars. Fortunately, many former staff and passengers still have very fond memories of grand liners like the *Himalaya*.

Gross tonnage: 27,955 (1949); 27,989 (1963); 28,047 (1969)
Length overall: 709 feet
Width: 91 feet
Machinery: Steam turbines, twin screw
Speed: 22 knots
Capacity: 758 first class and 401 tourist class (1949); 1,416 one-class (1963)
Built: Vickers-Armstrong Shipbuilders Ltd, Barrow-in-Furness, England, 1949
Demise: Scrapped at Kaohsiung, Taiwan, 1974–75

Above right *The newly-built* Himalaya *arrives at Circular Quay in Sydney with the famous Harbour Bridge in the background. The year is 1950* (courtesy of P&O Group).
Right *Under misty skies* Himalaya *departs London's Tilbury Docks in September 1969 just as P&O moved its liner operations to Southampton. She is bedecked in flags to signal this historic but rather sad occasion* (courtesy of P&O Group).

Above Himalaya *and* Iberia *together in Tilbury Docks for the last time* (courtesy of P&O Group). **Below** *In her final years* Himalaya *became an especially popular and beloved cruise ship sailing from Southampton as well as from Sydney* (courtesy of Mike Lennon).

Independence

For as long as I (WHM) can remember, my interest in the Hawaiian islands has been to cruise there in the traditional way: five days from California in one of those grand, white-hulled Matson liners. In 1973, part of the dream was crushed when Matson pulled out of the passenger business (they are still in freight) and passed their last two liners, the very popular *Mariposa* and *Monterey*, over to the Pacific Far East Line, another American shipping company, but one unaccustomed to passenger operations. Problems—especially financial ones brought on by expensive American labour and the rising cost of fuel oil—set-in quickly. By 1978, just as the US government discontinued its desperately needed subsidy monies, these last Hawaiian liners were withdrawn.

Two years passed without steamship service to Hawaii, despite it being one of the most logical cruise routes on earth. The American authorities insisted that only US flag tonnage could work the service, but since there were no available American liners left in service what was the rationale? Foreign cruise lines would have been more than happy to detour their ships, but instead had to sit this one out. Inter-Hawaiian is inter-American and, just as the Atlantic and Pacific coasts are affected, only American ships can carry passengers from one US port to another.

In 1980, a ray of hope came in the form of Mr C. Y. Tung, the Taiwanese freighter and tanker billionaire with strong American connections (including some astute, well paid resident lobbyists in Washington). Among other mothballed former liners, Tung had the *Oceanic Independence* sitting without work in a tiny alcove south of Hong Kong and was anxious to see her in service again, especially in the wide open Hawaiian market. But there were some initial problems.

The *Oceanic Independence* was the celebrated American Export liner *Independence* of 1951, a great favourite on the transatlantic circuit in the 1950s and 1960s. She and her sister *Constitution* were the Star Spangled alternatives on the otherwise Italian Line-dominated sunshine route to the Mediterranean. The American team worked a three-week express run, travelling between New York,

Algeciras, Naples, Genoa and Cannes. Exceptionally popular with American tourists, they also developed a strong following from the Italians, many of whom were immigrants and who wanted to cross the North Atlantic for the first time on a ship flying the red, white and blue. One Italian woman, who was leaving her native Rome in 1955, selected the *Independence*. 'The ship had an excellent reputation in Italy, but also, I wanted to practice my English before reaching New York.'

The *Independence* and *Constitution* were the first and only large liners built for the American Export Lines, a firm which ran a quartet of combination passenger–cargo ships in the 1930s and then the converted troopship *La Guardia* in 1949. They were, in fact, inspired by two post-war reasons. There was a huge gap in passenger liner service to the Mediterranean, especially since the Italians had only four surviving liners, two of which were destined for the South American trade. Obviously, there were very pressing needs. Furthermore, and possibly even more importantly, the US government was deeply impressed by the use of large liners as troopships during the Second World War. Feeling the threat of a possible third world conflict in the late 1940s, several liners were designed in commercial disguise, but actually as

Independence

201

high-capacity, readily convertible troopers. Amidst the streamlined design and functional decoration of the new American Export twins was the distinction of being convertible to 8,500-plus troopships within 48 hours. Fortunately, the call to duty never came.

The *Independence* was one of the most frequent sights in New York Harbor in her two decades under the US flag. She frequently appeared in newspaper photographs of groups of liners berthed along 'Luxury Liner Row'. Berthed at Pier 84, at the foot of West 44th Street, which was the southernmost of the 1,100-foot long finger piers, she was either the first or most distant of the grouped luxury liners. It all depended on the position of the aerial photographer.

The *Independence* (and *Constitution*) were also rather unique in that they were among the very few liners that were given their annual overhauls within New York Harbor. Each winter, they were berthed at the Bethlehem Steel Shipyards, at the foot of 56th Street in Brooklyn. Other American liners, such as *United States* and *America*, always travelled to the Newport News Shipyards in Virginia. In later years, the American Export sisters would use another Bethlehem facility, instead at Hoboken. Also, they often 'sat out' slack winter periods at the American Export freighter terminal in Hoboken. At the Third Street Pier, which was once used by the Hamburg America Line for their giant *Imperator* and *Vaterland*, the *Indendence* might be berthed for several weeks in empty silence. However, each evening, she was floodlit totally. Rising well above the pier sheds, she had a glittering majesty, the unmistakable quality of the huge ocean liner.

In later years, the *Independence*—like so many other fading transatlantic queens—began to cruise with greater frequency. Periodically, she appeared at such diverse ports as Casablanca, Istanbul and Odessa, and then Aruba, Nassau and St Thomas. It was not until the mid-1960s that the *Independence* began to show alarming losses, another victim of the unbeatable and defiant competition of the jetliner. Within three years, by the autumn of 1968, she would be out of service. There was even a last ditch effort to save her by offering 'go go cruises'—a mod' sunburst painted along her sides, the creation of 'Art Disco' interiors and seven-day

cruises to the Caribbean for $98 sans food! It failed quickly.

The *Independence* was sent to a quiet backwater of Baltimore and laid-up—forlorn, rusting, somewhat anachronistic in the new age of the cruise-ship. She was eyed by some wealthy Europeans (Chandris and the Lauro Line being among the group), all of them thinking of possibilities like cruising, the Australian immigrant trade or as a permanently moored hotel. However, it was Mr Tung who offered the first real downpayment in 1974. Shortly after, the ship raised steam (for the first time in some five years) and headed for Hong Kong.

She reached the East, however, just in time to catch the first major oil crunch. Once again, she was despatched to some offbeat anchorage. A year later, Tung had a brainstorm: cruising from South Africa to the Seychelles, South America and even the Far East. Except for a brief charter to the Portuguese government with some of the last Angolan colonials, the *Oceanic Independence* (as she had been renamed) did not impress the accountants. She went back to Hong Kong, for further lay-up and thought on her future. During 1976, some rich oil consortium wanted her for use in the Middle East as a hotel-recreation centre for its well paid, but tired drilling and rig crews. There would be movies, a bowling alley, even a full casino, and in readiness Tung renamed the ship as *Sea Luck I*. Then, at the last moment, the deal collapsed and the ship never left Hong Kong. What to do next?

The withdrawal of those last American cruise-ships from the Honolulu run seemed the perfect opening. But first, there were those legal problems. Most obvious, the *Oceanic Independence* was no longer an American ship, but had Liberian registry for tax and other purposes. That law about only American-flag ships being used on the Hawaiian service was not about to be changed and so, as part of the plan, Tung offered a completely refurbished ship (then nearing her 30th birthday) that would comply with every possible US Coast Guard safety and sanitary standard. The liner was despatched to the Kawasaki Shipyards at Kobe and was invaded by teams of American designers and Japanese work crews that spent months—and millions of dollars —on the rejuvenation. Huge containers arrived from the States filled with telephones and carpets, tableware and even the latest lifejackets.

Tung proceeded on the legal side by having the ship registered under his daughter's name, she being the American citizen required for ownership, to a specially created firm called the American Global Line. Quickly thereafter, American Hawaii Cruises opened an office in San Francisco for administration and passenger sales. But, Washington was still sceptical. It would be the first time that a major liner had left the American register, been foreign flag and then returned. The final instrument of persuasion seems to have been the promise that some 300 job-pressed US crewmen would suddenly have work. The offer was just too tempting. With great Union cooperation, the *Oceanic Independence* was allowed to re-hoist the Stars and Stripes.

The liner arrived at Honolulu for the first time in June 1980, to begin a new seven-day year-round service to Hilo, Kona, Kahului and Nawiliwili. A warm reception included a long line of local officials, flag waving spectators, fireboat sprays and even a formal Hawaiian blessing. Although the first three sailings were sell-outs, the initial gamble was substantial. The company expected to show losses as high as $5 million over the first two years, especially as 'teething problems' were worked out and a sound reputation developed.

I made the fourth cruise, with only 376 passengers aboard. Although I had visited the ship quite often in the 1960s, she was never quite as handsome or as well decorated as in this new service. The corridors were bright and made good use of cheery colours so as to appear even larger. The carpets were fresh and smelled so. There were handsome glass and brass lamps overhead. All the signs and cabin numbers included the new American Hawaii logo. The main foyer consisted of a reception area, some bold modern paintings and a stainless steel sculpture as a centrepiece. Colour and arrangement throughout made for a warm setting.

The public rooms totally defied the ship's actual age. Excellent quality contemporary furniture was placed about in a most gracious manner and the artwork included some traditional American scenes: Alexander Hamilton, historic Boston, Gold Rush clippers. One lounge had an antique Chinese table, which was surrounded by lacquered

Sailing as Oceanic Independence *for American Hawaii Cruises she is arriving at Honolulu for the first time in June 1980 (courtesy of American Hawaii Cruises).*

chairs with red velvet seats. The biege carpeting was overlaid by an exquisite Oriental rug. The bars were traditional trendy: multi-coloured velour or vinyl chairs, mirrored walls, sleek counters with stools and low-standing smoked glass tables.

The popularity of the *Oceanic Independence* soon rose and she began averaging 700 passengers per cruise well into 1981. In the following year, her sister-ship, also in Tung hands, was reactivated. Known as the *Oceanic Constitution*, she was revived as the *Constitution*, rekindling her glory days as an Atlantic liner. Shortly thereafter, the *Oceanic Independence* was renamed as *Independence*. Both ships now work the Hawaiian cruise trade full-time. A superb pair of liners have found new, profitable careers.

Gross tonnage: 30,293 (1951)
Length overall: 683 feet
Width: 89 feet
Machinery: Steam turbines, twin screw
Speed: 23 knots
Capacity: 295 first class, 375 cabin class and 330 tourist class (1951); 405 first class, 375 cabin class and 330 tourist class (1959); 950 one-class (1975); 721 first class (1980)
Built: Bethlehem Steel Co, Quincy, Massachusetts, 1951

Above *Her forward stack with American Export's new colours is hoisted into position at the fitting out berth of Bethlehem Steel shipyard.* **Below** Independence *(left) and* Constitution *stern first in Genoa.*

Above *In 1960 she was painted white. Her whistle is saluting as she passes the Statue of Liberty outward bound.* **Below** *Grotesque and horrible to many ship lovers, yet some people liked it. This is what Wall Street Cruises did to* Independence *when they operated her briefly.*

Kungsholm

The Swedish American Line first began to build their own brand-new passenger ships in 1925, with the *Gripsholm*. Three years later, they added the still larger *Kungsholm*. Handsomely decorated and comfortably furnished, these ships—having developed very strong followings on both the transatlantic trade and in one-class cruising—led to the company's biggest ship of all, the 29,000-ton *Stockholm* of 1938. But here the Swedes encountered a rather incredible stroke of misfortune. The new flagship was totally destroyed by fire while still at the shipyard.

A successor, with the very slightest refinements, was soon ordered, but she too never joined her intended owners. Soon after launching in March 1940, and with the Second World War underway, the ship was seized by her Italian shipbuilders and then finished as the troopship *Sabaudia*. She was later bombed and sunk at Trieste during an Allied air raid in the summer of 1944. For the Swedish American Line, new tonnage would have to wait, at least until after the war.

The Line was quite quick to order a new passenger ship (launched in September 1946), but, in fact, decided to limit their plans to a rather small 11,700-ton combination liner. She too was named *Stockholm*. Although a clever balance of passenger and freight, this vessel seemed far from the original intention of her owners. At best, she was a supplemental ship, built in the austere and conservative late 1940s. It was not until 1951 that the company again turned its attention to a sizeable new liner, a national flagship and a dual-purpose ship that could easily swing from some eight months on the North Atlantic to four months in tropical cruising. Like all of the Swedish American liners, with the exception of the smaller *Stockholm*, she could not be built in home waters, but instead had to be built at an overseas yard.

Among the Europeans, the Dutch were then sufficiently recovered from the devastation of the war and had resumed their large shipbuilding industry. They had recently completed the new flagship of the Norwegian America Line, the *Oslofjord* of 1949, and were soon to deliver two new transatlantic liners for Holland–America and three specialised migrant ships for the Argentines. Certainly, they could build a very high standard ship for Swedish American. The order with the De Schelde Shipyards at Flushing was signed and work on yet another *Kungsholm* was begun. The keel was laid on January 20 1951.

Named by Sweden's Princess Sybilla at the launching, on October 18 1952, the new liner was soon fitted out as one of the finest ships of that diminishing post-war era. While medium-sized, at 21,100 tons and exactly 600 feet overall, the ship had one of the finest profiles in this final era of twin-stackers (the ship's forward funnel was, in fact, a dummy ventilator). The forward of her twin masts was placed above the bridge, the bow was raked sharply and the ship painted overall in Swedish-American's attractive white and yellow colouring. The twin funnels included the blue discs that encircled three golden crowns. The Swedish flagship looked attractive from every angle.

Spread about the ship's six passenger decks, the public rooms had an almost pre-war dignity about them. There were glossy veneers, brass and crystal, wood murals and even a wood-burning fireplace. The first class rooms included a winter garden, drawing room, smoking room, verandah, cocktail bar, writing room-library, a club room, library and dining room. For tourist class, there was the main lounge, ladies' lounge (itself, a pre-war feature), library, smoking room, verandah and restaurant. There was also a 200-seat theatre and a health centre that included an indoor tiled pool, gymnasium and Swedish saunas. For her cruises, an outdoor pool was fitted into the aft cargo hatch.

Her passenger cabins were among the finest to be found on the 1950s North Atlantic route. They were all outside, a very distinctive 'first' for a transatlantic ship. All had adjoining private bathroom facilities (even in tourist class) as well as ship-to-shore phones and adjustable air conditioning. The rooms (again, even in tourist class) were quite large when compared to other liners.

Arriving at New York for the first time in December 1953, the *Kungsholm* crossed between

Gothenburg, Copenhagen, occasionally Bremerhaven and New York. Her first cruises were winter voyages to Bermuda and the Caribbean, but, beginning in January 1955, she made an annual three-month deluxe trip. With her capacity limited to 450 guests, she would alternate her itineraries from winter to winter: around-the-world, the South Seas and Far East, around Africa or even a combination of South America, Africa and Europe. She very quickly developed a devoted following, which included equal numbers of well known celebrities and millionaires. Her great popularity and profit soon prompted a successor, the similar-looking *Gripsholm* of 1957.

The highly reputed Swedish American Line had the *Kungsholm* fully refitted and modernised during a $1 million refit in the autumn of 1961. She had to be totally competitive, especially in the demanding, but enlarging cruise industry. As her transatlantic schedules decreased in the face of the jetliner, her cruise voyages were extended. In 1964, soon after returning from an 88-day around-the-world cruise, she set out on a new venture, a 'Spring-time in Europe' cruise, lasting 36 days and with fares that began at $1,250. Her ports of call were unusual: Villagarcia, La Coruna, Santander, Pauillac, Le Verdon, Lorient, Le Fret, Brest, Guernsey, Le Havre, Rotterdam, the Isle of Wight, Weymouth, Plymouth, Tresca, Waltham, Anchorage, Llandudno, Brodick, Ayr, Craigendoran and Tarbert. Immediately booked to capacity, the cruise was promptly made an annual Swedish American offering.

With its almost constant emphasis on new, more sophisticated tonnage, the Swedish American Line built yet another new *Kungsholm* in 1965–66. She would come from the John Brown yards on the Clyde and, with her twin domed funnels, was easily recognisable as an updated version of her predecessor. Unfortunately, the older ship became superfluous and had to go to the block. Very quickly, she was sold to the North German Lloyd (for some $8½ million), supposedly to replace their *Berlin*, the former *Gripsholm* of 1925. The Germans could not have bought a better ship.

Renamed *Europa* and introduced first in January 1966, the ship was to spend a few summer months on the North Atlantic run to New York, out of Bremerhaven, Southampton and Cherbourg, and then cruise mostly to the Caribbean for the remainder. She was again a very well-run, profit-making ship. However, the Atlantic sailings were soon cut to a mere two or three a year. In 1971, when the North German Lloyd merged with its one-time rival, the Hamburg American Line, to create Hapag-Lloyd, among the first decisions of the amalgamation was to end entirely the historic passenger run to New York. Thereafter, only cruises would be offered.

Captain Heinz-Dieter Schmidt, who served aboard the *Europa*, recalled this period of change: 'Our flagship, the *Bremen* of 1939, was burning 420 tons of fuel a day and therefore was becoming increasingly expensive, a problem complicated by the continuous breakdowns with her ageing French-built turbines. Most regrettably, soon after our final transatlantic sailing, in December 1971, we had to sell her, to the Chandris Group, who would sail her as their *Regina Magna*. We wanted to continue in American cruising with the beautiful *Europa*, but then ran head-on into new, very strict marine regulations with the US Coast Guard. The *Europa* could not pass. Another disappointment, but we had to withdraw from American service entirely.

'In 1973, we very much wanted to buy the financially-ailing *Hamburg*, a 24,900-tonner from 1969, to resume New York cruising and sell-off the *Europa*. Unfortunately, there was a last minute disagreement over the price with the German Atlantic Line and the ship went instead to the

Launching a ship which many believe to be the most beautiful of her era and which has been one of the most successful—the Kungsholm *of 1953.*

Soviets, becoming their *Maxim Gorki*. Ironically, she has been used ever since in the German luxury market, on year-round charters to the immense Neckermann Travel Company of Frankfurt. To this day [1984], she remains a very luxurious, superbly maintained ship.'

The *Europa* cruised mostly from either Bremerhaven or Genoa. Her voyages were as deluxe as they were long. In summer, she went northward to Scandinavia and the Baltic; for the remaining months, she travelled to the West Indies, South America, the Mediterranean, around Africa and even out to the Far East. Well into her third decade of service, she still maintained that impeccable image. Captain Schmidt recalled, 'We had a 70 per cent repeat factor with the *Europa*, which included a club-like atmosphere and even an inner circle of German millionaires. There were rumours that membership requirements included the wives having at least $1 million in jewels. However, in the mid-1970s we began a series of studies and tests for a new, deluxe liner. She was approved finally and became the *Europa* of 1981.'

The previous *Europa*, the former *Kungsholm*, was sold to Costa Line of Italy, but assigned to a special subsidiary company and registered in Panama. Renamed *Columbus C.*, in deference to the famed North German Lloyd liner *Columbus* of the 1920s and 1930s, the ship continued with her summer schedules out of Bremerhaven and then further voyages from Genoa and also in South America. Most unfortunately, this has been her last career. In July 1984, while attempting to arrive at the Spanish port of Cadiz in high winds, she rammed the outer breakwater. Seriously holed, she made the dock just in time to safely land her 1,000 passengers and crew, but then capsized against the open pier. While tugs eventually righted her, she then settled in an upright position. Damaged, flooded and surrounded in an oil boom, the *Columbus C.* was declared an economic loss. Her next voyage will most likely be to the scrapyards.

Gross tonnage: 21,141 (1953); 21,514 (1966)
Length overall: 600 feet
Width: 77 feet
Machinery: Burmeister & Wain diesels, twin screw
Speed: 19 knots
Capacity: 176 first class, 626 tourist class (1953); 122 first class, 721 tourist class (1966); later changed to 769 one-class
Built: De Schelde Shipyards, Flushing, Holland, 1953
Demise: Badly damaged at Cadiz, Spain, July 1984, and declared an economic loss

Above *The brand new* Kungsholm *at Flushing, Holland.* **Below** *A beautiful night time view of a very beautiful ship* (courtesy of Swedish American Line).

Above *Now called* Europa, *with white hull and blue bands around it as well as a new Hapag-Lloyd stack insignia, she was a cruise favourite.*

Left *Stern view of the ship, now in her third life as the Italian-owned, Panamanian-registered* Columbus C *of the Costa Line (courtesy of Luis Miguel Corriea).*

Bergensfjord (1956)

The Norwegian America Line was never quite in the 'big leagues' of North Atlantic passenger shipping. Instead, beginning in 1913, they opened a comfortable, moderate and rather slow service between Oslo, Bergen, Kristiansand, Halifax and New York. Their first passenger ships—the *Bergensfjord* and *Kristianafjord*—were a mere 11,000 gross tons. The 12,900-ton *Stavangerfjord* joined in 1918, but then 20 years elapsed before another liner came to the firm, this being the 18,600-ton *Oslofjord* of 1938. Overall, however, the company developed a fine reputation and a steady following.

Following the Second World War, the sole-surviving *Stavangerfjord* ran the transatlantic service singlehandedly for over four years. The new motorliner *Oslofjord*—carrying the same name as the 1938 version, but which became a war loss two years later—first appeared in late 1949. She was designed on contemporary patterns of the day: two-thirds of her year on the North Atlantic run and the remainder in sunshine cruising. The two ships, although quite unmatched in style and years, performed well and produced encouraging profits.

By the early 1950s, with the war becoming more and more of a distant memory, the European tourist business grew steadily. The Atlantic ferry was in its most successful period of all time. Passenger ships were filled on almost all voyages and in both directions. In addition, the American cruise business was growing steadily. The company felt—like many other shipowners—that even better days were yet ahead and ordered a new dual-purpose liner. The building order was signed with the famed Swan, Hunter & Wigham Richardson Yards at Newcastle (all Norwegian American

liners have, in fact, been built outside of Norway). It was formally announced that this new ship would replace the beloved, but ageing *Stavangerfjord* (a plan later scrapped as this latter ship survived until 1963, aged 45). Her Royal Highness Princess Astrid travelled to Newcastle for the launching and, on July 18 1955, christened Norway's new merchant flagship as the *Bergensfjord*.

The press were extremely enthusiastic about this new liner. She had the largest aluminium superstructure yet to be given to a European ship. Specifically, the use of aluminium reduced her tonnage by 500 tons and created greater passenger spaces. Her decorations and accommodation was of a particularly high standard, with a good use of blonde veneers and national artwork, but always in keeping with her owner's priorities for general comfort and warmth. The bulk of the passenger spaces—most unlike all previous company liners—were given over to tourist class, the ever-growing money-maker on the North Atlantic. There were 785 berths in tourist against a mere token 100 in first class. Furthermore, the tourist berths were hardly austere, certainly a far cry from the days of cramped, crowded below-deck quarters. All of the tourist cabins were fitted with private toilets and 90 per cent had either bath or shower. Additionally, the *Bergensfjord* was made fully air-conditioned (especially useful for warm weather cruising) and was given a set of fin stabilizers. The latter equipment was then just coming into fashion, particularly after successful installations on Cunard's giant *Queen Mary* and *Queen Elizabeth*. The Norwegian liner also had a good

Bergensfjord (1956)

sized indoor pool as well as a portable deck pool, which was fitted into an aft cargo hatch for cruising.

The *Bergensfjord* left Oslo—although her home port was, quite fittingly, at Bergen—on May 30 1956, on her maiden crossing to New York. She met with immediate praise and success. Six months later, she ran her first cruises: to Bermuda, Nassau and the West Indies. Later, with the appearance of the jet, these cruises became more diverse and more frequent: to the Mediterranean and Black Seas, the North Cape and Baltic, around South America or Africa, the Pacific and even special three-month trips around-the-world. She developed a special reputation in the cruising arena and became a familiar sight passing through Panama or Suez or crossing the Equator or the Arctic Circle. During her cruise trips, her capacity was reduced to an intimate 420, all first class. With her 18,500 tons, she became something of a large, cosy yacht.

Norwegian America's next flagship, the *Sagafjord*, first appeared in the autumn of 1965 and therefore relegated the *Bergensfjord* to 'second ship' status. More and more, as the older ship, she represented the changing conditions for ocean liners: less transatlantic service and more cruising. In the end, by the late 1960s, she sailed alone between New York and Oslo.

In early 1971, Norwegian America ordered yet another new liner, a 24,000-tonner that was, in fact, an improved version of the highly acclaimed *Sagafjord*. This new flagship was due in the spring of 1973, timed so that the *Bergensfjord* would then be sold-off. However, such plans were rather suddenly advanced.

The French Line had lost their *Antilles* by fire in the Caribbean, in January 1971, and were in urgent need of a replacement. Although listed in Norwegian America schedules and with her successor still two years off, the *Bergensfjord* was sold for a sum greater than her owners could refuse. She transferred to the Tricolour (in March 1971) and was renamed *De Grasse* (*Louisiane* had been the initial choice). Almost immediately, she entered a French shipyard for a six-month refit and refurbishing that included creating all new first class spaces for 581 passengers.

Unfortunately, soon after entering the regular liner service between Le Havre, Southampton and the Caribbean islands in November 1971, the ship met only with the slightest success. The old trade demands had fallen away, another lost battle with jet aircraft. The French Line worked hard, however, to create a more profitable alternative schedule, namely West Indies cruises out of San Juan, Puerto Rico. These sailings were heavily marketed in the United States. Furthermore, there were European cruises: summer Scandinavian trips from Le Havre and then Mediterranean, Black Sea and North African runs out of Cannes. Unhappily, none of these proved satisfactory either. The *De Grasse*'s fate was finally sealed by staggering fuel and labour costs. By the autumn of 1973, she was put on the sales lists.

At first, there was talk that she would become an Israeli hotel and casino ship. However, and most surprisingly, she was sold back to the Norwegians—her owners were listed as Thoresen Limited. She was registered at Singapore and renamed *Rasa Sayang* (translating to 'Flower of the East'). She was then the first and only liner in her owner's fleet and was intended to sail a new cruise trade. Manned by Norwegian officers, but with an Eastern hotel staff, she was assigned to 14-day voyages out of Singapore to Indonesian and South Pacific islands (later, her sailings were extended to include Hong Kong, Manila and Whampoa in mainland China).

The *Rasa Sayang*'s cruises became quite popular for a time and were linked to diverse air–sea packages not only from Europe but from North America as well. However, all was nearly lost when, on June 6 1977, she caught fire at sea and was seriously damaged after being abandoned by both passengers and crew. For a time, she was adrift, wallowing off Port Dickson, before a towline was arranged. She was later taken to a Singapore dockyard for repairs. Briefly, she resumed cruising, but the press received as a result of the fire killed off much of her remaining popularity and reputation. She was laid-up in June 1978, returning once again to the block.

The 22-year-old ship was bought by the voracious Greeks—a Cypriot-registered company called Sunlit Cruises Limited. Renamed *Golden Moon*, it was thought that she would be used in the Eastern Mediterranean. However, after arriving in Greek waters, she was sent to Perama Bay, to a lay-up berth alongside numerous other exiled liners. Nested in a row at a rather quiet dockyard, some of her immediate neighbours included the former United States Lines' *America*, the former Matson *Lurline*, the one-time Furness Withy *Ocean Monarch* and yet another rusting veteran across the bay, the bankrupt Greek Line flagship *Olympia*. Although a curious, intriguing collection of passenger ships, they represented a rather sad sight.

In the spring of 1979, the *Golden Moon* was to be chartered to a Dutch travel firm, who wanted her, as the *Prins Van Oranje*, for cruises from Rotterdam. This project never materialised. A year later, she was to be leased to the Soviet-owned CTC Lines, who wanted her for Pacific service out of Sydney under her earlier name of *Rasa Sayang*.

Evidently this charter was secure, but, on August 27 1980, while undergoing repairs, she was swept by fire. Her charred, twisted hull had to be towed to Kynosoura and deliberately sunk. Her half-submerged remains poke above the local waters to this time.

Gross tonnage: 18,739
Length overall: 578 feet
Width: 72 feet
Machinery: Stork diesels, twin screw
Speed: 20 knots
Capacity: 126 first, 726 tourist (1956); 590 first (1971)
Built: Swan, Hunter & Wigham Richardson Ltd, Wallsend-on-Tyne, England, 1956
Demise: Engine room fire on August 27 1980 and then deliberately sunk at Kynosoura, Greece

Heading for Norway to begin her maiden voyage (courtesy of Norwegian America Line).

Bergensfjord (1956)

Above *Steaming proudly into a fjord the new beauty shows off her superb lines to an aerial photographer.*

Left *Sold to the French Line, she became* De Grasse. *The French Line stack colours of black and cherry red fit her streamlined funnel to perfection.*

Left *In 1979 the former* Rasa Sayang *was laid up at Perama, Greece, in company with a mixed collection of merchant shipping, still looking streamlined and modern (courtesy of Antonio Scrimaldi).*

Rotterdam

Holland America - Line's 36,667-ton *Nieuw Amsterdam* of 1938 was one of the most popular, profitable and beloved ocean liners of all time. Initially, there was talk of a sister-ship or comparable running-mate. Such a plan was shelved, first because of the lingering economic woes of the Depression and then due to the outbreak of the Second World War. When commercial services resumed in the late 1940s, the Dutch company took a conservative approach in looking over the future of transatlantic liners. Instead of an equally-sized running-mate for the *Nieuw Amsterdam*, Holland America built twin 15,000-ton tourist ships, the *Maasdam* and *Ryndam* of 1951–2. That conservatism continued. Soon afterwards, a larger tourist ship was added, the 24,200-ton *Statendam* of 1957. It was not for 21 years, until 1959, that the superb *Nieuw Amsterdam* had a proper counterpart. This was the *Rotterdam*, Holland America's new flagship and, ironically, their last Atlantic liner.

Just as Her Majesty Queen Wilhelmina had named the earlier ship, her daughter, Queen Juliana, went to the same Rotterdam Drydock Company yards for the naming of this Dutch masterpiece. She went down the ways on September 13 1958. A year later, with a future queen aboard, Crown Princess Beatrix, the liner crossed to New York for the first time. After the Princess had been transferred in the Lower Bay to a waiting Dutch warship for the final few miles to Manhattan, the *Rotterdam* steamed majestically into port, surrounded by a flotilla of tugs, fireboats, ferries and pleasure craft. She was sparkling on a superb late summer's day: a well-shaped, all-grey hull, white upperworks, yellow lifeboats and a single radar mast above her bridge.

Her overall look was uniquely different, however. While Moore McCormack's *Argentina* and *Brasil* of the year before used twin aft uptakes and a dummy funnel, the *Rotterdam* used only the uptakes. She had absolutely no customary funnel device. A few ocean liner loyalists were quite shocked at first. A raised section of short decks, placed in the exact centre of the vessel's topmost section, seemed to be created for a large single stack. Many thought this was so and that the actual design was changed near to completion. This was not true. The *Rotterdam* was created from the start as an innovative, striking ship. She was the first Atlantic liner to do away with the funnel completely. This also meant that Holland America's familiar green, yellow and white stack colours were eliminated. The uptakes were painted in white with grey and black tips. Like Cunard's *Caronia*, which was coloured thoroughly in very distinctive shades of green and therefore always recognisable, the same could be said for the 'stackless' *Rotterdam*. As Moran tugs berthed the Dutch liner on that September afternoon, there were a number of significant changes ahead, both for the ship and her owners. First, and soon after disembarking her passengers, the ship was moved across the Hudson River, from the company's Fifth Street terminal in Hoboken, where they'd been for some 90 years, to a brand new three-berth pier that was still under construction in Lower Manhattan. This was the beginning of the slow transition and then decline of New York Harbor's ocean liner berths. Holland America left Hoboken permanently in 1963 and then remained at the new pier until 1974. Then, like all others in the cruise trades, they shifted to the six-berth West Side Passenger Ship Terminal, which opened in November 1974. When the *Rotterdam* first arrived in New York, there were 60 liner berths. Now, when she makes her annual winter world cruise call, there are only six.

The jet aircraft made its first commercial flight a year before the flagship's maiden crossing and within months, airlines secured 63 per cent of the trade and then steadily increased their grasp. While Holland America and others had considerable faith in the future of the Atlantic service, it was indeed fortunate that the *Rotterdam* was designed as a dual-purpose ship, with her off-season winters being spent on far more lucrative cruises. During her first winter (1959–60), and along with the usual Caribbean island sailings, the ship made two long cruises, one around continental South America and the other to three continents, Europe, Africa and South America. In January 1961, she established a more regular pattern: annual three-month world cruises.

At this time (1985), the *Rotterdam* has made more around-the-world luxury cruises than any other major liner. To date, she has made 23 such trips (the smaller *Veendam* was experimentally tried for one substitute trip in the mid-1970s but this has not been repeated). Overall, it is equivalent to nearly 2,100 cruising days. With passengers averaging $10,000 per person in fares over these years, the estimated revenue to ship is between $150–170 million. Quite understandably, these voyages now have something of a 'clubby' atmosphere about them, with many passengers joining the trip each year.

World cruising is perhaps the most demanding of all ocean travel. The high number of repeat passengers is coupled with an extremely well-travelled clientele. Consequently, the Holland America managers must revise the ship's itinerary each winter. While very popular ports are repeated, others must be deleted (or at least dropped for a few years) and new calls inserted. Added attractions off the more familiar routes have included Devil's Island, Safaga in Egypt, Pusan in South Korea and Cabo San Lucas in Mexico. For her January 1985 world cruise, the *Rotterdam* travelled for 87 days from New York and then Port Everglades, Florida, to Cartagena, Cristobal and the Panama Canal, Acapulco, Cabo San Lucas, Los Angeles, Honolulu, Manila, Hong Kong, Bali, Singapore, Kuala Lumpur, Colombo, Bombay, Safaga, Suez, Port Said, Haifa, Istanbul, Yalta, Odessa, Piraeus, Dubrovnik, Venice, Malta, Lisbon and then homeward to New York. For these voyages, her capacity is especially limited to 730.

In the early years, the *Rotterdam* was paired for her transatlantic sailings, between New York, Southampton, Le Havre and Rotterdam, with the venerable *Nieuw Amsterdam* and the handsome *Statendam*. They were known as the 'Big Three', making a New York departure each Friday afternoon, from April through October. However, by the mid-1960s, with the Atlantic seasons being cut more and more, and then just to the peak summer months, ships such as the *Rotterdam* increased their cruising schedules. Mostly, she has been used in a similar series of cruises, 10- and 11-days to the Caribbean and, in later years, seven-days to Bermuda and Nassau. The original 1,456 berths in two classes, first and tourist, has been rearranged to 1,109 berths, all one-class. Holland's flagship made her final visit to the homeland in 1969. Thereafter, she cruised year-round.

The *Rotterdam* has proved to be another strong, solidly-built Dutch liner. She has withstood a number of ferocious Atlantic storms, been nearly

The 'Ritz Carlton Room' on the new liner.

flooded and lost while in drydock at Lisbon and then was 'hammered' by a near-tidal wave at Casablanca. In 1984, as the ship approached her 25th birthday, her former Master proudly said that she had at least eight more years of service ahead.

The *Rotterdam* is presently the lovingly regarded '*grande dame*' of the world cruise-ship fleet. She has the two-deck high restaurants, the sweeping stair-wells, the luxurious Ritz Carlton Nightclub and a series of finely decorated public rooms that are all reminiscent of an earlier era in ocean travel. She was among the last big ships to make extensive use of rare and imported woods, national art and a rich ethnic overtone. She remains as the Holland America flagship, but of a vastly changed fleet. Her running-mates are two 33,900-ton twins, the *Nieuw Amsterdam* and *Noordam* of 1983–84.

While the *Rotterdam* continues with her annual world voyages, which will include her 'Silver Jubilee' sailing in January 1986, she spends her summers at Vancouver, cruising the Inside Passage to such Alaskan ports as Ketchikan, Juneau and Sitka. In the autumn, she sails from Port Everglades to the West Indies. Few passengers seem to come away disappointed. In a recent survey of North American cruise-ships, the 25-year-old *Rotterdam* scored in the first five. Certainly, she is one of the finest and most successful liners of all.

Gross tonnage: 38,645 (1959); 37,783 (1973)
Length overall: 748 feet
Width: 94 feet
Machinery: Steam turbines, twin screw
Speed: 20.5 knots
Capacity: Variable from 580 first class and 809 tourist class to 301 first class and 1,055 tourist class (1959); 1,109 all-one class (1969)
Built: Rotterdam Drydock Co, Rotterdam, Holland, 1959

View of Rotterdam *from a docking tug* (courtesy of Moran Towing).

Above *In March 1963 Holland-America moved to a new three berth terminal at Houston Street, Manhattan. Here the* Nieuw Amsterdam *is at the top, the* Westerdam *along the outer end and* Rotterdam *in the lower slip* (courtesy of Vincent Messina collection). **Below** *Holland-America's Silver Jubilee World Cruise in 1983—*Rotterdam *transitting the Panama Canal* (courtesy of Holland-America Line).

Leonardo Da Vinci

The Italians certainly produced some of the best looking (and most modern) ocean liners of the 1950s. It was a sensational rebirth for their greatly diminished fleet that survived the Second World War. The government owned Finmare Group controlled the four major passenger firms, the Italian, Adriatica and Tirrenia lines as well as the Lloyd Triestino, and consequently there are some similarities. A succession of beautiful ships began with the regally handsome *Augustus* and *Giulio Cesare* of 1951–52, then seven sisters and near-sisters for the Lloyd Triestino named *Australia*, *Neptunia*, *Oceania*, *Africa*, *Europa*, *Asia* and *Victoria*. Smaller than the transatlantic ships, they were superbly handsome with domed single stacks and masts perched above the bridge.

The exquisite sisters *Andrea Doria* and *Cristoforo Colombo* of 1953–54 reached for a new peak in ocean liner design. Assuredly, they are among the most attractive looking passenger ships ever built. As a refinement of the Lloyd Triestino design, the new Adriatica Line flagship *Ausonia* of 1957 had a modern majesty about her. However, perhaps the most beautiful and appealing of all these ships came, in fact, at the end of the decade. She was the *Leonardo Da Vinci*.

Laid down on June 23 1957, the *Leonardo Da Vinci* was an unintended ship, coming about primarily as a replacement for the tragic loss of the *Andrea Doria* 11 months before, on July 25–26. The Italian Line's Mediterranean–New York passenger business was booming and the sisters *Augustus* and *Giulio Cesare* had to be temporarily brought over from their South American run (to Rio, Santos, Montevideo and Buenos Aires) to fill the gap. Even the veteran *Conte Grande* and her near-sister, the *Conte Biancamano*, made peak season trips to New York. Italian Line directors realised the urgent need for a replacement for the *Doria*—in fact a need for an even bigger, more luxurious liner.

They re-examined the blueprints for the *Doria* and the *Cristoforo Colombo*. Though fine ships, some alterations were in order. Most obviously, the aft cargo space would be eliminated completely and used instead to create more popular lido deck space

with no less than six swimming pools, one of which was specially infra-red ray heated for cooler weather use. Also, there would be far more private stateroom plumbing. In fact, all of the first and cabin class rooms would have at least private showers and toilets while as much as 80 per cent of the tourist space would be similarly fitted. Although fitted with high power steam turbine machinery, the designers opted for a touch of what was thought to be the projected future. The *Da Vinci*'s engine spaces were said to be readily (and easily) convertible to nuclear power at 'some time in the 1960s'. In all respects, the new liner—the national flagship—was a floating showcase for Italian technology, design and decoration.

Launched on December 7 1958, from the Ansaldo Yards at Genoa (who had also built the *Doria* and *Colombo*), the *Leonardo Da Vinci* reached New York for the first time on a bright summer's morning in July 1960. There was an official escort to her West Side pier of tugs, fireboats, pleasure craft and harbour ferries. Whistles bellowed in salute. There was an official greeting, a ceremony-filled luncheon, a gala night-time banquet (which included huge floodlights being flashed on the ship from shore) and then an open house to the general public (a mere 50 cents was charged for the benefit of the Italian seamen's fund). The Italian Line was accurately proud of their exquisite new flagship. The tragedy of the sunken *Andrea Doria* was largely erased in the minds of Atlantic travellers.

The *Da Vinci* developed enormous popularity, in fact a loving rapport with her Mediterranean passengers, even as the 45,900-ton super-sisters

Michelangelo and *Raffaello* first appeared in the spring and summer of 1965. Having been on the express run between Naples, Genoa, Cannes, Gibraltar and New York, the *Da Vinci*'s itinerary was thereafter extended to include such other ports as Lisbon, Casablanca, Palermo, Boston (eastbound only) and Halifax (westbound only). Repainted with a white hull in February 1966, following the standard set by the two new larger liners, she was also sent on periodic winter cruises. Although made mostly to the tropic ports of the Caribbean, her most unique voyage was a 41-day trip in February 1971 that took her to the Caribbean, through the Panama Canal and out to Hawaii.

However, by the early 1970s, cruising had become more and more of her employment, especially as the Italian Line's transatlantic passenger figures began a swift, merciless decline. It was jet competition once again. Embarrassing news articles hinted of more staffmembers onboard than fare-paying passengers and all the while the Italian government, as owner of the entire Italian Line operation, was subsidising ships like the *Da Vinci* at a rate of $700 for every passenger carried. How could the job-pressed, financially-ailing Italian government in Rome continue with this irrational, impractical arrangement?

The *Leonardo Da Vinci* was selected to finally close out the Italian Line's transatlantic passenger run in June 1976. The passengers were all but gone completely. She sat idle for a time, awaiting some further reassignment. The government was pressured by the heavily unemployed region around Naples to restore the ship and thereby provide some 600 jobs. In July 1977, she was given over to the newly formed Italian Line Cruises International, a temporary offering at best, for the short-distance Miami–Bahamas trade. The management of the ship was passed to the Costa Line, a family-owned business based at Genoa that was fast becoming the biggest cruise operator in the Western World.

Little was, in fact, done to the *Da Vinci*'s original accommodation except that her overall capacity was reduced from 1,326 in three classes to 900 in a single, cruise class. However, the old sparkle, the glory and the prestige were gone. It was hardly the same. She proved far too big and

costly (her fuel bills were staggering) for such a service. Scarred in rust and with neglected maintenance, she was withdrawn. On September 23 1978, she was laid-up at an anchorage at La Spezia, south of Genoa and quite close to the biggest scrapyard in the Mediterranean.

She was, of course, the object of considerable rumour and many proposals. Some Italians wanted her as a national exhibition ship, others for use as a floating casino along the Thames and still others for a revived '1930s style' cruise-ship. It all failed to materialise. The ship sat—silent, lonely, rusting. There was continued pressure from the Italian seamen's unions to rebuild the ship for more lucrative cruising and thereby offer yet further subsidised employment.

Then, most tragically, on July 4 1980, the otherwise idle *Da Vinci* burst into flames. In four days, she was reduced to a scorched shell, a battered remnant of her former luxurious self. Caught in a rather morbid curiosity, thousands of Italians flocked to the shores of La Spezia to see their former flagship burn to death. The sky was covered in thick blankets of smoke as the fire reached the fuel tanks. Tugs were finally able to fix lines to the ship and then towed her to the outer harbour. She was deliberately scuttled in 40 feet of water, canting over at a 60 degree list. What a ruinous sight!

At the end of 1981, the ship was righted and carefully brought into La Spezia to be scrapped. David L. Powers Jr went aboard her remains in the following August. Some of his observations were described in a very thorough article entitled 'A Final Visit to the *Leonardo Da Vinci*', in the autumn 1983 issue of *Steamboat Bill*, the journal of the Steamship Historical Society of America:

'The *Leonardo Da Vinci* was a desolate sight, moored about 100 yards off shore, covered with rust, with a slight list. Already the crews were at work and sparks fell from their torches. It was now August and, from the bow to the bridge, the workers had cut their way down to the Foyer Deck, and from the bridge back, down to the Promenade Deck. The entire funnel casing was still standing, with exhaust pipes exposed and while the fore half of the funnel had already been removed. It was in this area that work was now being concentrated.

'I was taken out to the ship in a rowboat. The entrance to the liner was in a tiny cut on the B deck level and reached by a series of rickity ladders tied to the ship by several ropes. It did not look safe. I had a sickening feeling while climbing the ladder since I dread heights. But, the excitement and opportunity of being able to board the *Leonardo Da Vinci* overcame my nervousness. We inched our way upwards three decks to the Upper Deck through the forward crew's access stairway. It reeked of smoke and was cluttered with debris, including cans containing that special green paint that had been used to touch-up the green band on the white hull. Upon reaching the open deck, I was confronted with piles of rusting metal, crew bunks and assorted pieces of the massive anchor machinery. Walking aft, I peered down into the main cargo hold where each set of deck doors was standing in an open position. Here and there a porcelain shower or bathtub stood out of the ruins.'

By the end of 1982, the *Leonardo Da Vinci* was finished-off, the end to one of the finest looking liners ever built.

Gross tonnage: 33,340
Length overall: 761 feet
Width: 92 feet
Machinery: Steam turbines, twin screw
Speed: 23 knots
Capacity: 413 first class, 342 cabin class and 571 tourist class
Built: Ansaldo Shipyard, Genoa, Italy, 1960
Demise: Destroyed by fire, July 4–8 1980, at La Spezia, Italy; scrapped during 1982 at La Spezia

Her maiden arrival in New York.

Above left *Impressive view of* Leonardo Da Vinci *in drydock at Genoa.* Above right *An aerial view of the new ship.* Below *In 1977 she was used in the Caribbean under the colours of Italian Line Cruises International. These were ill-named and unsuccessful attempts to keep this costly ship sailing* (courtesy of Everett Viez collection).

Oriana

Britain's Orient Line had a long history of producing some very fine liners. In more recent memory are the handsome twin-funnel 'O Boats' of the 1920s, the *Orama*, *Oronsay*, *Otranto*, *Orford* and *Orontes*. But far more notable was a pair brought into service in 1935–37, the sister-ships *Orion* and *Orcades*. To the Australian service, they brought the decorative splendour of the North Atlantic liners. They were sumptuously fitted in then trendy Art Deco styles, using light woods, swirl carpets and sweeps of etched glass. They were by far the most modern liners on the 'Down Under' trade, even surpassing rival P&O's reputable *Strath* liners. So impressed was another competitor, the Shaw Savill Line, that they ordered something of a carbon copy—the beautifully furnished *Dominion Monarch* of 1939.

After the Second World War, the Orient Line seemed to pay slightly more attention to the externals of their new liners. The *Orcades* of 1948 was the first big liner to group her mast and funnel closely together and have them perched above the bridge. It was a handsome, practical and easily distinguishable arrangement. The *Oronsay* of 1951 used the same general concept, but perhaps even more attractively. Then, in 1954, for their flagship *Orsova*, the Orient Line decided to be totally innovative: the conventional mast was discarded completely. Wireless and necessary rigging was attached between the forward kingpost and the ship's large single funnel. In looking back over two decades of passenger ship design, between the mid-1930s and the mid-1950s, one might easily see the progression from the *Orion* (1935) to the *Orcades* (1948) to the *Oronsay* (1951) and finally to the *Orsova* (1954). Together, they made a very handsome fleet.

Soon after the *Orsova*'s delivery in May 1954, the respective boards of the P&O and Orient lines, which had begun to merge their passenger services, took a serious look at the future. Certainly, the Australian trade—particularly the tourist and migrant trades—had a very bright future. Then, there was the Pacific (the Far East, the North American West Coast and even the appealing Pacific islands), which to the twin firms

was 'the last frontier' of ocean liner travel. It was indeed time to build the biggest liners yet for a service other than the Atlantic. Design teams were put to work and bids sent out to various shipbuilders. Quite quickly, the Orient Line had agreed with an old friend, the Vickers-Armstrong Shipbuilders at Barrow, for the largest, fastest and, ironically, their last liner.

The general design was of another innovative, unique, easily distinguishable and, to some, an eccentric ship. Quite clearly, she was a successor to the *Orsova*. In fact, the earliest designs showed the new liner with one stack. She is, in fact, a single-stacker, but the aft ventilator (which is different in shape, being circular rather than oval) appears to be a second stack. More unusually, however, is that the forward funnel stands well above the aft ventilator/stack. Much like the *Orsova*, the funnel is therefore the highest feature of the ship. A stumped radar mast is placed forward, standing about eye level with the ship's bridge.

Everything about the new liner had to be very special. The name *Oriana* was selected, primarily because it had never been used in the Orient Line fleet before. Historically, it is the name given to Queen Elizabeth I by her court poets. She ranked as the biggest liner ever built in England (larger British ships had, in fact, come from either Scotland and Northern Ireland) and was given a royal launching, on November 3 1959, by Princess Alexandra of Kent. Her steam turbine machinery was such that she would be the fastest ever to

Australia. A year later, in November 1960, during her trials, she reached an amazing 30.64 knots as compared to her projected 27.5 knot service speed. Her trial speeds were, in fact, greater than those of Cunard's mighty *Queen Elizabeth*, then the largest liner afloat.

Quite accurately, it was estimated that the *Oriana* was the first new liner that could substitute for one of the Cunard *Queens* with absolute ease. She could quite readily make Southampton to New York in five days. On her maiden run, she cut the passage time between Southampton and Sydney via the Suez from four to three weeks and, in doing so, gained the coveted Golden Cockerel Award for the fastest passage to Australia. To this day, a golden cockerel is placed above the *Oriana*'s bridge. Much like the *United States* and the Blue Riband, it is most unlikely that another passenger vessel will take the honours.

The *Oriana* was designed for the swift delivery of tourists and migrants to Australia. Her decor and general styling were also considerate of other tourists, namely North Americans, who would be using the ship in the Pacific. The first class accommodation included a number of suites and spacious staterooms that were especially suited to passengers who might stay aboard for as long as two or three months. (At least one couple broke some records by living onboard for 15 months!) Designed not only for fast runs to Fremantle, Melbourne and Sydney, she was scheduled from the start to travel to such Far Eastern ports as Singapore, Hong Kong, Kobe and Yokohama, and then across the Pacific to Vancouver, San Francisco, Los Angeles and Acapulco. Alternatively, instead of returning to Britain via the Suez, she sometimes passed through Panama and called at Kingston, Port Everglades, Nassau and Bermuda before returning to Southampton.

She was especially designed for fast turnarounds in port and, in this consideration, was fitted with a rather limited cargo space. Even her lifeboats were different. They were placed in a position some 27 feet lower than on any other Orient liner and were stowed inboard, using under-deck davits. Beginning with her maiden trip, in December 1960, she made a fascinating sight: the yellow stacks, white upperworks and a sleek hull in Orient Line's distinctive corn colour.

P&O introduced their big liner a year later. She was, of course, the 45,700-ton *Canberra*, which came from the Harland & Wolff Yards. She was quite different: twin uptakes aft instead of conventional stacks, turbo-electric drive and a large sports and pool deck amidships. While the *Oriana* was always a dash faster, the *Canberra* was the larger and with a higher capacity. However, they were a team in a general sense. Just as the *Oriana* was delivered, the two firms merged their passenger services as the P&O–Orient Lines. This relationship lasted until 1966, when the last Orient Line houseflag was hauled down on the *Oriana*. Thereafter, all ships became part of P&O, which had reverted to its singular name. Presently, since all of the previous Orient liners are now scrapped, the *Oriana* is the sole survivor of that original fleet. A plaque commemorating this distinction is mounted aboard the *Oriana* in a foyer just behind the open-air stadium.

Like the *Canberra*, the *Oriana* had a very profitable first decade. However, in the early 1970s, with the startling intrusion of both the jumbo jet (which snatched most of her passengers) and the container-ship (which grabbed her cargo), she was suddenly out of work. Most of the older P&O and former Orient Line had no alternative but the scrapyards of Taiwan. Ironically, in later years, especially in the late 1970s, even the annual 'line voyages' to and from Australia were sometimes difficult to book fully. Times had indeed changed. Escaping the obvious possibility of the scrapper's torch, the *Oriana* (and the *Canberra*) were converted to one-class in 1973 (previously, both had been divided between first and tourist class) and transferred to a new corporate arm, P&O Cruises Limited. Thereafter, the two giant liners cruised mostly from Southampton, to ports in the Mediterranean, West Africa, the Canaries, Spain and Portugal, the Norwegian Fjords, the Northern Cities and even across the Atlantic to the Caribbean islands.

Co-author Miller was aboard what was perhaps one of *Oriana*'s most unusual cruises, which was set for August 1979. In three weeks, she travelled from Southampton to Reykjavik in Iceland, remote Cornerbrook in Newfoundland, Halifax in Nova Scotia and then down to American waters, to Boston and New York. She was given a fireboat maiden reception at New York and, following a two-day stay, then sailed directly homewards to Southampton. In the following year, she repeated a similar transatlantic pattern, but continued into the St Lawrence and visited Quebec City and Montreal. Now, nearly 25 years after their creation, there are very few world ports that have not been visited by the *Oriana* and *Canberra*.

At the end of 1981, the *Oriana* left England forever. She made her final 'line voyage' out from Southampton, through Panama, to the American West Coast and then southward to Australia. She has swapped places with the 27,000-ton *Sea Princess*, the former *Kungsholm* of 1966. The larger ship has been cruising from Australia ever since.

Ranking as the fourth largest cruise-ship afloat until early 1984, the *Oriana* has a special sense of enormity. Along with four outdoor pools (with one just for children) and a series of tiered decks, she has the open-air feel of a giant aircraft carrier. Vast deck spaces were, of course, a strong consideration of her original design, for sweltering passages in the Mediterranean, Suez, Red Sea and Indian Ocean.

In height, the *Oriana* appears to be a floating skyscraper. She's immense. She has 11 passenger decks: Tennis, Bathing, Stadium, Verandah, A, B, C, D, E, F and G. There's even an outdoor perch above the Tennis deck and positioned just above the bridge, which is especially delightful for port arrivals and departures, or more specifically, for dipping under the Sydney Harbour Bridge.

The Stadium deck includes the 'Lookout Bar', possibly the ship's best public room, with scoop swivel chairs that have a panoramic view of the bow and ocean ahead. Following, there's an open-air stadium, now used for impromptu Australian cricket and some serious deck quoits, and then an indoor card room and gymnasium. One large suite, known as 'the flat' which has its own doorbell, and several verandah cabins are also on this deck. Just below, on the Verandah deck, are the main public rooms: the library, 'Princess Room' (for lectures, demonstrations, bingos and quizzes), twin galleries, the 'Plymouth Room' (for night-time floor shows), the popular 'Monkey Bar' (with twin verandah alcoves) and the more informal 'Ocean Bar-Disco' (which face onto an open deck, a pool and the hamburger and beer bars).

The first class pool, one of four on Oriana *(courtesy of P&O Group).*

A deck includes cabins, including more special staterooms, the upper level of the theatre, the bureau and the 'Green Room'. B deck consists of the lower level of the theatre, the club-style 'Midships Bar', the 'Carnival Room' (for additional night-time shows and cabarets) and the 'Stern Gallery'. The rest of the passenger spaces are devoted to cabins. There are also four gift shops and three hairdressing salons. The slightly more formal 'Elizabethan Restaurant' (for passengers in cabins 1 to 171) is forward on E deck while the somewhat more casual, booth-style 'Drake Restaurant' (for passengers in all other, lower-priced cabins) is aft on the same deck.

Now engaged mostly in two and three-week cruises out of Sydney, the *Oriana* is enjoying renewed popularity as the South Pacific's biggest liner. Hopefully, there are some good years ahead.

Gross tonnage: 41,923 (1960); 41,915 (1973); 41,910 (1984)
Length overall: 804 feet
Width: 97 feet
Machinery: Steam turbines, twin screw
Speed: 27.5 knots
Capacity: 638 first class and 1,496 tourist class (1960); 1,700 one-class for cruising (1973); 1,550 one-class for cruising (1984)
Built: Vickers-Armstrong Shipbuilders Ltd, Barrow-in-Furness, England, 1960

Above *Just prior to her delivery to P&O in November 1960 the* Oriana *was drydocked briefly at Falmouth* (courtesy of P&O Group). **Below** *P&O maiden voyage at New York, August 22 1979* (courtesy of Moran Towing).

Shalom

The Israeli Merchant Marine developed quite rapidly following its creation in 1945. Especially interesting (and sometimes quite curious) was their unique assortment of early passenger tonnage: little passenger steamers, a converted Hudson River Day Liner and even some modified wartime landing craft. Their first deep-sea passenger vessel did not arrive, however, until 1953. She was the 11,000-ton *Jerusalem*, the former *Bergensfjord* of 1913 which is listed earlier in this work. Soon afterward, the Israelis took a giant leap forward. Through a West German reparations pact, four passenger ships were delivered between 1955 and 1957: the 9,800-ton passenger-cargo type sisters *Israel* and *Zion*, and then a 9,900-ton pair, the second *Jerusalem* and the *Theodor Herzl*.

The services of these ships, both within the Mediterranean and across the Atlantic to Halifax and New York, had a combination of purposes: for tourists, for immigrants, as a training ground for future Israeli seamen and also for the movement of cargo. Most importantly, however, such ships displayed the colours of the infant state of Israel. Maritime nationalism still prevailed, even in the late 1950s and early 1960s. This was the prevailing sentiment that prompted the decision to build a large, luxurious state flagship.

The Israelis turned to the French, to the famed Chantiers de L'Atlantique Shipyard at St Nazaire, for their new liner. Certainly, as a supreme shipbuilder, their expertise was intact. Having completed such ships as the *Ile De France* and *Normandie*, they had just finished the new 66,000-ton *France*. Meanwhile, the Dutch had just added their *Rotterdam*, the Italians had their new *Leonardo Da Vinci* and had just announced their plans for twin 45,000-ton super-ships and the Cunard Company was hinting of a giant successor for the ageing *Queen Mary*. Despite the appearance of the transatlantic jet in 1958, the forecasts—or at least the board room attitudes—were still bright and hopeful when this new Israeli flagship was ordered in 1960.

The Zim Israel Navigation Company Limited, which was more commonly known as the Zim Lines, wanted the new liner to not only represent their country on the Atlantic, between Haifa and New York, but to competitively represent them in the lucrative, ever-expanding winter American cruise trade to the Caribbean. In the latter, they had had noted success with the 487 foot *Jerusalem*, but now wanted a finer, better-equipped vessel.

A large team of designers and engineers were contracted to draw up the plans for the new Zim liner. Externally she was to be fashioned after Holland America's *Rotterdam* and P&O's *Canberra* in having twin aft uptakes instead of the customary funnel. Internally, she would be sleek and modern, with a sense of modern Mediterranean stylings that very much followed the high standards of the competitive Italian Line ships.

Costing some £7 million, the new ship was created quite quickly and floated out of her building berth (rather than launched) for the first time on November 10 1962. She was named *Shalom*, the Israeli word for greetings and peace, by Mrs David Ben-Gurion, the wife of the Israeli Prime Minister. It should be mentioned, however, that the new ship's name aroused considerable controversy. It was originally intended to follow a Biblical theme and use the name *King David*. This was later changed to *King Solomon*. However, the choice of *Shalom* seemed far more international in its tone and also appeared more contemporary.

The *Shalom* left the St Nazaire yard on her first sea trials on January 24 1964. Performing beautifully and accepted happily by her owners, she sailed several weeks later for her first visit to Haifa, her homeport. Following a series of inaugural

'show off' cruises in the Mediterranean, the liner then set off, on April 17, on her first crossing to New York. Her general routing was to work a 14-day passage, calling en route at such ports as Naples, Marseilles and Malaga.

I (WHM) was aboard one of the local Hudson River Lackawanna Railroad ferries on the day of the ship's maiden arrival. Although it was a grey, overcast morning, the tone of the reception was nothing less than joyous. There were fireboats, tugs, small craft and an outbound procession of liners. Norweigian America's *Bergensfjord* was the first to pass the inbound Israeli flagship. Whistles bellowed in official salute. Next to come were two American liners, the white-hulled *Independence* and the handsome *America*. Holland's *Statendam* followed and a final entry was the Grace Line combination liner *Santa Magdalena*, which was actually making a brief run from the Bethlehem Shipyards in Hoboken to her regular berth at Port Newark, also in New Jersey.

General understanding was that the *Shalom* was also paid for through a West German wartime reparations account. Years later, while visiting the Haifa headquarters of the Zim Lines in July 1982, I was assured that it was untrue. According to Mr M. Barzel, 'The *Shalom* was paid for totally by the Israelis. There were no German monies involved. We were especially proud of her for this reason.' Having a service speed of 20 knots, the Zim Lines publicised the *Shalom* as the fastest (and finest) liner on the run to Israel. However, during her first season on the Atlantic, it was noted that her first class quarters were inadequate and needed to be enlarged. Consequently, in the autumn of 1964, she was sent to Wilton-Fijenoord Shipyards at Schiedam in Holland to have 76 berths added to her first class accommodation. This increased the overall total to 148 beds.

When the *Shalom* returned to service, it was for her first season on the plush (and profitable) winter Caribbean cruise trade. Most unfortunately, while just hours out of New York, bound for her first cruise, she rammed the Norwegian tanker *Stolt Dagali* in thick fog. Being the night before the Thanksgiving holiday and with a capacity load of excited passengers aboard, the local press made sensational headlines out of the event. One headline ran: '*Shalom* Limps Back to New York in Tragedy'. Several feature stories hinted that the liner nearly sank, which was never the case.

However, the tanker suffered far more seriously. She was cut in half completely and the stern section went down. (Twenty years later, in August 1984, a local New Jersey diver reported that the stern section is still quite visible. The name *Stolt Dagali* was quite clear.) Sadly, there were 19 casualties. The *Shalom* returned to New York, on Thanksgiving Day no less, with a smashed bow and nearly $600,000 in damages. Her anxious passengers were sent ashore while the liner went to the Todd Shipyards in Brooklyn. A full investigation and inquiry followed. However, some months later, a crewman from the *Shalom* unofficially declared, 'We were simply going too fast in the fog'.

Although later returned to service, the *Shalom* was not a great success. While Mr Barzel has reported that she sailed at 80 per cent of full occupancy, she was a financial problem. Israeli crews were then among the highest paid in the world and this cut sharply into the ship's profits. More obvious was the problem of the Kosher kitchens. The rabbinate in Israel insisted that ships sail on the Atlantic only with her Kosher kitchens available. Otherwise, they threatened to pull their rabbis off the ship and therein create a frightening publicity scandal. However, to many passengers, particularly to Jewish travellers in America, the idea of having only Kosher cuisine was less than appealing. Her projected popularity on the Haifa run therefore never materialised. Furthermore, she was scheduled on a single-ship frequency, which created sizeable gaps between sailings. She could hardly be expected to be paired with the 313-passenger *Israel* and *Zion*, which were, in fact, sold off in the spring of 1966. Time was running out for the *Shalom*. Then, of course, there was the overall competition of the jet. Everyone was scrambling about to find passengers, including the rival American Export, Greek and Italian lines. The future looked dim from the Zim headquarters at Haifa.

There were some rather abrupt decisions. The *Shalom*'s 1967 Mediterranean sailing schedule was cancelled and the liner sent instead on a continuous series of 10–14 day cruises from New York to Montreal for that city's highly publicised 'Expo '67'. On some sailings, it was a most unique feature to have the 629-foot long ship sail around Manhattan island, along the East River and under several major bridges, and then proceed through Long Island Sound to the open Atlantic. Ordinarily, passenger ships would travel through Lower New York Bay, slip under the enormous Verrazano Narrows Bridge and then pass directly into Atlantic waters. The *Shalom* may well rate as the largest liner to have made the full East River passage.

The Montreal cruises were merely a temporary alternative. By the autumn of 1967, with little hope for a bright, profitable future, the *Shalom* was offered for sale. She was purchased almost instantly. The German-Atlantic Line, who had lost their *Hanseatic*, the former *Empress of Scotland* from 1930, at a New York pier fire in September 1966, were rather desperate for a new liner. While they ordered a brand new luxury ship, they also wanted an immediate replacement. The *Shalom* became the 'new' *Hanseatic*.

The Germans used the liner on a variety of services: transatlantic to New York, cruising to the Caribbean, cruising from Genoa to the Mediterranean and from Hamburg to Scandinavia, and later on long, luxurious trips such as around continental South America. However, her owners were hurt bitterly by the general economic recession and rapidly increasing fuel oil prices of the early 1970s. In August 1973, as the German Atlantic Line was quite close to full bankruptcy, the *Hanseatic* was sold to the Swiss-based Home Lines. Once again, she was in rather immediate need. The Home Lines had just lost their very popular *Homeric*. A replacement was needed urgently.

Although thought to be renamed *Homeric II*, she was rechristened as the *Doric*. Her interiors were greatly modernised and the accommodation restyled for 945 all-first class passengers. She entered Home Lines' service in January 1974, alternating between winters out of Port Everglades, Florida on 10–16 day cruises to various Caribbean ports to weekly seven-day cruises from New York to Bermuda between April and October. For some years, she was part of a rather regular foursome that departed from New York's Passenger Ship Terminal on Saturday afternoons. This quartet consisted of two Holland America liners, the *Rotterdam* and *Statendam*, and two Home liners, the *Oceanic* and *Doric*.

In 1981, as the Home Lines were building a brand new liner, the 1,179-passenger *Atlantic*, which was commissioned in April 1982, it was thought that the *Doric* would be transferred to the increasing American West Coast run. Instead, the Home Lines received a lucrative offer for the ship. In February 1982, she was handed over to the Greek-flag Royal Cruise Lines, which had developed a strong following and high reputation with their *Golden Odyssey* and now wanted an even larger vessel. Following yet another refit and modernisation (which included the installation of a funnel device quite similar to that of the *Queen Elizabeth 2*), the ship became the *Royal Odyssey*.

Once again, she divides her duties: winter cruising in the Caribbean, Mexico and Panama Canal, summers in Scandinavia out of London (Tilbury) and the autumn months in the Mediterranean. Now, at the age of 20 (in 1984), she is well into her fourth career. There has been one further historical notation, however. In July 1984, some 20 years after that collision outside New York Harbor, the former *Shalom* rammed the 4,600-ton Soviet freighter *Vasya Alekseev* in a sound between Denmark and Sweden. Sent directly to a Danish shipyard for repairs, she quickly resumed service. The Soviet vessel had to be run onto a sandbar, pumped out and then towed to Copenhagen.

Gross tonnage: 25,338 (1964); 25,320 (1967); 17,884 (1974)
Length overall: 629 feet
Width: 82 feet
Machinery: Steam turbines, twin screw
Speed: 20 knots
Capacity: 72 first and 1,018 tourist, then 148 first and 1,018 tourist (1964); 148 first and 864 tourist (1967); 945 all-first class (1974); 817 all-first class (1982)
Built: Chantiers de L'Atlantique, St Nazaire, France, 1964

Left *Newly purchased and refitted for the Home Line, the* Doric *is shown during a rare visit to Le Havre (courtesy of Le Havre Port Authority).*

Left *An artist's impression of what she was to look like with a massive new smoke-stack and a new name—Royal Odyssey.*

Below *A bow view of the reconstructed liner. The new single stack was a great improvement.*

Index

SCANDINAVIAN-AMERICAN LINE

SUPERIOR 3RD CLASS ACCOMMODATION

S.S. FREDERIK VIII.

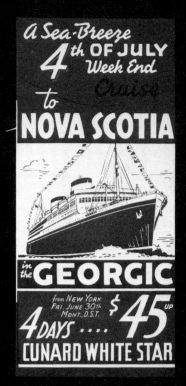

A Sea-Breeze
4th OF JULY
Week End
Cruise
to
NOVA SCOTIA
in the
GEORGIC
from New York
Fri. June 30th
Mdnt. D.S.T.
4 DAYS .... $45 up
CUNARD WHITE STAR

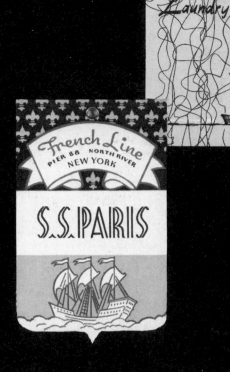

French Line
PIER 88 NORTH RIVER
NEW YORK

S.S. PARIS

Laundry Tariff

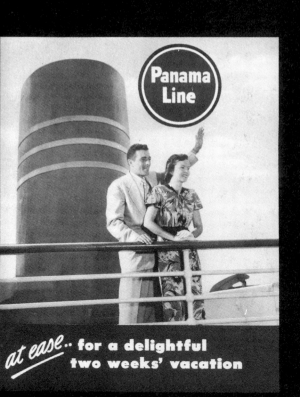

Panama Line

at ease.. **for a delightful two weeks' vacation**

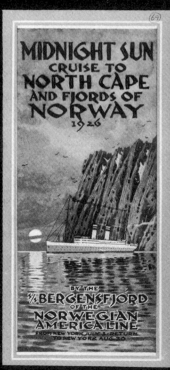

(69)

MIDNIGHT SUN
CRUISE TO
NORTH CAPE
AND FJORDS OF
NORWAY
1926
BY THE
S/S **BERGENSFJORD**
OF THE
NORWEGIAN AMERICA LINE
FROM NEW YORK JULY 3, RETURN
TO NEW YORK AUG. 20

SWEDISH AMERICAN LINE

GOTHENBURG DIRECT NEW YORK AND CANADA